GREAT BOOKS

~ OF ~

CHINA

GREAT BOOKS
≈ OF ≈
CHINA

From Ancient Times to the Present

FRANCES WOOD

BlueBridge

Published by
B l u e B r i d g e
An imprint of
United Tribes Media Inc.
Katonah, New York

www.bluebridgebooks.com

ISBN: 9781629190075

Library of Congress Control Number: 2016959624

Cover design by Cynthia Dunne
Cover art: Studying scholars in a garden (Hanging scroll).
From a private collection. Photo Credit: HIP / Art Resource, NY
Text design by Cynthia Dunne

Printed in the United States of America

10 9 8 7 6 5 4 3 2 1

Contents

Introduction

~ ~

The earliest significant body of Chinese writing is to be found on the "oracle bones" of the Shang dynasty (c. 1600–1046 BCE). These texts are records of divinations, questions concerning the outcome of such activities as military and hunting expeditions and childbirth; they are not literary but documentary and archival. The shoulder blades of oxen and turtle shells were used for divination by the Shang kings, whose territory centered on the eastern reaches of the Yellow River valley down to the Yangtse. The texts inscribed on the oracle bones were short and to the point, but the characters used were the ancestors of today's Chinese script, made more intelligible to us through the *Shuo wen jiezi* dictionary ("analysis and explanation of characters") of 121 CE. Traditional Chinese historiography traces a line of rulers through from the Shang to the Zhou kings, who came from west of the Shang territories and conquered the Shang in 1046 BCE. Recent archaeological discoveries, at Sanxingdui in Sichuan province, for example, have enriched the picture, demonstrating that there were other, and different, local civilizations flourishing in west and south China at the time, though not recorded in the traditional histories. It is from the Zhou that the first body of literature emerges (including the classics associated with Confucius and the Daoist classics), although the passage of millennia means that surviving texts may have considerably changed from their original state.

Zhou rule, which instituted a system of fiefdoms, collapsed in the fifth century BCE when its territorial control broke down into several distinct "warring states." Then, after hundreds of years of fighting, a vast area—from north of Beijing to near Guangzhou in the south, and from the eastern seaboard to the western area of today's Sichuan province—was united by the ruler of the state of Qin in 221 BCE. The ruler of Qin proclaimed himself emperor (thus he is known as "the First Emperor") and moved away from the aristocratic system of rule by fief, replacing it with the beginnings of the bureaucracy, a government staffed by trained officials armed with books containing the legal code and administrative regulations. Though the paramount importance of legal training weakened after the fall of the Qin in 206 BCE, the principle of bureaucratic rule was to continue until the early twentieth century.

The First Emperor unified the state that we now know as China by enforcing several methods of standardization, erasing the differences of the separate "warring states" by imposing a national standard of weights and measures, coinage and writing system. The form of coinage instituted lasted until the early twentieth century, but the standardization of the script was possibly the most significant element underlying the continuity of Chinese civilization and culture. Over the vast territory of China, then as now, many different dialects (or local languages) are spoken, but the written language is generally common to all, even if the characters might be pronounced differently in different areas. The Chinese script does not represent the sounds of the language today, as it is not a phonetic script but a series of up to 44,000 (the number included in the great *Kangxi Dictionary* [*Kangxi zidian*] of 1716) different characters. Though many non-sinologists still like to describe them as "pictograms," very few of today's characters are simple pictures of things: most are much more complex, made up of phonetic elements, phonetic loans, and combinations of these, now frequently combined so that many "words" consist of two syllables or two characters.*

The Qin dynasty, though hugely significant, was short-lived, barely outlasting its founding emperor. It was overthrown by the Han. The Han dynasty (206 BCE–220 CE) continued and further developed the bureaucratic system of government and largely maintained the same system of law and punishment that it deplored in the Qin. Han historical writing pioneered the line of moral justification by which each new dynasty wrote the history of the previous regime that it had overthrown. In order to justify this violent act and demonstrate the righteous assumption of the "Mandate of Heaven," it was necessary to vilify the preceding dynasty, thus the Han histories condemned everything about the Qin. It was during the Han that the precepts associated with Confucius (c. 551–c. 479 BCE) began to be associated with the concepts of moral rule and family worship.

The earliest extant texts (aside from the oracle bone inscriptions, which are divinations rather than literary texts) are those written on strips (or slips) of bamboo or wood during the Warring States period (475–221 BCE). These rare survivals include the earliest versions we have of the Confucian classics and Daoist classics.

The collapse of the Han dynasty in 220 CE was followed by over three centuries of disunion, with various small states and ruling houses competing and fighting for power: the eras of the "Three Kingdoms" and the Western Jin, followed by the "Sixteen Kingdoms" in the north and the Eastern Jin in the south, and then the Northern and Southern dynasties. At last the Sui dynasty reestablished central control in 581 CE. But the Sui rule did not last long and was overthrown in 618 CE when the Tang dynasty (618–907 CE) was established. The Tang is often regarded as a "golden age": the capital city, Chang'an (today's Xi'an, in Shaanxi province),** was the greatest in the world, boasting a rich and multicultural population, with merchants from all over Central Asia bringing luxury goods to the city and building mosques and Nestorian and Manichaean houses of worship alongside the Buddhist and Daoist establishments already there. A great age of poetry, many descriptions survive of the wealth, luxury, and splendor of the court (its furnishings and entertainments) and the contemporary fascination with Central Asian fashions in clothing, music, and dance.

Tang dynasty wall paintings from Buddhist cave complexes such as that near Dunhuang (Gansu province) reveal some of the earliest extant depictions of landscape, a subject that was to dominate Chinese painting for the next millennium. Paintings on paper and silk survive only through later copies that may not wholly reflect the appearance and style of the original. As with painting, an art to be learned and developed through constant copying of masterpieces, the art of poetry—developed to a high point during the Tang—often rested on the delicate and subtle interpretation of well-known themes and subjects, with frequent references to masters of the past.

———

Paper, invented in China in the second century BCE, came into more widespread use from the third century CE, and the earliest form of a book on paper was that of the scroll, imitating the format of the earlier bamboo and wooden strips, which were combined in bundles and then rolled up. Fragments of historical works, poetry, and popular literature, written on paper scrolls and dating mainly from the Tang, have been found among the mostly Buddhist texts preserved in Cave 17 at the Buddhist cave-temple complex near Dunhuang. There, too, was found the world's earliest surviving, securely dated, printed "book," a long paper scroll of the Chinese translation of the *Diamond Sutra*, dated to 868 CE.

Woodblock printing originated in China during the Tang dynasty, and may well have been largely inspired by the Buddhist practice of repetition as an activity that would gain merit and perhaps allow the practitioner to escape from the cycle of rebirths. As described in the *Lotus* and *Diamond* sutras, chanting the texts of the sermons of the Buddha would gain merit. Copying such religious texts would also gain merit, as would paying for the reproduction of Buddhist images. Woodblock printing—where a manuscript text was placed face down on a block of wood, the characters then carved onto the wood in reverse, before the block was inked and an impression taken on paper—enabled the mass production of Buddhist texts and images. Many tenth-century small block-printed sheets, with images of the Buddha or Bodhisattvas combined with a short prayer, were found at Dunhuang. In Japan, printing remained a religious activity, restricted to Buddhist temples until the twelfth century, but in China, the tenth century saw a massive growth in woodblock printing, with schoolbooks printed in large numbers as well as other useful books such as the almanac (*Tongshu*), which every household needed. The circulation of the almanac was technically an imperial monopoly but Chinese entrepreneurs, ignoring legal prohibitions, saw the economic potential of mass production through woodblock printing. The woodblock method, by which entire sheets of texts were carved onto a single block, remained the fundamental printing technology in China until the nineteenth century. Experiments with movable type made of wood, porcelain, or copper in the eleventh century never replaced the woodblock, since the nature of the Chinese script—with its tens of thousands of different characters—made movable-type printing impractical.

The beginnings of the transformation of the book format are also seen at Dunhuang, with two examples of "whirlwind binding," a format in which separate leaves of paper were held together in a piece of split bamboo but then rolled for storage (like a scroll). The name probably derives from the way that the separate leaves curled up when unrolled. This use of separate leaves anticipated the later codex format. During the Song dynasty (960–1279), printing flourished and books were produced in the codex format, with separate leaves sewn into a soft paper binding, which was to dominate until the twentieth century, when very different Western binding styles were introduced.

A complexity of the long history of texts in China is the survival of examples. Those of the Han were copied and recopied, possibly incorporating later additions, corrections, or errors; for example, the earliest surviving text of *The Grand Scribe's Records* (*Shi ji*) can be found in a Song printed edition. It is impossible for us to know whether the Song version of this significant text, written by Sima Qian in the first century BCE, preserves the original accurately.

The way in which texts were used in traditional China is also significant. Although patronage and recommendation was the most common way of entering the government administration, from the Han onward rigorous examinations, with questions on administration and the Confucian classics, began to form part of the procedure. Such civil service examinations became increasingly important throughout the succeeding centuries, and by the time of the Song there was a highly prestigious three-level examination system (with regional, provincial, and palace exams), and the palace exam presided over by the emperor. With some interruptions, this system persisted until its abolition in 1905. Beginning in the thirteenth century, the examinations were based upon knowledge of the Confucian "Four Books" (*Si shu*)—the *Analects* (*Lun yu*), the *Mencius* (*Mengzi*), the "Great Learning" (*Da xue*), and the "Doctrine of the Mean" (*Zhongyong*)—and the essays on set subjects taken from these works had to be written in a strictly regulated style, known as *ba gu wen* or "eight-legged essay."

———

The Tang dynasty—though imperiled by a rebellion in 755–763 CE led by An Lushan, a general of Central Asian origin—lasted until 907 CE when it was succeeded by another (brief) period of disunion, the "Five Dynasties" in the north of China and "Ten Kingdoms" in the south. This was ended by the establishment of the Song dynasty in 960 CE. Though historians downplay this apparent cycle of dynastic change, of disunion and reunion, it is firmly fixed in the popular imagination, exemplified by the opening lines of the fourteenth-century novel *The Story of the Three Kingdoms* (*Sanguo zhi*): "The empire long divided, must unite; long united, must divide."

The Song dynasty moved the capital away from Chang'an to Kaifeng (in Henan province), and it was a period characterized by an increasingly free economy as internal markets flourished (supplied by goods moved largely by waterways); a massive increase in the publishing industry based on the widespread development of woodblock printing; an interest in antiquarianism and a reexamination of Confucianism, which underpinned the ethos of both state and family. The flourishing economy led to the first issue of paper banknotes. It was, however, a period which also saw the rise of several warlike states of northern peoples (including the Liao dynasty founded by the Khitan people, and the Jin dynasty set up by the Jurchen people), resulting in the invasion and abandonment of the capital Kaifeng in 1127. Though the Song court reestablished itself in the beautiful lakeside city of Hangzhou (in Zhejiang province), threats of invasion from the north continued, and in 1279 the Mongols invaded China to found the Yuan dynasty (1279–1368). This was the first Chinese dynasty to be given an auspicious name, *yuan* ("primordial"). Previous dynasties had reflected personal or place names but the Mongols had no such associations or practices.

Though part of the massive Mongol expansion across Asia, Mongol rule in China was greatly adapted to Chinese ways. But although the first Mongol emperor of China, Khubilai Khan (1215–1294), assumed "an increasingly obvious facade as a Confucian Chinese emperor," he chose to rely on Central and West Asian advisors, avoided the employment of Chinese officers and ministers, and frequently failed to hold the bureaucratic selection examinations.*** Despite discriminatory laws, or perhaps because intellectuals were unable to follow their traditional path into the civil service, the Yuan dynasty saw a flowering of Chinese literature, most notably in the development of the drama and the novel. The last decades of the Yuan dynasty saw a rise in popular rebellions driven by disastrous floods in northern China and a crippling drought in the south. In 1368, the charismatic rebel commander Zhu Yuanzhang drove the Mongols out of China and established the Ming dynasty, which lasted until 1644. The Ming dynasty followed the Yuan in taking an auspicious name—*ming* ("bright, illuminated")—and it was a consciously "Chinese" dynasty, harking back to the glories of the Tang in particular, and reestablishing the old system of bureaucratic examinations. Zhu Yuanzhang, who became the Hongwu emperor, was an extraordinary character. Born into utter poverty, he was forced to take refuge in a Buddhist monastery until he left to join a rebel band through which he rose to ultimate power. Though initially a reformer, conscious of the need to help landless peasants rebuild agriculture and of the benefits of universal, free education, he became increasingly paranoid—and soon after his death in 1398, the Ming saw a second "founding" with the usurpation of the throne by his fourth son, who proclaimed himself the Yongle emperor in 1402. It was during the Ming that China engaged more fully with the outside world, first on its own terms with the massive convoys led by the eunuch admiral Zheng He (1371–1433) to Southeast Asia, India, the Persian Gulf, and East Africa, and later through the arrival of Portuguese traders at the beginning of the sixteenth century and of Jesuit missionaries such as Matteo Ricci (1552–1610). Literature flourished during the Ming with novels, poetry, and books of essays on good living as well as a growth in writing about science and travel.

A series of emperors with little interest in the affairs of state and the growth of corruption, together with natural disasters, led to peasant uprisings in the mid-seventeenth century and a state of chaos that provided the opportunity for another northern group, the Jurchen from Manchuria, to sweep down and take the country, ending Ming rule. In 1644, the Manchu Jurchen established the Qing ("pure, clear") dynasty, which lasted until 1911. Before their conquest, the Manchus had absorbed something of the Chinese system of administration, and unlike the Mongols who kept Chinese scholars away from the administration, the Manchus adopted Chinese methods and traditions while still retaining their own identity through their social organization, belief systems, language, script, and dress.

During what is called the "long eighteenth century," covering the reigns of the Kangxi emperor (r. 1661–1722), the Yongzheng emperor (r. 1722–1735), and the Qianlong emperor (r. 1735–1796), the Qing seemed magnificent and flourishing; but by the nineteenth century, internal pressure from massive popular rebellions (including the Taiping Rebellion, and later the Boxer Rebellion) and external pressure from the increasingly determined commercial adventurers from Europe and America caused a steady decline. British attempts to trade with China for tea, which had become a staple, led to an imbalance in trade as the Chinese had no interest in British trade goods. This trade deficit was addressed by the export of opium from British India which led to dramatic social problems in China and a massive outflow of silver to pay for the illegal drug. Official Chinese attempts to stop the trade led to two Opium Wars (1840–42, 1856–60) and humiliation for China as ports were forced open to foreign commerce and residence.

The Qing government stumbled toward reform in the late nineteenth century, setting up modern (Western-style) shipyards and arsenals, the beginnings of a more modern legal system, and establishing schools and sending students abroad to study, but the reforms were too little, too late.

In 1912, after a rather muddled uprising, China saw a truly dramatic change with the establishment of a republican government—after two millennia of imperial rule. Though the new government began with high ideals—it did its best to initiate modernizing reform and modern institutions—the difficulties of escaping from traditional ways and the legacy of a number of local armies (set up in the last years of the nineteenth century) soon saw fragile central power break down into warlord rule, with bitter battles fought between local despots. At the same time, Japan was doing all it could to exploit China's fragmentation with a view to invasion. The warlords aside, two political parties were competing for power: the Nationalist Party (Guomindang/Kuomintang) led by Chiang Kai-shek, and the Chinese Communist Party, founded in 1921. Though encouraged by Soviet Russia to cooperate, relations between these two Chinese parties broke down when Chiang Kai-shek, leading an expedition northward—ostensibly to regain control of the country from the warlords—in 1927 turned on the Communists who had seized control of Shanghai in advance of his arrival. The massacre of workers there and a series of failed uprisings in China's cities led the Communist Party to turn from urban insurrection to work in the countryside (against Soviet advice, which held that a revolution could only be led by the urban working class). Mao Zedong, who fought his way to the top of the Communist Party, led this rural campaign, establishing the Jiangxi Soviet in southeastern China in 1931. Turning away from the campaign against the warlords, Chiang Kai-shek ordered five massive attacks, forcing the Communists to abandon Jiangxi in October 1934 and embark upon the Long March, finally arriving in Yan'an in distant Shaanxi province a year later.

Japan seized control of Manchuria in 1931 and began a full-scale invasion of China in 1937, an invasion characterized by acts of terrible cruelty such as the massacre known as the Rape of Nanjing in 1937 when over 100,000 civilians were killed and many women and girls attacked with deadly savagery. In its distant northwestern base, the Communist Party led effective, wide-scale guerrilla resistance to the Japanese, attracting support from the local peasants and, increasingly, intellectuals and city dwellers, shocked at the corruption of Chiang Kai-shek's government and its failure to join the Communists in a united front against Japanese invasion. Defeat in World War II ended Japan's ambitions in China, and a civil war between the Nationalists and Communists ended in Communist victory and the establishment of the People's Republic of China in 1949.

Chinese literature of the republican era reflected a new internationalism and awareness of the outside world, with many works reflecting the influence of Western writers such as Ibsen and Gogol. The most dramatic change in literature, however, came about with the May Fourth Movement of 1919, a political protest against China's treatment at the Versailles Peace Conference which was transformed into a "self-strengthening" movement with a strong emphasis on literary reform. The old, difficult Classical Chinese style of the highly educated was abandoned by writers who saw the vernacular—closer to the current spoken language—as the best vehicle for literature that could free China of the shackles of the past. Writers of the period struggled with censorship, but this struggle continued with greater ferocity in the post–1949 period, which saw a series of anti-intellectual campaigns. The Communist Party line that literature should be for the masses, rather than for the intellectual elite, severely restricted subject matter and, at times, even attempted to control style. Nevertheless, many writers managed to create new and impressive works despite restrictions.

———

When I started work in the Chinese section of the British Library, there was a rule in place that no translations of literature were to be acquired, as readers were expected to read the original. This antiquated regulation must have dated back to the foundation of the British Museum and its library in the mid-eighteenth century when gentlemen were expected to be able to read Latin, Greek, French, and German, but it did not make much sense in the twentieth-century Chinese section of the British Library. Quite apart from the fact that few readers at the library were able to immerse themselves in *The Water Margin* (*Shuihu zhuan*) or *Dream of the Red Chamber* (*Hongloumeng*) in Chinese, the titles that were chosen for translation, whether from Chinese to English or vice versa, were in themselves interesting. Who made the choices? Why did they choose one book over another?

In my own work, though I have read many texts, I have translated one work of fiction, a modern novel—Dai Houying's *Stones of the Wall* (*Ren a ren!*)—because, in the early 1980s, it was the only post–Cultural Revolution (1966–1976) novel that I had found difficult to put down. Most I found hard to pick up, let alone translate, but Dai Houying's novel was quite gripping and constructed in what, for China, was a new and interesting style.

Since I was fascinated by the Chinese language from the moment I began to learn it in 1967, I have always tried to share the fascination, for through language and literature it is possible to grasp something of China's cultural history and current preoccupations. China is too important to be ignored, and while its politics may not please many, the complexity and depth of China's culture is there to be explored, partly through translations of the great books of China.

In the preface to his *Anthologie de la littérature chinoise classique*, Jacques Pimpaneau writes, "To create an anthology is to commit a crime, to select some authors and send others, even if they are not without interest, to the hell of oblivion. And it is a mutilation of the texts from which one selects a single passage . . ."† Yet he continues to reflect that it is through anthologies and selections that we begin to appreciate our own literature at school and that an approach to Chinese literature may necessarily involve this same process of reading short passages in order to gain an idea of the literature of the world's most significant continuous culture. He recounts a meeting with a tourist guide in China who was keen to discuss *Madame Bovary* and comments that it would be unlikely to find a tourist guide in France who was familiar with the eighth-century Chinese poetry of Du Fu and Li Bai.

Using another example, a full translation of Shakespeare's plays was published in China in 1954. Charles Dickens, Arthur Conan Doyle, and a number of major French and other European authors were also translated into Chinese in the last hundred or more years and, perhaps more interesting, enjoyed considerable popularity. I remember a taxi driver in Shanghai clutching a battered copy of the Chinese translation of *The Adventures of Sherlock Holmes*, a sight that would be highly surprising in London—not to mention a copy of a translation of the *Dream of the Red Chamber*.

Guilty of the same process of offering a selection of Chinese literature through which some great authors and great works have been excluded, I am hoping that interested readers can make use of existing translations of the works described. Many other translations of Chinese works are listed in the wonderful *Indiana Companion to Traditional Chinese Literature* (Vol. 1, 1986; Vol. 2, 1998), edited by William H. Nienhauser, Jr. There are also some fine and useful modern anthologies, including Pimpaneau's and *The Columbia Anthology of Traditional Chinese Literature* (1994), edited by Victor H. Mair, and *The Columbia Anthology of Chinese Folk and Popular Literature* (2011), edited by Victor H. Mair and Mark Bender.

I have chosen sixty-six works, from the *Book of Songs* (*Shi jing*) compiled over 2,500 years ago to late-twentieth-century novels. While I have tried to give a fairly comprehensive overview of types of writing

—from poetry, drama, and fiction to science and travel—I have been limited, not only by my own preferences but by the availability of translations into Western languages that will enable readers to pursue the texts for themselves. Mainly for reasons of space, a number of works could not be included, such as the oeuvre of the poet Tao Qian (also called Tao Yuanming, 365–427 CE), including his prose work *Peach Blossom Spring* (*Taohuan yuan*), a phrase that has come to mean "utopia" in Chinese; the epic ancient poetry collection *Songs of the South* (*Chu ci*), translated by David Hawkes (1985); Han Shaogong's extraordinary novel *A Dictionary of Maqiao* (*Maqiao cidian*) (1996), translated by Julia Lovell; and pieces such as my favorite Chinese poem, "sung at the burial of kings and princes," which is included in Arthur Waley's *One Hundred and Seventy Chinese Poems* (1918):

> How swiftly it dries,
>
> The dew on the garlic leaf!
>
> The dew that dries so fast
>
> Tomorrow it will fall again,
>
> But he who we carry to the grave
>
> Will never more return.

———

I have used the pinyin system of romanization, which was introduced in China in 1958 and adopted as an international standard in 1982. Unfortunately, many of the translations I have listed use the old (nineteenth-century British) Wade-Giles romanization system or the even more complex French romanization. The Buddhist site known in pinyin as Dunhuang, pronounced "Doon-hwang" however you romanize it, was Tun-huang in Wade-Giles and Touen-huang to the French.

In pinyin, though many of the letters are used in the same way as we do in English, some letters differ. The following rough guide lists the problematic letters, where pronunciation needs to be noted or where pinyin and Wade-Giles differ (and Wade-Giles consistently uses an apostrophe after certain letters to indicate aspiration):

a: "ar" as in "bar"
b: as in "bar" (Wade-Giles: p)
c: as an initial consonant, "ts" as in "its" (Wade-Giles: ts)
d: as in "dog" (Wade-Giles: t)
e: "er" as in "her"
g: as in "go" (Wade-Giles: k)
i: varies according to the preceding consonants: pronounced "ee"
   unless preceded by c, ch, r, s, sh, z, zh, when it is pronounced "er"
   as in "her"
j: as in "jingle" (Wade-Giles: ch)
k: as in "kill" (Wade-Giles: k')
o: with a slight "r," or as in "lord"
p: as in "pick" (Wade-Giles: p')
q: "ch" as in "chick" (Wade-Giles: ch')
r: an unrolled "r" (Wade-Giles: j)
s: as in "smile" (Wade-Giles: s, ss, sz)
t: as in "tuck" (Wade-Giles: t')
u: either "oo" as in "fool" or, with an umlaut, as the German "*ü* "
x: between "ss" and "sh" (Wade-Giles: hs)
z: "ts" as in "its" (Wade-Giles: ts, tz)
zh: "j" as in "jingle" (Wade-Giles: ch)

A complication in the pinyin system is that vowel combinations such
as "i" and "a" (as in *tian*, "heaven") are not pronounced as individual
sounds ("i" and "a") but as a combination, pronounced "yeh." Thus
tian, with its "i" and "a," is pronounced "tien." Similarly, the "o" in
guo ("country") is pronounced in the standard manner, but when followed by "ng," as in *zhong* ("middle"), is rather longer—thus *zhongguo*
(China) is pronounced "joong guor."

Book of Songs
Shi jing

(c. 1000–c. 600 BCE)

AUTHOR UNKNOWN

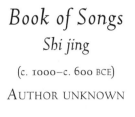

The *Book of Songs* (*Shi jing*), also called *Classic of Poetry* or *Book of Odes*, is one of the Confucian classics revered since the Han dynasty (206 BCE–220 CE). It is a collection of 305 poems (or songs) dating back to c. 1000–c. 600 BCE. Later tradition holds that Confucius was instrumental in gathering and forming the collection, which is doubted, but it is certain that he enjoyed the collection and made frequent references to it in his conversations recorded in the *Analects* (*Lun yu*): "Why is it none of you study the *Songs*? A quotation from the *Songs* may stimulate the imagination, show one's breeding, settle difficulties, and express complaints." Or, "If a man has studied the three hundred *Songs* yet fails in his administrative duties . . . what use are the *Songs* to him?"

However the collection was compiled, it survived in several versions into the Han dynasty and was found inscribed on wooden strips in a tomb dated to 165 BCE in Anhui province, and also inscribed on a set of stone tablets in 175 CE and another set dated 837 CE. Quite a number of the poems survive on paper in the great corpus of (mainly Buddhist) manuscripts dating from c. 400–c. 1000 CE in the cave-temple complex near Dunhuang.

The *Book of Songs* is divided into four parts: one hundred sixty "Songs of the [Northern] States," which describe in quite lyrical terms the life cycle of the common people, their festivals and daily lives, with much reference to flora and fauna; seventy-four "Lesser Songs" describing upper-class life, with some poems interpreted as complaints against the state regime; thirty-one "Greater Songs" on the Zhou (1046–221 BCE) and the overthrow of the Shang dynasty (c. 1600–1046 BCE), with more criticism of contemporary politics and references to the mythology of earlier periods; and the remaining forty songs of praise on rituals, rites, festivals, and music practiced in various Chinese states. The connection with ritual is important: many songs may have been performed during rituals which were of huge significance to the ruling elite.

Though the poems (or songs) originally rhymed, the rhymes have largely been lost due to changes in the pronunciation of modern Chinese. Many of them contain repetition, characteristic of their folk or ritual origins.

Among the first group, the following poem contains typical references to wildflowers and wildlife interspersed with a lament about separation:

> "Guan," "guan" cry the ospreys on the island in the river
> The graceful lady is a suitable wife for the lord.
> Scattered grows the yellow-heart duckweed, here and there
> The graceful lady is a suitable wife for the lord.
> Waking and sleeping he sought her, sought her and did not
> find her
> Waking and sleeping he thought of her, grieving, grieving,
> tossing and turning.
> Scattered grows the yellow-heart duckweed, here and there
> The graceful lady is a suitable wife for the lord.
> He must woo her with lutes.
> Scattered grows the yellow-heart duckweed, here and there,
> With drum and chimes he must delight her.

There is a similar use of bird and flower motifs in another poem:

> How the tuberose fills the valley: its leaves are thick, thick.
> The yellow oriole flies and perches in the thicket and calls.
> How the tuberose fills the valley, its leaves are dense, dense.
> I cut it and I boiled it to make fine cloth and coarse,
> Clothes that I will always wear.
> I have told the housekeeper,

I have told the housekeeper that I am returning to my
    parents.

I wash my clothes, I rinse my clothes,

Which to wash, which not?

I am going to stay with my parents.

The secure daily round of agricultural life is contrasted with a woman's worry about her absent husband. He is away on compulsory military service, but men were also expected to take part in corvée labor, a form of taxation which might involve the construction of defensive walls or road-building in a distant and, perhaps, dangerous place. The wife longs to care for him and ensure that he is properly fed:

My husband is away on military service,

I don't know when he may return.

Where is he?

The chickens roost in their coop,

Oxen and goats come down from the hill.

My husband is away on military service

How can I not think of him?

My husband is away on military service

Not days but months.

When will he return to me?

The chickens roost in their coop,

Oxen and goats come down from the hill.

My husband is away on military service,

Without food or drink.

A simple wish for family continuity is often expressed, here through the sounds made by locusts, themselves emblematic of huge numbers:

> The locust wings say "numbers, numbers,"
> May your sons and grandsons be many, many.
> The locust wings flap, flap,
> May your line of sons and grandsons extend forever,
>   forever.
> The locust wings extend, extend,
> May your sons and grandsons be united, united.

There are themes of hunting and warfare:

> The hare nets are impressive, impressive,
> Ding, ding, the noise of the hammers.
> The warrior's head is held high,
> Shield and wall to his prince.
> The hare nets are spread across the paths,
> The warrior's head is held high,
> A good companion to his prince.
> The hare nets are spread in the middle of the forest,
> The warrior's head is held high,
> Stomach and heart to his prince.

Animals and humans are compared in the context of what were to become major themes of Confucian virtue such as righteousness, correct conduct, and respect for the rituals that held communities together:

> Look at the rat,
> A rat has its skin,
> A man without righteousness,
> A man without righteousness,

What should he do but die?

Look at the rat,

A rat has its teeth,

A man without control,

A man without control,

Why should he not die?

Look at the rat,

A rat has its bones,

A man without respect for ritual,

A man without respect for ritual,

He should die quickly.

One very simple poem that still retains its rhyme at the end of each line (and makes great use of the repetition that is also seen in some of the much later *Nineteen Old Poems* [*Gu shi shijiu shou*]) is the eighth in the "Songs of the [Northern] States":

Thick, thick grows the plantain

We go to pick it

Thick, thick grows the plantain

We go to collect it.

Thick, thick grows the plantain

We pick with our fingers

Thick, thick grows the plantain

We gather handfuls.

Thick, thick grows the plantain

We fill our aprons

Thick, thick grows the plantain

Full aprons tucked into our belts.*

The *Book of Songs*, as the only work of literature mentioned by Confucius, was to become one of the "Five Classics," adopted during the early Han period as the basis, or curriculum, for a "Confucian" education system designed to train government officials. The Five Classics (*Wu jing*) are: *Book of Songs*; *Book* (or *Classic*) *of Changes* (*Yi jing*), a divination manual; *Book* (or *Classic*) *of Documents* (or *History*) (*Shu jing*), a book of government documents and proclamations purporting to date from the semilegendary Xia dynasty onward; *Book of Rites* (or *Ritual*) (*Li ji*), a book of ritual, incorporating discussions on ritual by Han dynasty scholars; and *Spring and Autumn Annals* (*Chun qiu*), annals of the state of Lu, from 722 BCE to 481 BCE.

The significance of these five works is that they formed the basis of Confucian education and the training of government officials not just during the Han dynasty—when they had some relevance—but right up to the end of the nineteenth century.

Book of Changes
Yi jing

(first millennium BCE)

AUTHOR UNKNOWN

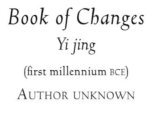

I n the Han dynasty (206 BCE–220 CE) an ancient divination text was incorporated into the Five Classics and given the name by which it is still known, *Book* (or *Classic*) *of Changes* (*Yi jing*, or, in the old Wade-Giles romanization system, *I-ching*). It derived from the *Zhou Changes* (*Zhou yi*), a manual for divination that may have been compiled as early as the ninth century BCE, during the Western Zhou period (or, as some suggest, as early as the eleventh century BCE). The addition of a series of explanatory texts dating from about the third century BCE resulted in the compilation we now know as the *Book of Changes*. Recent archaeological excavations of parts of the text of the *Book of Changes* inscribed on bamboo or wooden strips during the subsequent millennium demonstrate its popularity.

The *Book of Changes* consists of interpretations of sixty-four hexagrams. Each hexagram is composed of six horizontal lines stacked one above the other, with each of the six lines either being solid (unbroken) or broken into two halves, thereby creating sixty-four possible combinations. The two most important hexagrams are the first one, *qian*, with six solid lines, which is glossed as "heaven," "creative principle," *yang*; and the second one, *kun*, with six broken lines, which is glossed as "earth," "passive principle," *yin*.

Among the sixty-four hexagrams are "peace" (*tai*), with three broken lines above three solid lines, and "stagnation" (*pi*), with three solid lines above three broken lines. Some of the others are "argument or conflict" (*song*), "fellowship" (*tongren*), "contemplation" (*guan*), "return, or turning point" (*fu*), and "retreat" (*dun*).

The ancient primary interpretations of the hexagrams are brief, but the accompanying later commentaries are often very long. For example, the ancient text of the first hexagram, "heaven," is only a few lines long, but in later centuries it was accompanied by several pages of commentary to expand the gnomic response.

The work reflects the cosmological theories of the late Warring States period with its stress on the *yin-yang* dialectical theory and the division of all things into the Five Elements (water, fire, wood, metal, and earth, which were thought to be the basis of composition of all things). Their interaction accounted for the formation of the earth and the shifting fortunes of humans and nature and could be seen to create "change." The question of how much human beings could influence or react to changes of circumstances underlay the act of divination. Much of the *Book of Changes* commentary seeks to expand the significance of the work beyond personal divination to a Confucian explanation of the workings of the cosmos. As such it was used by later scholars, provoked by the popularity of Daoist cosmology, to create a Confucian alternative.

The method of divination is highly complicated, and the instructions are mysterious and imprecise. It was traditionally done with fifty yarrow stalks, i.e., long, dry sticks. According to the *Book of Changes*, ritual associated with divination started with the care of the text which should be kept wrapped in clean silk and stored on a high shelf (which was not, however, to be higher than a man's shoulder). When opened, the text should be laid upon its protective wrapper. The fifty yarrow stalks, one to two feet long, should be kept in a plain but elegant box which was not to be used for other purposes. To begin the divination process, the question is raised, not about what might happen but what should be done—should a certain action go ahead? The text is placed on a table in the center of the room, facing south; and on a lower table, to the south of the main table, the sticks are placed beside an incense burner. The questioner faces north and performs three full kowtows (*ketou*, meaning "knock head"), bowing low and placing his forehead on the ground three times. Then he puts burning incense in the burner. Taking the sticks in his right hand, he waves them three times through the smoke rising from the incense, rotating his hand clockwise, and returns one stick to the box. Taking the remaining forty-nine sticks, he bunches them together and then divides them into two piles. These sticks are then sorted and resorted until the questioner arrives at certain numbers that correlate to the solid and broken lines of the hexagrams in the *Book of Changes,* which are still not easy to understand, let alone interpret. (At a later time coins were also used, in combinations of "heads" and "tails." Apparently this method saves time and was used by professional fortune-tellers. Three coins are thrown six times and the results—combinations of tails-tails-tails, heads-heads-heads, tails-tails-heads, and heads-heads-tails—correlated to hexagram lines.)

In the interpretation of the hexagrams, "nine" stands for a solid line and "six" for a broken line; and lines are read from bottom to top. For the first hexagram, "heaven," the statements for the six (solid) lines are:

"Nine in the bottom line": "The hidden dragon does not act."

"Nine in the second line": "A dragon is seen in the field; it would be profitable to visit a great man."

"Nine in the third line": "The superior man is alert all day and in the evening. If there is danger, he is not at fault."

"Nine in the fourth line": "If the dragon jumps over a chasm, he is not at fault."

"Nine in the fifth line": "There is a flying dragon in the sky; good to see a great man."

"Nine in the top line": "The dragon regrets."

And "for all six lines": "Crowds of headless dragons, good luck."

For the second hexagram, "earth," the statements for the six (broken) lines are:

"Six in the bottom line": "The hoarfrost means that real ice is coming."

"Six in the second line": "Straight and wide: without exertion, everything will profit."

"Six in the third line": "He restrains his talent in the king's service, though unfinished, final success is assured."

"Six in the fourth line": "A sack tied up, no blame, no praise."

"Six in the fifth line": "A yellow jacket: ultimate good luck."

"Six in the top line": "Dragons fighting in the wilderness, their blood is black and yellow."

And "for all six lines": "The power of endurance."

In general, some of the text lines connected to the sixty-four hexagrams have a very clear message. For example, "Now is the time to set armies marching to subdue the cities and countries of the empire." Or, "The time is favorable for legal processes." But other lines are more mysterious: "The ablution has been performed but not the sacrifice"; "The ridgepole sags"; "The inn has burned down"; "A cow is lost through sheer carelessness." The hexagram "development" (*jian*), for one, relies upon the activities of wild geese: "The wild goose moves gradually to the river bank" means "the younger son is in trouble," while "The wild goose moving to dry land" means "the husband goes out and never returns."

Of course the significance of the gnomic interpretations depended very much on the question that was posed. This would naturally influence the action that might be undertaken.

Classic of the Way and of Virtue
Daode jing

(sixth to fourth centuries BCE)

LAOZI (c. sixth century BCE)

Zhuangzi

(c. fourth century BCE)

ZHUANGZI (c. fourth century BCE)

≫ ⁄≪

These two works are viewed as the origin of Daoism, a complex phenomenon in Chinese culture.* In the *Classic of the Way and of Virtue* (*Daode jing*) it is stressed that the *dao*, often translated as "the Way," is ineffable and ungraspable—too great, too significant to be described. It might be glossed as the underlying principle behind the cycle of life and death, the creative force behind the universe and its creation, the source of everything and the relationships between all things.

Since the Han dynasty (206 BCE–220 CE), there were two major strands of Daoism, philosophical and religious. Religious Daoism, associated with major temples across China, served the population through ritual and ceremony, offering a series of deities to worship and beg for favors. Philosophical Daoism offered an alternative to the very worldly, political aspects of Confucianism, with an attempt to understand the world and one's place in it through a concentration on nature and natural phenomena—rather than the Confucian observance of ritual and social conventions. Put at its most simple level, there was a saying that people in China were "Confucian in office, Daoist in retirement, and Buddhist as death approached"—for Confucianism permeated the ethos of government and Buddhism offered a comforting prospect of paradise and a series of rituals that conducted the soul there, while Daoism offered the prospect of unity with nature, and acceptance.

"Daoist in retirement" described the ideal of retreat to a country estate or urban garden once free from the restrictions of Confucian official life. The construction of gardens with their miniature mountain scenes and carefully chosen plants, which could be appreciated according to the seasons, was an expression of the way that Daoism formed part of the traditional culture. Poetry and painting reflected the same desire to escape from bureaucratic office life into the majesty of nature where one could "study the *li* ['pattern'] of the bamboo" and marvel at the way that it grew, equal segment by equal segment, in a pattern ordained not by humans but by nature.

The text itself, with its early origins, presents problems of transmission (as does the *Zhuangzi*). Stone-carved versions of the *Classic of the Way and of Virtue* survive from 708 CE and 738 CE, the latter an "official version" carved at the order of the Xuanzong emperor of the Tang (r. 712–756 CE). It is a short text in about five thousand characters, comprising eighty-one sections that are most commonly arranged in two parts: one part on the *dao*, "the Way"; the other on *de*, which is traditionally translated as "virtue" but is considered by many to be closer to the Latin *virtus* (meaning "strength" and "vigor"). Though traditionally referred to as the *Daode jing*, the recent discovery of the text written on silk in a tomb at Mawangdui (Hunan province) dated to 168 BCE revealed a different order, a *Dedao jing*.

The *Classic of the Way and of Virtue* is traditionally assumed to have been compiled by Laozi (literally, "the old man"), allegedly an older contemporary of Confucius and described in Sima Qian's *The Grand Scribe's Records* (*Shi ji*) as a native of the state of Chu (in the south) named Li Tan or Li Er, who served as archivist to the Zhou court. Though there are stories about Confucius consulting Laozi, scholars tend to agree on the largely fictional nature of Laozi. (Early Chinese texts, including the *Classic of the Way and of Virtue* and the *Analects* [*Lun yu*] of Confucius, have been described by experts such as A. C. Graham as compilations gathered by disciples, rather than being unique compositions by the "original" author. Such compilations, perhaps from a variety of different sources, were subject to addition and subtraction, particularly as time passed.)

The *Classic of the Way and of Virtue* is enigmatic. In the *Daode jing* version, it begins: "The Way that can be spoken of is not the eternal Way; the name that can be named is not the eternal name. The unnamed is the beginning of heaven and earth, the named is the mother of the ten thousand things [everything]. Eternally without desire, one can observe the mystery. Eternally desiring, one can see its form. These two have the same origin but their names are different. The origin is spoken of as primordial, primordial of primordial, the gate of mystery." Section 14 says: "Look and you cannot see it, it is said to have gone. Listen and you cannot hear it, it is beyond hearing. Grasp and you cannot hold it, it is ungraspable. These three cannot be grasped, therefore they are joined into one. Above it is no brightness, below it no dark; a thread without name, it returns to non-existence. It is described as formless. Form without substance, its appearance is dim. Face it and there is no beginning, follow it and there is no end. The ancient way is powerful and present, knowing its beginning is called knowing the Way."

———

By contrast, the text of the *Zhuangzi* consists of a series of anecdotes and reflections not unlike the *Analects*, but much more playful. The *Zhuangzi* is traditionally ascribed to Zhuangzi ("Master Zhuang"), also called Zhuang Zhou, who is described in *The Grand Scribe's Records* as a contemporary of the Hui King of Liang and the Xuan King of Zhou, who were rulers in the fourth century BCE. We know next to nothing about Zhuangzi; he might have lived in the state of Song, and around the time of Mencius.

The *Zhuangzi*, too, has long been recognized as a compilation rather than the work of one person. It seems to have consisted of fifty-two sections at one time but survives as thirty-three sections, and though it was first printed in 1445, sections have been found in the corpus of manuscripts from the fifth to eleventh centuries CE discovered at the cave-temple complex near Dunhuang; there is also a partial manuscript from the Kozanji temple near Kyoto (Japan) founded in the eighth century and restored in the twelfth century.

Zhuangzi, as revealed in the text, is a paradoxical and playful character. One of the most famous passages relates to fish. In section 17, "Zhuangzi and Huizi were walking on the bank beside the Hao river. Zhuangzi said, 'Look at the little fish swimming as they please. That is what fish enjoy!' Huizi said, 'You are not a fish. How do you know what they enjoy?' Zhuangzi said, 'You are not I, how do you know I don't know what fish enjoy?' Huizi said, 'I am not you so I definitely do not know what you know. But you are definitely not a fish, so you still don't know what fish enjoy.' Zhuangzi said, 'You asked me how I know what fish enjoy: you knew I knew when you asked the question. I know it by standing here beside the river.'"

According to the *Zhuangzi*, when Zhuangzi's wife died, Huizi went to see him and found him squatting on the ground, banging on a basin and singing. Feeling that this was going a bit far, Huizi remonstrated with him, reminding him that the couple had been together for a long time and that she had brought up their children. Zhuangzi disagreed, saying that he had been desolate at first but he had considered his wife's life and its changes, from before existence, through the existence of body and soul, to the end. "It is like the natural progression of the seasons. Now she is lying down peacefully in the Great Inner Room. If I were to follow her, crying and howling, it would show that I did not understand [this natural progression]."

Not all the stories are about Zhuangzi. For instance, "The Official in Charge of Ancestor Worship, dressed in his black robes, looked into the pigpen and asked the pigs, 'Why do you object to dying? I'm going to feed you up for three months, then I will fast for ten days and make preparations for three days, put down white mats and lay you on the sacrificial altar. Don't you consent?' If he had been talking on behalf of the pigs, he'd say it was better to eat bran and stay in the pigpen. If he were talking for himself, he'd rather be honored in his lifetime as a high official and lie on a fine hearse when he died. The pigs would certainly refuse that plan. Why were his ideas so different from those of the pigs?"

Many of the stories have entered the Chinese language, such as that of the frog in the well who was convinced that the entire universe consisted of the tiny circle of blue sky above his well—which has come to stand for narrow-mindedness. Other images are similarly well-known, such as that of Zhuangzi refusing office by comparing a long-dead tortoise venerated in a temple to a turtle alive and well, saying he'd rather be like that live turtle, happily dragging his tail through the mud. In the *Zhuangzi*, Daoism stands for nature, spontaneity, and simplicity, against Confucian ritual and complication.

Analects

Lun yu

(fourth to third centuries BCE)

CONFUCIUS (c. 551–c. 479 BCE)

≈ ⁄≈

T he *Analects* (*Lun yu*) or "sayings" of Confucius contain most of what little we know about the philosopher whose ideas formed the core of "Confucianism" (a Western term), which lay behind the beliefs about state and society that underpinned the Chinese imperial system for two thousand years, from the Han dynasty (206 BCE–220 CE) to the fall of the Qing in 1911.

Despite his enormous significance, not much is known about the life of Confucius, a latinized name given by seventeenth-century Jesuit missionaries in China. Born Kong Zhongni, supposedly in 551 BCE, he lived for much of his life in the state of Lu (in present-day Shandong province). As a young man he is said to have held minor offices as Keeper of Granaries and Director of Public Pastures, but his ambition to achieve higher office through his wisdom was never realized, and he traveled from state to state with a group of disciples in search of a sympathetic ruler who would admire and follow his teachings. He lived during a time now known as the "Spring and Autumn." The centuries of "Spring and Autumn" and "Warring States" were also a time known as the "Hundred Schools of Thought," when the proponents of different philosophies (including Confucianism, Daoism, Mohism, and Legalism) sought to impose their views. Confucius was one of many thinkers at the time.

The *Analects* is supposed to have been created by Confucius's disciples but was probably composed long after his death by the disciples of disciples. Though the entries are all brief, it is uneven in content and is seen as a compilation from differing sources. Early references suggest that the *Analects* had existed in various forms and the surviving version is that of Zheng Xuan (127–200 CE), a noted commentator on the Confucian classics. Unlike many early texts that survived only in manuscript copies until woodblock printing became commonplace during the Song dynasty (960–1279), parts of the *Analects* were inscribed on stone in around 175 CE. (The Xiping Stone Classics were carved at the instigation of scholars who wanted to establish a permanent version of the text to prevent arguments about variant texts.) Fragments of the text, probably dating from the Tang dynasty (618–907 CE), have also been found among the great corpus of paper documents dating from the fifth to eleventh centuries CE hidden away at the Buddhist cave complex near Dunhuang.

The text mainly takes the form of brief exchanges or anecdotes: "The master said, 'Do not concern yourself with government matters unless they are the responsibility of your office'; 'When the master was with a mourner, he ate modestly [not till he was full]'; 'If on one day he wept, he did not sing on the same day.'" There are quite a few references to Confucius's behavior and habits, particularly in book 10 (there are twenty brief chapters, or "books," in the *Analects*): "If his mat was not straight, he would not sit on it";* "He did not talk when eating, nor did he talk in bed," and in eating, he sought to balance rice with meat, made sure that gifts of fine meat were not kept too long in case they spoiled, and enjoyed the taste of ginger, although not to excess. In his clothing, he seems to have considered purple and strong red colors unsuited to "the superior man" and so he avoided these colors, even in informal dress. "In summer, he wore an unlined garment but always over an undergarment. He wore a black jacket over a lambskin, an undyed jacket over fawn skin, and a yellow jacket over fox fur. His informal fur robe was long with the right sleeve short. His robe for sleeping in was twice as long as his body and he lay on thick fox and badger skins." The deference of his demeanor, especially in the presence of a duke, but also when in "the vacant place of a prince," was emphasized. He bent low on entering a palace gate, stood respectfully to one side rather than occupy a central position, and he was careful what he wore when on condolence visits.

The main significance of the *Analects* lies in what is conveyed about learning, moral development, leadership, and the relationship between heaven and humans, particularly those in high office. Confucius is not considered an innovator since he reflected many views that were widely held during his time, such as the need to follow "the Way," an undefined path, which Raymond Dawson describes in the Confucian context as "an ideal ethico-political system" rather than the Daoists' "Way of nature."** Another ancient Chinese concept that lies behind the conduct of government in particular is that of the "Mandate of Heaven" (*tianming*), the idea that a good ruler governs with heaven's support—which can be withdrawn if he behaves in an immoral or unjust manner. The confusion and strife of the period in which Confucius lived caused him and others to look back on the early days of the Zhou dynasty (established 1046 BCE) as a golden age of virtuous rulers. In the *Analects*, Confucius says, "I am ruined—I no longer dream of the Duke of Zhou," one of the architects of the Zhou dynasty venerated by Confucius for his nobility and self-sacrifice. And, "I transmit but am no innovator. I am trustworthy and I love antiquity." The sense that innovation is not necessarily helpful to good government is expressed in Confucius's response to a question about good government: "Let the ruler be a ruler, let the minister be a minister, let the father be a father, and the son a son." Being a ruler, or a father, carried the firm implication that the person in question carried out his responsibilities in a just and moral manner. His stress on the status quo is also reflected in his view of *junzi*, the "superior man" or "gentleman," as opposed to the "small man." It is clear from many references that in Confucius's view, the "superior man" can improve himself through study (which Confucius frequently emphasized), but the "small man" is not receptive to learning and will never achieve higher status.

Confucius's conservatism was also characteristic of the era in that he paid no attention to the lowly status of women; indeed, he appeared to consider them as lower than the "small man." One of his rare references to women concerns King Wu, who boasted of having ten competent officials—to which Confucius responded, "As one of them was a woman, there were in fact only nine . . ."

On the basis of the *Analects* alone, with its brief anecdotes of a fundamentally unsuccessful would-be official, it is quite hard to understand how "Confucianism" became the underpinning of the Chinese system of education and bureaucracy. But in the early Han period, the scholar Dong Zhongshu (c. 179–c. 104 BCE) advised the emperor Wudi to establish an imperial academy to train officials, and the "Five Classics" (*Wu jing*)—*Book of Songs, Book of Changes, Book of Documents, Book of Rites, Spring and Autumn Annals*—formed the curriculum. These five works were only loosely associated with Confucius, and it was not until the Song period that official education became more strictly "Confucian" through the use of the "Four Books" (*Si shu*), which were more closely associated with him. These four texts are the *Analects*, the *Mencius* (the work of Confucius's major disciple, Mencius), and two chapters from the *Book of Rites*: "Great Learning" (*Da xue*) and "Doctrine of the Mean" (*Zhongyong*).

Confucius's influence on traditional Chinese society is seen in many ways which go beyond the anecdotes in the *Analects* and his (loose) association with the Four Books and Five Classics. While long-entrenched social concepts such as family loyalty and filial piety, traditionally ascribed to him, antedate the philosopher, the traditional veneration for education can certainly be seen in his works.

Mencius

Mengzi

(fourth century BCE)

MENCIUS (c. 372–c. 289 BCE)

≈ ⁄

L ittle is known about the life of the Confucian philosopher Mencius
(a latinized name), or Mengzi, but he is traditionally described as
the major disciple of Confucius (though he lived over a century later,
during the Warring States period). Like Confucius, he traveled from
state to state, attempting to counsel various rulers. The work ascribed
to Mencius, which bears his name, is one of the Four Books, traditional Confucian texts (including the *Analects* [*Lun yu*]) chosen by the
great philosopher Zhu Xi (1130–1200) during the Song period as fundamental to understanding Confucianism and to passing the imperial
bureaucratic exams. Apart from Mencius's ideas, expressed in his text,
there are a somewhat confused and confusing biography of him in Sima
Qian's *The Grand Scribe's Records* (*Shi ji*) and anecdotes, particularly
referring to his mother who was sufficiently admired to be included
in a first-century BCE compilation, *Stories of Exemplary Women* (*Lie
nu zhuan*). A widow living with her young son in the state of Zou (in
today's Shandong province), she was said to have moved house three
times in an attempt to find a suitable home for him. She moved away
from a house beside a burial ground because the little boy was getting
too interested in funerals and playing at being a grave digger. The next
house was near a market but she soon found him playing at being a
street hawker, which was also unsuitable, so she found a house by a
school where he absorbed more appropriate rituals to emulate. Later she
also intervened in a quarrel between Mencius and his wife, who was so
upset at his criticism that she threatened to return to her parents. Mencius had apparently entered their bedroom without warning and found
her scantily dressed (in another version of the story, she was sitting in
an inappropriate way) and scolded her. His mother reminded him that,
according to proper ritual, a person should announce his arrival at the

gate, should raise his voice when approaching a room (in order to give the inhabitants time to get dressed or sit up straight), and lower the eyes in the room and not stare angrily as Mencius had done. (In another version of the story, it concludes with a mysterious quotation from the *Book of Songs* [*Shi jing*], "When gathering turnips, pay no heed to the roots . . .")

Mencius's ideas are often bracketed with those of another great Confucian philosopher, Xunzi (c. 312–c. 230 BCE), and they are usually described in opposition to each other—with Mencius's view being that humans are born good, although they must still aspire to improvement, while Xunzi declared that human nature was fundamentally bad and needed firm control through education. The argument was fiercely fought at the time and Xunzi (whose book of essays is called *Xunzi*) influenced some of his contemporary thinkers who developed the Legalist school. This was most influential during the brief Qin dynasty (221–206 BCE), when the population was controlled by a carefully compiled legal code (rather than moral exhortation). Xunzi's influence continued through the Han dynasty but effectively disappeared thereafter, never achieving the status of Mencius nor inclusion in the Four Books.

Though the *Mencius* is very much preoccupied with the same concerns as Confucius in the *Analects*—education and self-cultivation, good government and proper reverence for ritual—its composition and style are different. Like the *Analects*, it consists of records of conversations between the philosopher and his contemporaries, but the episodes in the *Mencius* are longer and allow for fuller exposition of ideas. (The *Analects* is very much concerned with the character of Confucius, and the short passages are often somewhat obscure.)

Mencius's ideas about human nature comprise the distinction between humans and animals, for though both have "base" natures or desires, humans also have hearts which can think (the heart being seen as the "thinking" organ) and which distinguish them from animals. In one chapter of the *Mencius*, he debated this with another philosopher, Gaozi, who held that man was fundamentally amoral and this was man's nature. Seeking to separate humans from amoral animals, Mencius argued by analogy, using the definition of "white": Were all white things the same? Was the whiteness of white feathers the same as the whiteness of white jade? Or white snow? And by extension, was the nature of man the same as the nature of a dog or an ox? Mencius thought not.

A long passage in which Mencius is actually discussing the importance of cultivating the "good" heart—but where he uses the analogy of the deforestation of a famous mountain—has often been quoted to demonstrate both changes in the ecology of fourth-century BCE China and the damage that humans could do to their environment.

"The trees on Ox Mountain were once beautiful. But because they were close to a great city, chopped down with axes and hatchets, how could they remain beautiful? But with the rest they got through the days and nights, watered by rain and dew, they were not without new shoots. But then oxen and sheep were brought to graze on the mountain and it became completely bare. Now when people see its bareness, they assume that it was never covered in trees. But is that the nature of the mountain? And when it comes to man, can he be completely lacking in benevolence and righteousness? If he lets go of his good heart, it is like the action of the hatchets and axes on trees. If they are chopped away at every day, can they be beautiful? If a man, despite the rest he gets day and night, the freshness of morning air, in his likes and dislikes is not like other men, it is because he wastes what he has gained. If this happens repeatedly, then the restorative night air will not be sufficient to preserve his good nature. Then he is not very different from animals and people will think he never had much worth. Is this really what man is like? Given its proper care and nourishment, there is nothing that will not grow. Without such nourishment, everything will decay."

The length and depth of exposition of the ideas in the *Mencius*, as well as Mencius's supposed closeness to Confucius, assured the position of the work in the Confucian canon as used from the Song dynasty onward.

Master Sun's Art of War
Sunzi bingfa
(c. 544–c. 496 BCE)
SUN WU (c. 544–c. 496 BCE)

≈ ⁄

In one form or another, *Master Sun's Art of War* (*Sunzi bingfa*), despite its antiquity, is probably one of the best-known Chinese books. It is available in a number of English-language editions and has also been taken up in books by business strategists and management gurus. Earlier applications of the text related more closely to its original intention. Mao Zedong praised the work for its practical application to guerrilla warfare—"forage from the enemy"; "attack where the enemy does not expect you"—and stressed its perennial usefulness to the military. Though the first Western translation was made by a French Jesuit, Jean-Joseph-Marie Amiot (in 1772), later translations included those by military men such as Captain E. F. Calthrop of the British Royal Field Artillery (made between 1905 and 1908).

Recent archaeological discoveries in China have elucidated many of the mysteries about *Master Sun's Art of War*. It had been known from woodblock-printed editions dating from the Song dynasty (960–1279), some 1,500 years after the original compilation, but the discovery of sets of bamboo slips in Han tombs dated to c. 140–118 BCE revealed a very early version of the work. The bamboo slips found at Yinqueshan in Shandong province include the thirteen-section text known from the Song dynasty, as well as five sections that had been lost. The text was found with other military works, including Sun Bin's *The Art of Warfare* (*Sun Bin bingfa*). Until recently there was some confusion between Sun Wu (also called Sunzi), literally Master Sun of Wu, and Sun Bin (c. 380–c. 316 BCE), but it is now clear that we have two separate works, one by Master Sun of Wu and one by a descendant of his, Sun Bin.

Little is known about the life of Sun Wu, who might have been a contemporary of Confucius. There is a description of his activities in Sima Qian's *The Grand Scribe's Records* (*Shi ji*), in which Sun

Wu, serving as an advisor to King Helü of Wu (r. 514–496 BCE), demonstrated the drilling of troops by using the king's women of the court. He lined them up, appointed commanders, and ordered them to drill, "Eyes right! Eyes left!" but they just collapsed with laughter. To the king's horror, Sun Wu ordered that the two women in command (favorites of the king) be executed. After that, the women of the court obeyed his orders. Though early commentators have cast doubt on the story and the cruelty of the exposition, the Yinqueshan bamboo slips bear it out.

Further archaeological discoveries have also elucidated aspects that were previously thought to be anachronistic. The use of crossbows, which transformed Chinese military techniques, has now been pushed back to c. 500 BCE. When the two texts by Sun Wu and Sun Bin were still confused, contradictions about tactics (such as the question of whether or not to attack a fortified city) were problematic, but we can now begin to understand that changes in fortifications as well as modifications of weapons were responsible for the differences, or developments, in the authors' approaches.

Apart from military technology, philosophical concepts form a background to *Master Sun's Art of War*. Ancient Chinese theories of *yin* and *yang* and the Five Elements pervade the text. Soft and hard, weak and strong, these ideas form the basis of analyzing the condition of the enemy and the topographical challenges upon which strategic decisions are to be made, with the proviso that each situation is unique and requires flexibility. The somewhat heterodox and contradictory nature of the text can be explained, as with other early Chinese texts, by its origin as a compilation rather than being one person's work.

While the thirteen sections of *Master Sun's Art of War* vary between the practical and the philosophical, the emphasis on practicality underlies most of the propositions. The question of waging war in distant places and the consequent need to ensure a chain of supplies for an army far from home—which involves considerable expense and difficulty—is discussed at length, with the suggestion that a clever army can supply itself by foraging from the enemy. Such foraging is a tactic, but the most significant preparations are made before any engagement is undertaken, and the outcome of battle should be predictable to a well-prepared general.

Preparation involves "temple calculations" where, it would seem, army commanders meet (in a temple) to assess their chances and weigh the balance of possibilities before engaging in battle. *Master Sun's Art of War* constantly reminds generals that astrology, past history, and omens are not useful indicators of success or otherwise. The commanders need to consider the relative strengths of their own and the enemy's army as well as the advantages of the topography, and various sections of the book describe good and bad situations for different military maneuvers: open areas, hills, valleys, and the multiple varieties of such formations. There are also many references to the relative significance of the "ruler" and the general. *Master Sun's Art of War* comes down firmly on the side of the general—"if the way of battle guarantees you victory, it is right for you to insist on fighting even if the ruler does not want you to" (but also not to engage if success is unlikely)—because the exemplary general is aware of all the circumstances.

Many of the pieces of advice given are effective couplets: "Where you are capable, seek to appear incapable; when you are ready, seek to appear unready; when near, seek to appear far; if the enemy appears to have an advantage, use it; if he seems to be in chaos, take advantage . . . if he is rested, harry him . . . attack when he is unprepared . . . go where he does not expect you." But the general should bear in mind that a fortified city with a defensive moat but no supplies could not be held by any of the great fighters of history. And in the section on "Waging War," the difficulties experienced by ordinary people are spelled out: "maintaining an army at a distance causes poverty," and "when an army is nearby, prices go up and the people's livelihood suffers." The conclusion is that "there is no example of a country profiting from prolonged warfare."

The last section of the book deals with espionage—which provides the essential preparatory foreknowledge underpinning a successful campaign (rather than omens and astrology). There are five different types of spy listed: local spies, inside agents (i.e., recruited enemy officials), double agents, as well as expendable spies (whose lives may be sacrificed) and non-expendable spies who work within the army or outside the army and who furnish real information or supply false information to the enemy. Spies of all sorts are described as a key element in warfare and, indeed, they underpin the message of *Master Sun's Art of War*: preparedness is key.

Almanac

Tongshu

AUTHOR UNKNOWN

~≈ ≈~

Unlike January 1, which marks the beginning of the new year in the Gregorian calendar, the Chinese New Year is a movable feast, celebrated somewhere between mid-January and mid-February. And while the twelve astrological signs of the Western zodiac divide one year into twelve periods, the Chinese zodiac has a twelve-year cycle of animals—including Tiger, Dragon, Horse, and Monkey. Each new year is signified by one of these animals in turn (and they are also used to designate the twelve hours of the traditional Chinese day).

The Gregorian calendar is solar, and the Islamic calendar is lunar; China, on the other hand, for thousands of years has used a lunisolar calendar (i.e., in relation to sun *and* moon). It consists of twelve months, with the New Year fixed as the second new moon after the winter solstice. The solar year is just over 365 days, while the lunar year is circa 354 days. In a lunisolar calendar like that of the Chinese, a whole leap month (not just certain leap days) has to be inserted about every three years. (In Lu Xun's story "My Old Home" ["*Gu xiang*"], the little boy Runtu was born in a leap month [*run*], which was noted in part of his name.) Though the Gregorian calendar was officially adopted in China in 1912 with the advent of the republic, the traditional calendar is still popularly followed and the Chinese New Year remains the major festival of the year.

Because of the complexity of lunisolar calculations, the Chinese calendar and its associated almanac (*Tongshu*) became important household possessions. So significant was the establishment of the annual cycle that from the ninth century CE onward (if not before), private publication of calendars was prohibited by law; setting out the annual calendar was an imperial activity and its publication an imperial monopoly.

The traditional date for the adoption of the lunisolar calendar is 2265 BCE, and calendrical references are found on the inscribed oracle bones used to record divination by the Shang kings (c. 1600–1046 BCE). The significance of calculation lay not only in the need to fix the New Year and subsequent important festivals but also in controlling the agricultural cycle. The agricultural aspect of imperial control was seen in the custom, during the Ming and Qing dynasties, whereby the emperor would follow his New Year observations at the Temple of Heaven in Beijing by proceeding to the Altar of Agriculture next door and plowing the first ceremonial furrow to initiate the new agricultural season.

Imperial astronomers, whose activities are known in detail from the Han dynasty (206 BCE–220 CE) onward, worked out the date of the New Year and predicted other astronomical events such as eclipses, and the calendar was written out for official distribution throughout the country at the start of the year. When Jesuit missionaries first arrived in Beijing in the last years of the sixteenth century, they specifically used their astronomical skills to ingratiate themselves with the Ming emperors. Matteo Ricci (1552–1610) arrived in Beijing in 1598 and was appointed as a court advisor on the strength of his skill in predicting solar eclipses. Ricci was followed by Johann Schreck (1576–1630), who arrived in China in 1619 to continue the work as court astronomer; and he, in turn, was followed by Adam Schall von Bell (1592–1666). Though they incurred the enmity of the previously dominant Muslim court astronomers, Jesuits continued to work in the imperial court after the fall of the Ming in 1644, acting as court astronomers to the new Qing dynasty.

The lunisolar calendar, fixing the dates of significant annual festivals, was only part of the traditional household almanac called *Tongshu* (which literally means "book of all things"). Interestingly, in the collection of paper documents dating from the fifth to the eleventh centuries CE found in the cave complex near Dunhuang, there were a number of manuscript almanacs and even three printed versions, two of these datable to 877 CE and 882 CE—which makes them very early examples of woodblock printing. These early woodblock-printed popular almanacs were illegally produced despite the imperial monopoly, but obviously a lot of money could be made through the sale of such an essential household item.* They list the days of the year that are auspicious or inauspicious for various activities, such as traveling or construction work, and the seasons of the agricultural year: "the start of spring, spring rain, awakening of insects, grain rain, start of summer, full grain, small heat, great heat," and so on. The 877 CE printed almanac from Dunhuang includes a diagram of a house with a garden at the rear, agricultural implements to the western side, a privy to the east, the whole surrounded by a diagram of a geomancer's compass. The cycle of twelve animals is also charmingly depicted.**

Consultation of the almanac is recorded for example in Cao Xueqin's novel *Dream of the Red Chamber* (*Hongloumeng*), where the (eventually unsuccessful) examination candidate prepares to make his trip to the capital by looking up an auspicious day for travel. And in H. Y. Lowe's *The Adventures of Wu* (1940/1941), which describes life in Beijing in the first half of the 1900s, the family almanac is consulted and the day is found to be a good day for entering school, making sacrifices, shaving, commencing building works, and buying property, but a bad day for crossing rivers.

Elements in the almanac of popular use are the combinations of the ten "heavenly stems" and twelve "earthly branches," which are used to form a sixty-year cycle (often used traditionally for dates) and to predict a child's fortune by examining the stem-and-branch combinations for the year, month, day, and hour of the birth. The twelve animals, which designate subsequent years, are also popular in fortune-telling. Their characteristics, briefly, are as follows: Rat: "clever, home-loving"; Ox: "gambles but generous and patient"; Tiger: "loyal but quick to anger"; Rabbit: "clever and talented"; Dragon (the best sign): "powerful"; Snake: "quick to seize opportunities"; Horse: "hardworking"; Goat or Sheep: "patient and gentle"; Monkey: "quick-witted and clever"; Rooster: "reliably punctual"; Dog: "not a leader"; and Pig: "loves comfort."

Much of fortune-telling and divination was a specialist trade, but the modern almanac still contains sections on prognostication by facial features and handreading; fortune-telling by physical sensations such as eye tics, ringing in the ears, or burning ears; tables of auspicious and inauspicious dates; good and bad days for particular activities; and plenty of charms consisting of magical Chinese characters to ward off various evil spirits or unhappy events.

There are also strange sections left over from the past, such as the charming story of Confucius and the child Chong Ni, in which the child gets the better of the great philosopher. One section discusses how to tell if a cat is any use: it should have a loud voice to frighten rats but if it has a long body, it will leave to live with another family. And there is a guide on how to run the home: Rise at daybreak and water the dust in the courtyard, then sweep it away. You should keep your house tidy. Do not hire handsome servants, but reward all servants appropriately and be nice to your neighbors. Beware of people who move like crabs as they are not straightforward.

Sold to this day in vast numbers throughout the Chinese world, almanacs with their red covers and auspicious pictures remain a key element of the Chinese year (although only certain sections would be consulted on a regular basis today, except perhaps by the superstitious). However, important elements remain the listings of the dates of major festivals such as the Double Fifth (on the fifth day of the fifth lunar month, near the summer solstice), a day of danger but one on which dragon boat races are held, and the Mid-Autumn Festival (on the fifteenth day of the eighth lunar month), when it is good to climb a hill and drink wine with friends while admiring the great globe of the harvest moon.

Proper Ritual
Yi li

(Western [or Former] Han/206 BCE–9 CE)

AUTHOR UNKNOWN

～ ∕

Confucius was preoccupied with ritual and its proper observance, as the constant references in the *Analects* (*Lun yu*) show. Throughout China's imperial history, at every social level, from the imperial court to the peasant family, ritual remained crucial. According to traditional Chinese cosmology, the correct ordering of human affairs—expressed by the performance of the correct rituals, whether in the home or at court—would please heaven and thus ensure the safety and prosperity of the state.

The importance of ritual at the Qing court (1644–1911), for example, can be seen in the many paintings of ritual events such as the annual reception of foreign ambassadors at court, the annual ceremony of plowing the first (ceremonial) furrow in the Temple of Agriculture, and the several tours of southern China by the early Qing emperors and their massive retinues.* The paintings show how palace officials and servants were ranged in rows, bearing pennants and placards of different colors; how the emperors were carried in imperial yellow sedan chairs, with yellow silk parasols held above their heads, through ranks of soldiers; and how animals were laid out for sacrifice. The Qing court also published a multivolume illustrated work, *Illustrated Compendium of Ritual Objects for the Court* (*Huangchao liqi tushi*) (1766), which depicts the different ceramic vessels, bamboo baskets, ritual weapons, and court uniforms appropriate for each season and each ceremony. That such paintings and publications appeared during the Qing may relate to the fact that the Qing emperors were not Chinese but Manchus from the far northeast, and they were particularly concerned to demonstrate their mastery of Chinese protocol and ritual in their government of the country. (Earlier versions of such paintings and manuals of ritual and ritual implements may well have existed but none have survived.)

Though there were revivals of ritual—such as those enacted for Confucius's birthday in the Confucian temple in Qufu in Shandong province (witnessed by Linqing, the author of *Tracks of a Wild Goose in the Snow* [*Hongxuan yinyuan tuji*] in the mid-nineteenth century)—the establishment of a Communist government in China swept aside most traditional rites and ceremonies. The continuing importance of ritual is most evident in other East Asian cultures such as Japan but also, to a lesser extent, in Taiwan. The long-held practice of thrice refusing an offer of a government appointment, for example, with the assumption that the offer will be agreed after three polite refusals, still persists.

The *Proper Ritual* (*Yi li*), a book that has also been translated as *Etiquette and Rites* or *Ceremonies and Rituals*, was probably compiled during the Western Han dynasty but based on a corpus of earlier texts describing ceremonial and ritual practices. It is one of the "Three Ritual Classics" (*San li*), together with the *Rites of Zhou* (*Zhou li*) and the *Book of Rites* (*Li ji*; this is also one of the Five Classics), both similar compilations of a similar date. The earliest surviving fragments of the *Proper Ritual* were found in a first-century CE tomb at Wuwei in the northwestern province of Gansu (in 1959), and the earliest printing of the text was in the tenth century CE.

In China there has always been a love of classification and numerical listings, and the Confucian classics underwent various categorizations. In addition to the Five Classics (*Wu jing*) and the Four Books (*Si shu*), a grouping of "Thirteen Classics" (*Shisan jing*) was devised during the Song (960–1279). The "Thirteen Classics" consist of: the Five Classics (*Book of Songs, Book of Changes, Book of Documents, Book of Rites,* and *Spring and Autumn Annals*—which was subdivided into three parts); the *Analects* and the *Mencius*; the *Proper Ritual* and the *Rites of Zhou*; as well as the *Book of Filial Piety* (*Xiao jing*, dating probably to the Western Han) and the *Er ya* ("Approaching Correctness," a lexicographical work dating to circa the third century BCE).

The *Proper Ritual* differs slightly from the other two ritual texts in that it is concerned almost entirely with the behavior and rites of officials of different rank and in a variety of formal situations, rather than the history of rituals or details of the implements used. The seventeen chapters of the *Proper Ritual* include: Capping rites marking the end of childhood for the son of a common officer; Nuptial rites for a common officer; Rites for common officers attending a meeting; Rites of a district symposium; Rites of a district archery contest; Banquet ritual at state (not imperial) level; Rites of great archery contests; Rites of courtesy calls (state to state); Rite of the "gong" feast for a great officer; Rites of imperial audience; Mourning dress; Mourning rites for a common officer; Post-burial rites for a common officer; Rites of a simple food offering; Rites of a [more complex] double food offering; and Servants clearing the way. This last rite was an important part of official meeting and travel protocol: whenever an official left his office, his way would be cleared, according to his rank, by servants, standard bearers, and soldiers.

As stated in the *Proper Ritual*, the banquet offered by the prince to an envoy from another state begins with an invitation to enter the palace (which has to be politely declined several times), much kowtowing by the envoy, and the preparation of food cooked in great tripods. Finally, the envoy reaches the banquet hall and kowtows twice:

The tripods are brought in and the stands filled:

Ordinary officers take up the tripods, leaving the covers outside the gate and, entering the door in order, lay them to the south of the tablet, facing south and arranged in importance starting from the west.** The men on the right draw out the poles and, sitting down, lay them to the west of the tripods, afterward going out by the west of the tripods. The men on the left then await the order to set the meat on the stands.

Then the cooks bring in the stands and set them out to the south of the tripods; the pantrymen, facing south, put the ladles into the tripods and withdraw.

Then the great officers, in order of precedence, wash their hands, standing to the southwest of the water jar, and facing west, in rank order, starting from the north. They go forward and wash in turn, the man withdrawing meeting the other man coming forward in front of the jar. When their washing is finished, they go forward in turn and, facing south, ladle out the meat.

Those who set the meat on the stands face west.

When the fish and dried game are cooked, they set the joints on the stands with the underside foremost.

The fish are seven in number, laid lengthwise on the stand, and resting on their right sides.

The set of entrails and stomachs are seven in number and occupy the same stand.

There are seven sides of pork on one stand.

The entrails, stomachs, and sides of pork are all laid across the stands, and hanging down at either side.

When the great officers have finished the ladling, they place the ladles in the tripods and, withdrawing in the reverse order of their coming, return to their places.

Laying out the principle set of viands [the main dishes]:

The prince goes down to wash his hands and the envoy descends also, the prince declining the honor. When the washing is finished, the prince, with one salute and one yielding of precedence, goes up the steps, the envoy going up also.

Then the understeward brings the wet hash [stew] and sauce from the east chamber, and the prince sets them down. The envoy, declining and with his face to the north, removes them and sets them down on the east in their proper place.

Then the prince takes his stand on the inside of the inner wall, looking west, and the envoy stands to the west of the steps in an expectant attitude.

Then the understeward brings out from the east chamber six holders [dishes] and places them to the east of the sauce, and arranged in importance starting from the west. There are pickled vegetables and, on their east, the pickled hashes. Then come pickled rush-roots, with, to their south, elk flesh hash with the bones in; and on the west of this, pickled leek flowers, with deer flesh hash following.

Then the officers place the meat-stands to the south of the holders, and arranged in importance starting from the west. The beef comes first, then the mutton, and then the pork. The fish is to the south of the beef, and is followed by the dried game and the entrails and stomachs, the sides of pork being by themselves on the east side.

Different types of millet are served in dishes with tortoise-shaped covers and "the wine for drinking" is poured into a goblet. Offerings from these dishes are then made, with much kowtowing before the prince invites the envoy to take his mat and eat some millet porridge.

It can be seen from this small section of the description of one type of official banquet that the guests did not attend for the food which would have been cold, to say the least. What was all-important was the ritual.

The Grand Scribe's Records
Shi ji

(first century BCE)

SIMA QIAN (c. 150–c. 86 BCE)

≈ ⁄

Sima Qian was the son of Sima Tan (d. c. 108 BCE). Sima Tan was "Prefect of the Grand Scribes" under the Han emperor Wudi (r. 141–87 BCE), and his official duties were "the supervision of sacrifices and the calendar, the management of astrological questions, and the care of the imperial library." According to Sima Qian, it was his father who began to compile a volume setting down all of China's history from the beginning to his own time, using the resources of the imperial library. Sima Qian, succeeding his father in office, was determined to continue the project. When he offended the emperor by defending an army commander who had been betrayed while fighting the Xiongnu tribes in the north, he was sentenced to either death or castration. He chose the latter so that he could continue his father's work. Sadly, he could have avoided both punishments had he had enough money to pay a large fine.

Sima Qian's universal history, *The Grand Scribe's Records* (*Shi ji*), was of huge significance to Chinese historiography. Written in a clear and straightforward manner, making use of imperial archives to record events in a largely chronological sequence—but with the addition of appendices on ritual, music, the calendar, astronomy, sacrifices, economics, and biographies of notables—it set the style for subsequent histories. His work covered some 2,500 years of Chinese history, from the time of the legendary Yellow Emperor down to Sima Qian's own lifetime, the reign of Wudi. No previous historical writing in China had been so extensive in scope, either in terms of time span or coverage of topics such as biography and astronomy. Earlier historical works such as the *Book of Documents* (*Shu jing*) and the *Spring and Autumn Annals* (*Chun qiu*) were collections of documents and commentary, and in the case of the latter restricted to events in the single state of Lu.

China's history after *The Grand Scribe's Records* was recorded in much detail in the great "Twenty-Four Histories," each covering a single dynasty. These were compiled by successor dynasties, many decades or centuries after the fall of the dynasty described, and are often prejudiced—for the victorious dynasty needed to justify the overthrow of its predecessor—but their basis in archives means that they are still useful. The first "dynastic" history book after *The Grand Scribe's Records* is the *History of the Han (Han shu)*, covering the period from 206 BCE to 23 CE. It was completed in 111 CE and it noted that the purpose of history was based on the approach of two earlier compilations: "The *Book of History* [or *Documents*] broadens one's information and is the practice of wisdom; the *Spring and Autumn Annals* passes moral judgement on events and is the symbol of good faith."* Thus chronological description was important but essentially somewhat secondary to the didactic and improving nature of historical writing. Reflecting the increasing veneration of Confucius during the Han, it was believed (inaccurately) that Confucius arranged the *Spring and Autumn Annals* and wrote the prefaces to the *Book of Documents*—thus Confucius's views on the conduct of rulers and the existence of a past golden age of perfect rule were intrinsic to the writing of later histories.

Sima Qian recorded his father's dying words, which included praise for the current Han dynasty that had "put in order the laws" and "settled questions of rites and ceremonies." The Han had overthrown the short-lived Qin (221–206 BCE), which was accused of discarding and destroying such works as the *Book of Songs* and the *Book of Documents* by order of the First Emperor. In this context it was essential that official historians clarified the Han right to rule by vilifying the regime it had overthrown (despite the fact that Sima Qian himself had incurred imperial wrath). Vilifying the Qin helped to prove that the good Han dynasty was not destructive but had received heaven's approval, the Mandate of Heaven, to rule.

Sima Qian's account of the reign of the First Emperor (who ordered the creation of the massive "buried army" of terracotta warriors, to be placed beside his tomb) is told chronologically. In 221 BCE, the year in which the ruler of Qin ended his conquests by uniting all of China, he issued edicts about his new rule and decreed that since (according to the cycle of the Five Elements) the Zhou dynasty had been under the element of fire, "Qin must be able to conquer fire, so now came the era of water. The start of the year was changed to the first day of the tenth month . . . Black was decreed the imperial color for garments and flags, and six became the paramount number . . . carriages were to be six feet wide and the emperor's carriage was drawn by six horses." This decree conjures up the impressive sight of an imperial procession, with black pennants flying from the carriages filled with black-clad officials passing through villages of peasants in undyed cloth garments.

One of the most notorious acts of the First Emperor, set out in detail by Sima Qian to underline the emperor's refusal to accept Confucian beliefs, was his "burning of the books." His prime minister, Li Si, is recorded as suggesting "that all historical records, except those of Qin, be burned. If anyone who is not an official court scholar dares to keep ancient songs, historical documents, or the works of the Hundred Schools [of Thought], they should be publicly executed . . . If thirty days after this order they have not had these books destroyed, they should have their faces tattooed [a punishment] and be condemned to hard labor on the Great Wall."

One of the biographies in *The Grand Scribe's Records* is that of Confucius, which may be compared with the description Sima Qian recorded of the appearance and character of the First Emperor. Confucius is accorded a very long biography, and Sima Qian's detailed account forms an important part of the Han dynasty elevation of Confucius from unsuccessful advisor to preeminent thinker. It begins with his birth in around 551 BCE after his mother, far younger than his father (who had contracted an "unusual marriage" with such a young girl), prayed for a child on Ni Hill, a sacred hill near Qufu. Confucius's filial piety is evident in the care he took to bury his mother in a temporary grave until he could find his father's remains and unite his parents in a single grave. Described as being over two meters tall, his career is first set out in a breathless rush before a more detailed account. Promoted from his office in charge of saddlery and harnesses, he "left Lu; he was chased out of Qi, rejected in Song and Wei, endangered between Chen and Cai, and then returned to Lu." A further breathless list of names and events follows: "When Confucius was thirty-five, on account of a cockfight Ji had had with Hou, Ji was regarded as the guilty party by Duke Zhao of Lu. Duke Zhao led his soldiers to attack Ji, but Ji, massing his family forces with those of Chen and Zhou, defeated Duke Zhao who fled to Qi. Soon after there was a revolt in Lu and Confucius went to Qi to serve Guo in the hope of thus making contact with Duke Jing. He discussed the music of Qi and listened to songs. He studied them and abstained from meat for three months. He was praised by the people of Qi. When Duke Jing asked Confucius about government, he replied, 'In order for there to be good government, the ruler must be a ruler, the subject a subject, the father a father, and the son a son.' Duke Jing replied, 'Well said.'"

Apart from his height, little is said about Confucius's personal appearance, although remarks about his proper behavior (taken from the last section of the *Analects* [*Lun yu*]) abound in *The Grand Scribe's Records*. By contrast, the physical description of the First Emperor takes the form of a report by Wei Liao, who came to advise the emperor in 237 BCE, during the period in which he was undertaking the conquests leading up to 221 BCE. Despite the fact that "he treated Wei Liao as an equal, sharing clothes, food, and drink with him . . . Wei Liao said, 'The King of Qin has a nose like a wasp, the breast of a chicken, and a voice like a jackal. He is merciless and has the heart of a tiger or a wolf. He may humble himself when he is in difficulty but when he is successful he swallows men up without scruple . . . If he succeeds in conquering all, we shall all be his captives . . .'"

Even though many subsequent dynasties carried out ruthless censorship and literary purges, and despite the lack of contemporary records corroborating his supposed horrible deeds, Sima Qian's account of the First Emperor helped to set him up as a demonic figure, a reputation which persists to this day.

Nineteen Old Poems
Gu shi shijiu shou

(Eastern [or Later] Han/25–220 CE)

AUTHOR UNKNOWN

≈ ⁄

The *Nineteen Old Poems* (*Gu shi shijiu shou*) are thought to have been composed during the Eastern Han dynasty. They survived through their inclusion in the *Selections of Refined Literature* (*Wen xuan*), a famous anthology of model forms of poetry and prose writing (featuring over 700 text pieces by over 100 writers) that was compiled between 520 and 530 CE by Xiao Tong, son of the emperor Wu of the Liang dynasty (502–557 CE). During the Song dynasty (960–1279) this anthology became a very significant source for all those wishing to succeed professionally, particularly in the first stage of the examination system that enabled entry into the imperial bureaucracy. A popular rhyme noted that "if you master the *Wen xuan*, you are halfway to your licentiate."

Though the *Nineteen Old Poems* are anonymous, it is often assumed that they were written by an aristocrat, because the poems' themes and descriptions are of a rich lifestyle, of abandoned women and traveling men, and contain political allusions relevant to imperial courtiers (although these themes were common, almost intrinsic, in a great deal of earlier and later Chinese poetry).

Significantly, in terms of form the *Nineteen Old Poems* are in fact not "old" but represent a radical departure from the previous *shi* poetry style, which was almost invariably cast in regular lines of four characters (including the poems in the *Book of Songs* [*Shi jing*]). The *Nineteen Old Poems* have regular five-character lines instead, thus forming a new *shi* style, often with a caesura or break after the first two characters. (The total number of lines in each poem varies.) Though in later centuries poems using seven-character lines became more common (with the caesura after the fourth character), both types—lines with five characters, and seven-character lines—reveal a rhythm that Perry Link has described as deeply embedded in modern Chinese, used even in traffic directives and slogans.

The *shi* form of poetry has a long history, deriving from the *Book of Songs* and developing into verses composed of lines of four, five, or seven characters. The *fu* form, on the other hand, described as "rhymed prose" (i.e., longer pieces with varying line lengths), developed during the Han dynasty (206 BCE–220 CE).

In many of the *Nineteen Old Poems*, in the first few lines the caesura is preceded by duplication, which creates a strong pattern that is not always reflected in translations. A characteristic example of the format is the second poem, with its equally characteristic theme of abandonment:

> Green, green, the grass on the riverbank
>
> Thick, thick, the willows in the garden
>
> Fine, fine, the lady in the tower
>
> Pale, pale, by the window
>
> Fair, fair, her rouged face
>
> Fine, fine, her outstretched hand.
>
> Once she was a singing girl
>
> Now the wife of an unfaithful man.
>
> The philanderer left and has not returned
>
> How hard it is alone in this empty bed.

The tenth poem is similar in theme and form but refers to folk tradition rather than a personal history:

> High, high, the herdboy's star
>
> Bright, bright, the girl by the river
>
> Clack, clack, the shuttle of her loom.
>
> At the end of the day she has not finished the pattern
>
> Her tears fall like rain.

The river is clear and shallow

The distance between them is short.

Full, full the river between them

Looking, looking, unable to speak.

The "herdboy's star" is Altair, and Vega is known in Chinese folklore as "the weaving maid's star." They stand on either side of the "heavenly river," the Milky Way. According to Chinese legend, the two lovers, the herdboy and the weaving maid, can only meet once a year when a flock of magpies forms a bridge that enables them to cross the "river" on the seventh day of the seventh lunar month.

The sixth poem also dwells on separation:

Passing the river, I gather lotuses

In the lotus marshes there are many fragrant plants

For whom do I pick them?

My love is far away

I turn and look back to my home village

The road is long, limitless and endless,

Hearts united yet living apart

A painful sadness until we grow old.

Here, the narrator appears to be a man, and though the separation would seem to be from his wife or mistress, the theme of separation and distance is also used to indicate political distance from a ruler and the theme of exile, from court or from home.

A similar idea is expressed in the first poem:

Traveling on, on, again on,

I am alive yet separated from you

Over ten thousand miles lie between us

Each on one edge of the sky
The road is difficult and long
Who knows if we will meet again?
The barbarian horse turns to the north wind
The bird from Yue perches on southern branches
It is a long time since we parted
Daily, my clothes and belt hang looser
Floating clouds hide the bright sun
The traveler does not wish to return
Thinking of you makes me grow old
Months and years past, suddenly it is evening
But let us not dwell on this
Try to eat and thrive.

That separation does not mean death is emphasized in the second line and recurs in the last line, where there is a determination to survive the ordeal. Some have seen this slightly odd emphasis as referring to the earlier *Songs of the South* (*Chu ci*)—an anthology of poems associated with the southern state of Chu and attributed to Qu Yuan (c. 340– c. 278 BCE)—which includes odes addressed to the spirits of the dead, hoping to call the spirits back to the world.*

Here, however, the main character stresses the fact that he is still living. Distance is emphasized in the lines about the horse and the bird. The horse, associated with northern tribes, is described as "barbarian," and Yue was the name of an area in the south of China. The distance and the differences between north and south China, including their different inhabitants, perhaps express some of the fears of the period in which the nineteen poems were written—the Han dynasty was weakening and the threat of invasion and disunion was growing. The line "Floating clouds hide the bright sun" anticipates a popular poetic trope: the "bright sun" stands for the emperor and "clouds" for political problems—often poor advisors—preventing the emperor from seeing clearly. This poem can therefore be understood as a lament about separation from loved ones—but also as the grief of the sage separated from his ruler.

The ninth poem is a simpler lament, set in an enclosed domestic courtyard:

> In the courtyard grows a marvelous tree
>
> A profusion of flowers among the strong green leaves
>
> I reach for a branch and pick a wonderful flower
>
> I will send it to the one I love.
>
> The sweet scent fills my breast and sleeves.
>
> The road is long, how shall I send it?
>
> The flower in itself is not worth it
>
> But I am saddened by the time we have been separated.

These themes of love and separation, as well as carefully concealed hints of political problems, remained characteristic of Chinese poetry throughout the centuries.

Records of the Buddhist Kingdoms
Foguo ji
(fifth century CE)

FAXIAN (c. 337–c. 422 CE)

~~~~

Faxian was a Buddhist monk from Shanxi province who in the year 399 set out on foot from China to India in search of Buddhist scriptures. *Records of the Buddhist Kingdoms* (*Foguo ji*) is the account of his journey and of what he saw in India and Sri Lanka. Faxian's work was very influential both in the development of Chinese Buddhism, through his collection of Buddhist scriptures and their subsequent translation into Chinese, and also through the rediscovery in the nineteenth century of Buddhist monuments in India recorded in the account of his travels.*

Buddhism (in a variety of concepts and practices) came to China from India sometime around the first century CE, brought along the series of ancient commercial routes (known as the Silk Road) that ran along the northern and southern edges of the Central Asian deserts. Originally an ascetic, monastic tradition, over centuries Buddhism was gradually transformed in China, for the monastic tradition ran counter to China's older belief systems that stressed family cohesion and family worship. The possibility of salvation in paradise through Buddhist practice, a concept lacking in Chinese religion and philosophy, may have offered some hope to many Chinese during the difficult period of disruption and division after the fall of the Han in 220 CE. Despite occasional persecutions during the Tang period (618–907 CE)—largely due to the great economic wealth of the major Buddhist temples at the time—Buddhism remained a significant aspect of Chinese culture and belief.

The first translations of Indian Buddhist texts into Chinese were made by the Parthian monk An Shigao around 148 CE, followed by a series of translations by the Gandharan monk Lokaksema c. 164–c. 186 CE. These translations were of sutras (sermons or discourses of the Buddha) and commentaries but not of the *vinaya*, texts dealing with rules for Buddhist monks and nuns. Faxian wrote, "When I was in

Chang'an [today's Xi'an] I regretted the lack of the Buddhist rules, so in 399 I agreed with Huijing, Daozheng, Huiying, Huiwei, and others to go to India to seek out the *vinaya*."

This group of monks set out northwestward on the Silk Road toward the great Central Asian deserts that lie between China and India. Beyond Dunhuang, Faxian said, "in the desert [literally, the 'river of sand'] there are evil spirits and hot winds that kill all men who encounter them. Above, no birds fly; below, no animals move. Looking in all directions for a route to cross the desert, as far as the eye can see, there is nothing that can be perceived except dead men's bones marking the route." They traveled to the oasis town of Khotan (today's Hetian), where the inhabitants followed Mahayana Buddhism; further west, in the oasis of Kashgar (Kashi), near where the northern and southern Silk Roads met (and where a route led through the mountains to Afghanistan and India), they encountered the variant tradition now known as Theravada Buddhism. They reached Gandhara, ruled by a descendant of the great patron of Buddhism, Emperor Ashoka, and the group divided. Some of the monks were ill and some stayed to care for them; others went elsewhere, leaving Faxian traveling on his own to "the place of the Buddha's skull" in Nagarahara (today's Jalalabad, Afghanistan). "In the country of Nagarahara, in the city of Xiluo, is the Buddha's skull bone, now covered with gold and the seven precious jewels.[**] The king deeply venerated the skull bone and feared that it might be stolen, so he ordered eight men of notable families to hold a seal each and these seals were used to seal up and protect the shrine. Every morning the eight men went together and each inspected their own seal and then the door was opened. When the door was opened, they washed their hands in scented water. The Buddha's skull was brought out and placed on a high platform . . . The skull bone is yellowish, a rounded square, about four inches long and slightly convex. Every day when it is brought out, the protectors of the skull climb a high tower and beat huge drums, blow on conch shells, and clash bronze cymbals. On hearing this, the king comes out to offer flowers and incense and make obeisance. Every day he enters the precinct through the East Gate and leaves by the West Gate."

Faxian appears to have stayed in India for ten years or more, visiting such sites as Kapilavastu, the Buddha's childhood home; Bodh

Gaya, the place of his enlightenment; Varanasi, near where the Buddha preached his first sermon; and more Buddhist sites such as Vaishali and Ramagrama, and Ashoka's pillar at Sarnath.

For two years he then visited Sri Lanka, which he described as "the country of the Buddha's tooth"; he saw the shrine of the Buddha's tooth at Kandy and, more significantly, obtained a copy of the *vinaya* and other Buddhist scriptures, "all in Sanskrit," as he wrote. Eventually Faxian returned to China by sea. The trip was dangerous for the ship was frequently tossed by gales and seems to have been blown off course to Java. He described how he had boarded a merchants' ship which was dangerously overloaded with more than two hundred people. During a gale, the merchants ordered many things to be thrown overboard to lessen the weight of the vessel. Faxian threw his water pitcher into the sea and, "fearing that the merchants would throw his sutras overboard, prayed with all his heart to the Bodhisattva Guanyin that he might return to China." (Chapter 25 of the *Lotus Sutra* contains a long passage in which it is recommended that all in peril, whether from robbers, falling rocks, childbirth, fire, demons, or dragons, should call on Guanyin, whose name in Chinese means "the one who hears the cries of the world.") Faxian wrote of his prayer, "I have traveled very far in search of the dharma, let me get home to spread the dharma everywhere." Then a great wind blew for thirteen days and nights and they came to an island and were able to find the place where the boat was leaking. According to the *Records of the Buddhist Kingdoms*, Faxian on his long journey "had traveled through more than thirty countries . . . [and afterward] he recorded his experiences on bamboo slips and silk."

When Faxian returned to China in the year 421, he brought with him the *Mahasanghika Vinaya* from Pataliputra in Central India (which he translated into Chinese before his death) and the *Mahisasaka Vinaya* from Sri Lanka. The massive work of translation of Buddhist texts to which Faxian contributed had another lasting effect: because Buddhism remained a significant religion in East Asia for many centuries while it declined in South Asia, many Sanskrit sutras have survived only in their Chinese (and Mongolian and Tibetan) translations.

Lotus Sutra
Saddharmapundarika sutra
(translation into Chinese third to fifth centuries CE)

AUTHOR UNKNOWN

Diamond Sutra
Vajracchedikaprajnaparamita sutra
(translation into Chinese fifth century CE)

AUTHOR UNKNOWN

~ ~

Buddhist images and Buddhist texts were brought to China from South Asia to serve as models for temple art and for translation from Sanskrit (and Prakrit) into Chinese. Over hundreds of years, numerous Chinese monks, including Faxian (c. 337–c. 422 CE) and Xuanzang (c. 602–664 CE), traveled to India in search of sutras (sermons or discourses of the Buddha) and other Buddhist texts. (Xuanzang, born in Henan province, set out for India in 629, against imperial orders, and returned in 645 to devote the rest of his life to translating the many sutras he had brought back with him.) The translation industry in China was such that many sutras now exist only in their Chinese version, while the originals were lost as Buddhism declined in its homeland. The whole process of translation was elaborate because Sanskrit texts contained not only a strange vocabulary related to the Buddha's life and faith practice in India, but new and complex ideas for which there was no existing vocabulary in Chinese. It seems that the early translators decided to use a version of Chinese that was close to the vernacular, so that many people could understand it. They often had to work in teams, with Chinese alongside non-Chinese interpreters such as An Shigao (fl. 148–180 CE), who was a Parthian; Zhu Fahu (also called Dharmaraksha, fl. c. 233–c. 310 CE) of Indo-Scythian origin; and Kumarajiva (334–413 CE), who had a Kashmiri father and a Kuchean mother.*

One of the most popular Buddhist sutras in China was the *Lotus Sutra* (*Saddharmapundarika sutra* [or, in Chinese, *Miaofa lianhua jing*], meaning "The Sutra of the Lotus of the Wonderful Law"). First translated by Zhu Fahu in about 286 CE, the most popular version was that made by Kumarajiva in 406 CE. In this sutra the Buddha addressed his followers through a long series of very varied parables, hoping to lead them to Buddhahood, to freedom from illusion. Some parables are straightforward: the one on the dragon king's daughter shows that women, too, can achieve enlightenment; that on medicinal plants shows that plants grow in different ways despite receiving the same basic nourishment. Other parables are more complex. There is the man, for example, who sews a valuable jewel into his friend's garment when the latter is asleep. Unaware, the friend wanders through life in poverty, despite the jewel in his possession.

In China, the most popular part of the *Lotus Sutra* is chapter 25, in which the Buddha describes the efficacy of the Bodhisattva Avalokitesvara. (Bodhisattvas are beings who have achieved the possibility of nirvana but who choose to remain in the world to lead others to salvation.) Avalokitesvara's name was rendered in Chinese as Guanshiyin, usually shortened to Guanyin, which in its full form means "hearing/paying attention to the sounds/cries of the world." As the chapter makes clear, the Bodhisattva does not just hear the cries of those in trouble, he responds and saves: "The Bodhisattva Inexhaustible Significance got up, faced the Buddha, uncovered his right shoulder and asked the Buddha, 'World-Honored One, what is the reason for the name of the Bodhisattva Guanshiyin [the one who hears the cries of the world]?' The Buddha replied to Inexhaustible Significance, 'Good man, if any of the innumerable hundreds of thousands, ten thousands of living beings who are suffering hear about the Bodhisattva Guanshiyin and recite his name with a full heart, the Bodhisattva will immediately hear their voices and they will be rescued. If a person holding to the name of the Bodhisattva Guanshiyin enters a great fire, the fire cannot burn him because of the Bodhisattva's awe-inspiring spiritual power. If a person is tossed about on a great lake and calls out the Bodhisattva's name, he will find [the safety of] a shallow place. If the hundreds of thousands, ten thousand living beings who look for gold, silver, lapis lazuli, mother-of-pearl, carnelian, coral, pearls . . . embark upon the great sea, an evil wind might blow their ship to the country of the evil spirits. But if even one of them calls the name of the Bodhisattva Guanshiyin, they will be saved from the peril of the evil spirits. This is the reason he is called Guanshiyin.'" (Faxian for one prayed to Guanshiyin/Guanyin during his dangerous sea voyage back to China.) The chapter continues: "'If a person who is in danger calls out the name of the Bodhisattva Guanshiyin, the knives and sticks will be broken into pieces and he will be saved . . . If a person, whether guilty or not, has been imprisoned in a cangue [a great square board, like the stocks, that was placed around the neck of criminals in traditional China] or has his body bound by chains, if he calls out the name of the Bodhisattva Guanshiyin, his fetters will break and he will be freed . . . If there is a woman who wants a male child, who worships and makes offerings to the Bodhisattva Guanshiyin, then the birth will go well and the good fortune will be achieved . . .'"

Interestingly, while in India the Bodhisattva Avalokitesvara was male (like all other Bodhisattvas), in China Guanshiyin underwent a gradual, though incomplete, transformation into a woman. This was presumably because his merciful powers were associated with female characteristics. We have depictions of a bearded and mustached deity in the Tang (618–907 CE), but later images of Guanyin, especially the popular Blanc-de-Chine porcelains of the Ming (1368–1644), definitely suggest the female form, although her feet were never bound.

Another very popular sutra in China was the *Diamond Sutra* (*Vajracchedikaprajnaparamita sutra* [or, in Chinese, *Jingang banruo poluomiduo jing*]), particularly in Kumarajiva's translation of c. 401 CE. There was a later version by Xuanzang (in the early 660s), but Kumarajiva's remained a favorite for recitation. It is usually called the *Diamond Sutra* in English after the translation made by Max Müller in 1894, although it should probably be more accurately entitled "The sutra of the perfection of wisdom which cuts like a thunderbolt."** The sutra begins, in the time-honored way, with the Buddha seated in a garden, surrounded by monks, in this case answering the question posed by an elderly monk, Subhuti, who wants to know how someone wishing to follow the Bodhisattva path should proceed: "How should he control the mind?" The question is posed several times and the

Buddha's answers discuss the doctrine of emptiness through paradoxical argument, but also emphasize the repetition of the text of the sutra—not the amassment of wealth or even the practice of charity. "Incalculable, immeasurable" merit, worth more than heaps of jewels, can be gained by frequent recitation.

Buddhist "merit," which could transform a person's position in the cycle of rebirths or on the path to Bodhisattvahood—achieved by recitation of the Buddha's words or by repetitive painting of Buddha images (creating "Caves of the Thousand Buddhas")—probably had a significant role in the invention of printing in China some five hundred or more years before Gutenberg. As mentioned, the world's earliest surviving, securely dated, printed "book" is a copy of the *Diamond Sutra* (Kumarajiva's translation) printed in China in 868 CE. The colophon explains that it was commissioned by Wang Jie, "on behalf of his parents," as he hoped that printing multiple copies of the sutra for free distribution to temples would enable his parents to escape the cycle of rebirths.***

The complexity of argument within the *Diamond Sutra* contrasts with the simplicity of its message: to learn it and recite it will bring the comfort of infinite merit.

Poems

(eighth century)

LI BAI (701–762)

Poems

(eighth century)

DU FU (712–770)

≫ ⚞

L i Bai (or Li Po, in the older Wade-Giles romanization) and Du Fu (Wade-Giles romanization: Tu Fu) are popularly considered China's greatest poets. Their collected poems, however, were not published until long after their deaths. Examples of their works are included in the enduringly popular collection *Three Hundred Tang Poems* (*Tang shi sanbai shou*) (c. 1763). As with so many Chinese texts dating back to the manuscript era before the invention of printing, with texts written most commonly on the fragile medium of paper—and in the case of Li Bai and Du Fu, given the turbulent times in which they lived, when the great An Lushan rebellion (755–763) took place—poems have been lost, and among surviving poems many variants exist. (We know of about 1,000 poems written by Li Bai, and of around 1,500 poems by Du Fu.)

The two poets only met a couple of times, in 744 and 745. They had very different personalities and led very different lives, but they retained a sense of brotherhood. A number of poems addressed to each other survive. Li Bai wrote "Sent to Du Fu as a Joke":

I encountered Du Fu by Rice Grain Mountain

In a bamboo hat with the sun at high noon.

He has got very thin since our parting,

It must be the struggle of writing his poems.

Li Bai appears to have been born in Central Asia (an area in which Chinese culture was dominant at the time) but was brought up in

Sichuan province, near Chengdu (where Du Fu settled in later life). Li Bai never braved the imperial examinations but attempted to obtain posts through patronage, in which he was rarely successful.

Du Fu, born in Henan province, came from an established family of bureaucrats, but even though he took the imperial examinations several times, he never managed to pass. On one occasion when he tried, in 746, all the candidates were failed by the prime minister who apparently feared the possibility of rivals.

With the support of an influential Daoist priest, in 742 Li Bai was summoned to the court of the Xuanzong emperor, and though the emperor treated the poet with great respect, personally handing him his soup, it was not a lasting success. This may have been because Li Bai was famous for his love of wine, although he was said to have been quite capable of conducting himself correctly when drunk. Given his eccentric reputation, it is not surprising that there is a famous (though distinctly posthumous) depiction of him by the wonderful, and equally eccentric, painter Liang Kai (c. 1140–c. 1210, also known as "Madman Liang"). In 744, Li Bai left the capital for a mountain retreat.

Du Fu, after his second failure in the exams, had to resort to petitioning powerful figures for an official position. He held several posts but was never very successful. Appointed as commissioner for education in Huazhou, in Guangdong province, he wrote, "I'm about to scream madly in the office / They keep bringing more papers to pile on my desk . . ."

The devastating years of the An Lushan rebellion affected them both. The Tang dynasty (618–907 CE) was almost ended when the besotted Xuanzong emperor allowed his famous "fat concubine" Yang Guifei and her family and friends, including the general and military governor An Lushan, far too much power. In late 755, in the first weeks of the rebellion, An Lushan's troops conquered Luoyang, the eastern capital of the empire, and he proclaimed himself emperor of a new dynasty. His soldiers then marched toward the main capital, Chang'an (at the time the greatest city in the world), and the Xuanzong emperor had to flee. His concubine Yang Guifei was killed by the emperor's bodyguards at the village of Mawei outside of Chang'an. Though the Xuanzong emperor survived the uprising he officially retired in 756, and one of his sons became the new emperor, Suzong. According to legend, Xuanzong spent the rest of his life wandering through his palace mourning Yang Guifei. Though there are no official figures, some millions may have died as a result of the rebellion, which also caused massive population displacement.

Du Fu was briefly captured by the rebel army but escaped to join the court of the Suzong emperor. He fell out of favor for supporting a disgraced minister and eventually moved his family to Chengdu, where he built a thatched cottage (a replica of which remains a major tourist attraction in the city today). His poem "A Guest Arrives" may reflect his rural retreat:

> North and south of the cottage, spring waters everywhere,
>
> All I can see is a flock of terns that come every day.
>
> The flowery path has not been swept for guests,
>
> Only today did I open the gate for you.
>
> The market is far away, our supper dishes lack variety,
>
> Our family is poor, the wine flask holds only home brew,
>
> But if you are willing to drink with the old man next door,
>
> I'll call across the fence for him to share the last cup.

During the rebellion, Li Bai unwisely associated himself with one of the Xuanzong emperor's other sons, who failed to take power. Li Bai was sentenced to death, although this was commuted to exile in far-off Guizhou province in the southwest. He was eventually pardoned, and is said to have drowned in a river while drunk and inviting the moon to drink with him. This is probably a case of extrapolation from his most famous poem, "Drinking by Moonlight":

> Between the flowers, a cup of wine,
>
> I drink alone with no friends nearby.
>
> Raising my cup, I invite the bright moon
>
> Together with my shadow it makes three people.
>
> The moon, sadly, doesn't drink

My shadow just follows me around.

Together with moon and shadow

We must make merry before spring ends.

I sing and the moon flickers

I dance and my shadow goes crazy

Sober, we share the fun,

When I'm drunk, each goes its own way.

I take an oath to travel free of feeling

And that we will meet on the Milky Way.

Li Bai's poetry is described as old-fashioned, harking back to Han (206 BCE–220 CE) and Wei (220–265 CE) styles and forms, full of references to friends, to the sadness of their departures and the joy of their arrival, mountain scenery and nostalgia for home, with a constant sense of displacement. It has always appealed for his simple obsessions with the moon and drink:

This illusory world is a great dream,

I won't waste my life laboring,

So I was drunk all day,

Lying helpless by the columns of the hall.

When I woke I blinked in the courtyard,

A single bird singing in the flowers.

What has the weather been like?

The spring wind was asking the oriole.

Moved, I felt like singing,

Turning to the wine, I filled my cup,

Wildly singing, I waited for the moon.

At the end of the song, I was senseless.

One of Li Bai's shorter poems still involves the moon and the frost-like light it casts but also, lightly, refers to his exile:

> Moonlight before my bed
> Looks like frost on the ground.
> I lift my head and look at the moon,
> I lower my head and think of home.

Du Fu has always been regarded as a more engaged poet. Though Li Bai did write about fleeing from the An Lushan rebellion, Du Fu described the sufferings of others: the misery of conscripts and their fear of dying far from home in "The Ballad of the Army Carts"; the poor who wove silks for the rich and those who starved to death outside the great red gates of the houses of the rich, both in "Lament after Traveling from the Capital to Fengtian." But he also wrote of the paintings of the imperial horses called Night Shiner, Curly, and Lion in "On Seeing a Horse Painting by Cao Ba in the House of the Recorder Wei Feng," and of loneliness and separation in "Thinking of My Brothers on a Moonlit Night." Here, the (migratory) wild "goose" is a symbol of a letter home from an exile and the "old home" is the ancestral, eternal *gu xiang* (which, in the 1920s, Lu Xun also described in his story "My Old Home" ["*Gu xiang*"]), where family and ancestral spirits are united:

> War drums interrupt travel,
> On the frontier in autumn, the sound of one goose,
> From tonight, the dew will be white.
> The moon shines with the same brightness on my old
>   home,
> My brothers are all scattered,
> With no home, I cannot find out if they are dead or alive,
> The letters we send never get through,
> It will be worse as war goes on.

Poems

(ninth century)

LI SHANGYIN (c. 813–c. 858)

≈ ≈

Li Shangyin came from a family of lowly officials in Henan province where his family, though claiming ancestral residence in Huaizhou (present-day Qinyang), was based in nearby Zhengzhou. (It is still common in China to find people who have lived in one area for several generations nevertheless referring to another location as their "ancestral home.") He was born into a turbulent time. After the Tang dynasty (618–907 CE) was almost brought down during the An Lushan rebellion, it saw a brief recovery at the beginning of the ninth century under the Xianzong emperor (who reigned from 805 to 820). But his successors were more interested in hunting, polo, and feasting, and left the increasingly powerful court eunuchs to run the state, with disastrous consequences. Five ineffective emperors ruled during Li Shangyin's adult life, and he spent a lot of it attempting to pass a series of imperial examinations, some dependent upon the whim of the emperor or powerful officials.

The examinations Li Shangyin took were part of a more complex and less regulated system than was established later, during the Song dynasty (960–1279). There were three main exams, the first consisting of essays on state policy, the next on the Confucian classics (which was largely a test of memory), and the third was a literary exam. There were also occasional exams presided over by the emperor, intended to search out men of talent. The actual selection of officials (what Arthur Waley has called "the placing exam") was a separate process designed to sort out men who were "tall and imposing" and who demonstrated powerful and beautiful calligraphy and "superior literary style and reasoning."

Despite apparently showing literary talent since an early age, Li Shangyin failed the literary exam in 833 and 835 but passed in 837. Though he was rejected for high office several times, he finally obtained a post in the Imperial Library in Chang'an, the capital, working on literary texts. But he was then demoted and sent off to serve as a local administrator in the circuit of Hongnong. There he managed to offend his superiors, whereupon he was reappointed to the Imperial Library in 842, but at a lower level. With interruptions such as the death of his mother, also in 842—which meant that he had to return home for the customary three years of mourning (the death of parents and the length of the compulsory Confucian mourning period interrupted most official careers until the end of the nineteenth century)—the rest of his career saw many moves, partly the result of political maneuverings by others and partly due to bad luck.

After the death of his mother, Li Shangyin also embarked on a complex action of Confucian filial piety by burying, or reburying, five family members: his mother, his elder sister, his uncle (who had given him his first lessons in the Confucian classics), and a young niece were all buried in Zhengzhou, but his great-grandmother was reburied in the old ancestral home in Huaizhou, in accordance with the complicated proprieties. He seems to have been fond of his wife (who died in 851) and attracted to Buddhism.

Li Shangyin's poetry does not appeal to all. A character in Cao Xueqin's *Dream of the Red Chamber* (*Hongloumeng*) says, "I hate Li Shangyin's poetry!" and it can be difficult, seemingly requiring more footnotes and explanation than in other cases. His reputation, however, grew in the twentieth century and he is now admired for his imagist poetry. He wrote a series of short poems on Chinese history, including one commemorating the capital city of Xianyang built by the First Emperor of the Qin dynasty (221–206 BCE):

> The towers of the Xianyang palace,
>
> The terraces and mansions of the Six Kingdoms,
>
> Are bright with silk gauze.
>
> It was noticed that in those days, the King of Heaven
> was drunk,
>
> No matter that Qin had mountains and rivers.

The First Emperor's palace was legendary for its luxury and splendor. Built high on an earthen mound concealed by towers and terraces, it was also said to include rebuilt mansions from different parts of China that had been incorporated into his empire by conquest, as tangible evidence of the scale of his territory. Despite the vastness of the Qin empire (with its mountains and rivers demonstrating not only the scale but the ease with which it was naturally defended), the dynasty was short-lived, unprotected by the "King of Heaven" who withdrew the mandate to rule.

Another short-lived regime was that of the Sui dynasty (581–618 CE), whose founding emperor Wendi was viewed as cruel and wasteful —although he had reunited a divided China. Li Shangyin also chose the palace of the Sui emperor to characterize the dynasty:

> The palace halls of the Purple Spring are enclosed in mist and clouds,
> He wanted to seize Weed City as an imperial dwelling.
> The jade seal was returned and the brocade sails spread to the horizon.
> Today there are no fireflies in the rotting grass,
> At twilight crows haunt the ancient willows.
> If in the underworld, he meets the king of Chen,
> It would be inappropriate to ask again for the dance of "Flowers in the Back Courtyard."

The palace of the "Purple Spring" refers to Chang'an (present-day Xi'an, in Shaanxi province), the primary capital of the Han emperors (206 BCE–220 CE) before the Sui. But the Sui emperor Wendi felt this was unlucky for him so he developed (at great expense) the old secondary capital of Luoyang (in Henan province). "Weed City" was a place (near Yangzhou, in Jiangsu province) that became his secondary capital. (One of the Wendi emperor's more successful projects was the construction of the Grand Canal that linked Yangzhou and Luoyang.) The construction of the city near Yangzhou (and his tomb) was criticized as wasteful, and during the subsequent Tang dynasty the capital reverted to the old Han pattern of Chang'an as the main capital, with Luoyang as the secondary capital ("the jade seal was returned" means that the emperor had returned). The Wendi emperor's extravagance extended to the use of expensive silken "brocade sails" for his pleasure boats and he apparently collected fireflies to release into the area around Yangzhou. He was said to have dreamed of a legendary dancing girl famous for her performance of "Flowers in the Back Courtyard" at the court of the last ruler of Chen, one of the smaller ruling houses of the pre-Sui division known as the Northern and Southern dynasties (420–581 CE).

Li Shangyin wrote a poem about the death of the Xuanzong emperor's concubine Yang Guifei in 756, at Mawei (during the An Lushan rebellion), and the appalling situation of an infatuated emperor (a popular theme that was also addressed by the poet Bai Juyi [772–846], a near-contemporary of Li Shangyin):

> Horses from Qi and armor from Yan came shaking
>   the earth.
>
> Her pink powder was buried and she became ash.
>
> If the ruler had understood that she could topple
>   kingdoms,
>
> How would the jade carriage have passed Mawei slope? . . .
>
> Never again, the cockerel announcing the dawn,
>
> On this day the Sixth Army stopped all their horses . . .

Qi and Yan were the names of old states near Beijing, where the rebel leader An Lushan had built up his military power; the pink-powdered lady met her end at the hands of the imperial bodyguard (or Sixth Army) at Mawei.

Another gloomy poem celebrates Wang Zhaojun (born c. 50 BCE), the famous beauty of the Western Han dynasty. Wang Zhaojun, along with Yang Guifei, Xi Shi (c. seventh to sixth centuries BCE), and Diaochan (c. third century CE), are known as the "Four Beauties." Xi Shi was so beautiful that fish sank to the bottom of the pond when they saw her reflection, Diaochan's beauty eclipsed the moon, Yang Guifei's beauty shamed flowers, and Wang Zhaojun caused birds to drop from the skies. She was also said to have been too poor to bribe the court painter, and therefore he produced a hideous portrait of her. Seeing the portrait, the Han emperor decided not to keep her in the palace but to send her off as a bride and diplomatic gift to the ruler of the nomadic Xiongnu people who threatened China's western borders. Before her departure, the emperor did notice her great beauty, but it was too late. She "traveled ten thousand miles on horseback carrying her *pipa* [lute]" and, dying far from home, is one of the eternal Chinese symbols of the horror of exile and separation.

The Story of Yingying
Yingying zhuan
(early ninth century)

YUAN ZHEN (779–831)

Master Dong's Western Chamber Romance
Dong shi Xi xiang ji zhugongtiao
(late twelfth century/early thirteenth century)

DONG JIEYUAN (flourished c. 1189–c. 1208)

Romance of the Western Chamber
Xi xiang ji
(late thirteenth century/early fourteenth century)

WANG SHIFU (c. 1250–c. 1337)

≫ ⟋

Through these three works we can follow a story that has remained popular for hundreds of years and was told in different literary forms. The first version of the story, *The Story of Yingying* (*Yingying zhuan*), is in the novella form, a genre known as *chuanqi* ("tales of the unexpected") that first became very popular during the Tang dynasty (618–907 CE). (The late-seventeenth-century short stories, or novellas, in *Strange Stories from the Liao Studio* [*Liaozhai zhiyi*] by Pu Songling follow the same format and contain many of the same elements of love—especially love between "a scholar and a beautiful woman"—and supernatural intervention.)

The second version, *Master Dong's Western Chamber Romance* (*Dong shi Xi xiang ji zhugongtiao*), is in a very particular format called *zhugong-tiao*—sometimes translated as a "medley" or "*chantefable*"—in which the story is told mainly in verse, with short prose passages intervening.

One of the characteristics of the *zhugongtiao* is the high number of different verse forms used.

The final version, *Romance of the Western Chamber* (*Xi xiang ji*), is a proper Yuan dynasty (1279–1368) drama, known as *zaju*, with alternating sung verse and spoken prose enacted by a cast of several different actors with a musical ensemble. Despite the Yuan being an alien dynasty, with China ruled by Mongol emperors, this was the period in which drama flourished as a new genre, sometimes with subtle anti-Mongol messages.

Yuan Zhen's story opens with a young man, Zhang, who is preparing to take the imperial examinations in the hope of achieving high office (in other words, a typical hero of this type of love story between "scholar and beautiful woman"). Zhang appears to be principled and lacking experience with women. On his way to the capital (where the examinations will take place), he lodges at a Buddhist monastery where he meets the widowed Madame Cui, who is staying there with her young son, her daughter Yingying (a beautiful, chaste young woman), and her maid, Hong Niang. Zhang discovers that he is distantly related to Madame Cui. The monastery is suddenly threatened as mutinous soldiers plan to attack it. Fortunately, Zhang knows the local military commander and makes sure the monastery is protected. Madame Cui is filled with gratitude and asks her children to pay their deep respects to Zhang. Meeting Yingying, Zhang is overcome by her beauty and—despite her maidenly reluctance—on the advice of Hong Niang he woos Yingying with a love poem, and she reciprocates. He boldly takes her poem as an invitation to visit her at night in her Western Chamber, and climbs over the garden wall to meet her. Hong Niang, the maid, is startled by his visit and fetches Yingying. But Yingying is stern and upset and accuses Zhang of lewdness. Her poem, she says, was only intended to summon him so that she could reprimand him in person. Zhang is dumbfounded and leaves.

But a few nights later, Hong Niang comes into Zhang's room, carrying bedding with her, and then Yingying arrives. The next morning, he can hardly believe he has spent the night with Yingying but her perfume lingers on his gown and her face powder still gleams on his sleeve. Though she exhibits a new reluctance, he persuades her to relent with a poem, "Rendezvous with a Fairy," and for a month or so they continue to meet each night.

Eventually, Zhang has to continue on his way to the capital to take the examinations, which he fails. He is compelled to stay there for a second year, to try the examinations again. During this time, Yingying writes him a long letter stressing her deep love for him but also her unworthiness to be the wife of a high official. In Yuan Zhen's story, the affair ends there. She finally marries another and so does Zhang. The tale remains one of young love, without a future but still unforgettable. The position of Yingying seems particularly sad as she pours out her heart in her long letter, while Zhang decides to end the relationship and gets on with his life with tactless speed.

The contrast between the life of Zhang and that of the author, Yuan Zhen, could not be greater. Unlike Zhang who had to try twice to pass the imperial examinations, Yuan Zhen passed a special examination in 806, coming first at the head of a distinguished list of examinees and achieving appointment to the Legislative Bureau. Though official life in the early ninth century was fraught with political struggle, Yuan Zhen achieved much, producing his literary work as well as a 300-volume compilation of legal rulings.

The second version of the story is by Dong Jieyuan, or Master Dong, whose personal life is little-known. Here, Madame Cui promises Yingying to Zhang if he passes his examinations. When he does so, after some delay, he returns to the monastery to find Mr. Zheng, Yingying's original fiancé, there. He discovers that Madame Cui has now promised Yingying to Zheng. However, through the intervention of the local military commander, matters are set right and Zhang marries Yingying. One poem, "Adorning Crimson Lips," describes Yingying as a rather difficult young woman:

> The beautiful Yingying looked at Zhang, then lowered her
> head without a word.
>
> Her handkerchief, even her sleeves, were wet with tears.
>
> A frown contracted her leaflike eyebrows.
>
> Her golden-lotus feet were sore from stamping,
>
> Her scallion-stalk fingers were red and raw . . .

There are two songs set to the tune of "A Speckled Woodpecker." The first song describes the happiness of the young lovers but also their separation:

> At the end, Yingying came to me secretly,
> We made love behind silk curtains for months.
> She'd come at night and leave at dawn,
> Our tryst was discovered—Madame was persuaded to
> betroth her to me,
> But the allure of fame and wealth enticed me away from
> my love.

In the second song, the "difficult" Madame Cai, "her petulant temper unaltered" and "disregarding her indebtedness," breaks off Zhang's engagement to Yingying but eventually all ends happily.

The same long-delayed happy ending is found in Wang Shifu's famous drama. Little is known about the life of Wang Shifu, who was born in the Mongol capital of Dadu (today's Beijing). He is thought to have written fourteen dramas of which only three survive, but the popularity of *Romance of the Western Chamber* has never waned and it continues to entertain through film and television adaptations.

Here the dilemma of Yingying, knowing that meeting a man before marriage is improper, is played out at greater length. Her character, too, is developed further. From making her bound feet sore through stamping petulantly, we now learn that she once knocked a man's teeth out with the shuttle of her loom. And while Zhang gloomily thinks that "beauties bring ill-fate," Yingying explains her fear of being "seduced and abandoned" when Zhang goes off to the capital and worries that a "union without the usual proprieties cannot but result in disgrace . . ."

The continuity of the tale of Yingying and Zhang through the centuries, and through the variety of literary treatments, testifies to its enduring familiarity and popularity.

Poems

(twelfth century)

Li Qingzhao (1084–c. 1150)

≈ ≈

Li Qingzhao's poetry has been immensely popular in China for centuries. She was born in the northern province of Shandong toward the end of the Northern Song (960–1127). Her father was a high official who had passed the highest examinations and was described as the best prose writer since Sima Qian, the great Han historian. Her mother, who died when Li Qingzhao was young, was the eldest daughter of a prime minister, and her stepmother was the granddaughter of another famous man—he made first place in the palace examinations in the year 1030 when he was only eighteen. Li Qingzhao, at the age of seventeen, married Zhao Mingcheng, himself a student in the imperial academy and the son of a future prime minister. However, such political prominence on both sides of the family was to cause problems. Li Qingzhao's father was an associate of the great poet-essayist Su Shi (also known as Su Dongpo, 1037–1101) and politically associated with conservatives at court, for which he was banished, while her father-in-law, a reformer, gained more power until a struggle within the reform party led to his dismissal as prime minister and his subsequent death.

As a result, Li Qingzhao and her husband lived very quietly for a while in Shandong province and, despite his weakness for singing girls, she left a charming account of their intellectual diversions. "Whenever we'd finished dinner, we'd sit in our hall named 'Returning Home' and brew tea. Then, looking at the books on the shelves, choosing a particular event, we would try to guess which line in which chapter of which book contained the relevant passage, and see who was right." The winner could drink the first cup of tea. "When I guessed right, I would lift up my teacup and laugh so much that I spilled tea down the front of my dress . . . How I wish we could grow old living like that."

Zhao Mingcheng was appointed to serve as a magistrate in their home province of Shandong, first in Laizhou (bordering the Yellow

Sea), then further inland in Qingzhou. But in 1127 the invading Jurchen Jin troops—on the way to driving the Song emperor out of his capital, Kaifeng, and southward to Hangzhou—took Qingzhou. In the battle, much of Zhao Mingcheng's library, which filled ten rooms in their house, was burnt. The couple fled southward to Nanjing but Zhao Mingcheng, after being disgraced for having abandoned Nanjing during an attempted coup, died in 1129. His widow moved unhappily around southern China, weighed down by the remains of their collection of books and scrolls. As she wrote, "After I had buried Mingcheng, I had nowhere to go. At the time I still had 20,000 books, 2,000 folios of inscriptions on bronze and stone, and enough utensils and bedding for 1,000 guests. Much of this I sent to my brother-in-law in Hangzhou, but Hangzhou was sacked. All I had left [then] were a few small calligraphic inscriptions; manuscript copies of [the Tang poets] Li Bai, Du Fu, Han Yu, and Liu Zongyuan; a few mounted rubbings of Han and Tang inscriptions; ten bronze vessels from the Three Dynasties [the ancient Xia, Shang, and Zhou]; and a few cases of other manuscripts. All these were eventually lost through thieves, tricksters, and gifts to the emperor . . ." As this list of possessions reveals, Li Qingzhao and her husband had indeed been a highly intellectual couple.

Li Qingzhao remarried, which was unusual because, according to Confucian tradition, a widow should remain chastely faithful, but the actual legal prohibition on the remarriage of "titled wives" (upper-class widows) had been withdrawn during the reign of the Shenzong emperor of the Song (r. 1067–1085). However, she discovered that her new husband had falsified his qualifications in order to obtain an official post and she revealed this fact to the authorities. Since traditional Confucian ethics held that a wife should always be subservient to her husband, Li Qingzhao was sentenced to two years in prison for violating this code. Fortunately, she was released after nine days through the intervention of one of her first husband's relatives, a highly placed official. She then lived alone for the subsequent two decades.

To honor her first husband, Li Qingzhao published his posthumous account of their collection, *Records of Bronze and Stone [Inscriptions]* (*Jin shi lu*), and added a postface in which she also described their life together. The great neo-Confucian philosopher Zhu Xi (1130–1200)

approved: "How could a woman ever think up lines like these?" The
loss of her first husband was also a theme of some of her poems:

> The wind has dropped,
>
> The flowers have all faded.
>
> There is a lingering scent of petals
>
> In the earth.
>
> Evening, and I cannot comb my hair.
>
> Things remain but all is lost
>
> He is gone.
>
> Tears prevent words.
>
> I hear that spring is sweet
>
> At Twin Streams.
>
> I'd like to row in a light boat.
>
> I only fear that at Twin Streams my grasshopper-light boat
>
> Could not bear
>
> Such heavy grief.

Many of her poems have been lost or survive only in part. Many do
not demonstrate a necessarily female point of view but sit within the
(male-dominated) poetic tradition. There is, for example, a pair of short
poems intended to be sung (as was common for various poetic forms),
both entitled "As if in a Dream":

> Last night, the rain was soft, the wind strong
>
> Heavy sleep has not dispelled my drunkenness
>
> I ask the maid as she rolls up the blinds
>
> And she tells me the geraniums are still the same
>
> Does she know?
>
> Does she know?
>
> Surely there should be more green and less red.

I remember the hut beside the water in the evening
We were too drunk to find the way home
Saturated with pleasure, we turned back late,
Lost in the thick growths of lotus, we rowed
As fast as we could
As fast as we could
All along the banks,
Gulls and herons flap upward in panic.

Two other "poems to be sung," from a series entitled "Washing the River of Sand," do have a female voice:

I must do my hair! Sadness of spring, what languor!
The spring wind penetrates the courtyard! The prunus
    flowers have fallen!
Pale clouds, blown this way and that, cover the
    transparent moon.
In the duck-shaped jade incense burner, burning camphor
The red curtain is pulled close, its fringes trailing
Could a rhinoceros horn drive away the cold?*

Washing the river of sand: after a dream
The cup was so full of amber-colored wine
That my heart drowned there before I could get drunk
The evening wind is getting up.
The scent of camphor from Borneo disappears as I wake
A narrow gold hairpin holds my hair in place
I wake, what can I do in the bright candlelight?

The Orphan of Zhao
Zhao shi guer

(c. thirteenth century)

ATTRIBUTED TO JI JUNXIANG (c. thirteenth century)

～～

Born in Beijing, little is known about Ji Junxiang. Although he is thought to have written six dramas, only *The Orphan of Zhao* (*Zhao shi guer*) survives, a famous example of *zaju* drama developed during the Yuan period (1279–1368). It tells the story of an orphan's revenge for the mass murder of his entire family, the Zhao clan. Based on an event in the state of Jin in the Spring and Autumn period (770–476 BCE), the drama has gained significance outside China through its several translations and adaptations, including by the French Jesuit missionary Joseph Henri Marie de Prémare (1666–1736) and by Voltaire (François-Marie Arouet, 1694–1778); by the Irish playwright Arthur Murphy in 1759; as well as by the English poet James Fenton, with the sinologist and translator Brian Holt, in 2012.

The Orphan of Zhao includes themes that are characteristic of very many historical dramas in China. It harks back to ancient history; it stresses the bitter rivalry of court officials, all striving against each other for royal or imperial favor; it upholds the primacy of family and family loyalty; and the tension arises from the theme of revenge—here, as in many cases, revenge pursued beyond the grave. The drama recounts the story of the king of the state of Jin who had two major officers, his minister Zhao Dun and his general Tu'an Gu. Zhao Dun is a paragon of virtue who angers the king by criticizing him for putting to death a cook who had served an underdone bear's paw. Zhao Dun has become something of a hero to the culinary staff because he also gave food to a man he found collapsed from starvation under a mulberry tree. The man survived and became a cook in the royal kitchen. Tu'an Gu, as a rival official hoping for royal favor, hates Zhao Dun and decides to eliminate his entire family. One newborn Zhao child escapes the massacre, hidden away by a doctor whose own baby is sacrificed as Tu'an Gu embarks upon a Herodian killing of all baby boys. The orphan survives and grows up, assuming he is the son of the doctor, but he eventually learns the truth and kills Tu'an Gu in revenge.

The Orphan of Zhao was the first Chinese drama to be translated into a European language. In eighteenth-century Europe there was a fashion for all things Chinese, which developed into Chinoiserie, a decorative style widely seen in European interior furnishings and garden design. At the same time philosophical interest in China, which began with information derived from Jesuit missionaries there, gave rise to a view of China as a rational and advanced society. Both strands of interest were served by translations from the Chinese.

Prémare, who was a missionary in China in the early 1700s, translated the dialogue of the drama but he omitted the verse, an essential part of the mixture of opera, drama, and acrobatic movement that defines the *zaju* format. Prémare gave his 1731 draft to two friends to take from China to France, where it was intended for Étienne Fourmont, a scholar of Chinese. Fourmont, with an enormous amount of largely unacknowledged help from the Chinese Jesuit convert Arcadius Huang, had catalogued the Chinese manuscripts in the French royal collection. Prémare's text, however, never reached Fourmont but was instead acquired by the Jesuit Jean-Baptiste du Halde, who (to Fourmont's fury) included it in his four-volume *Description de la Chine* (1735)—a work that much influenced Europe's view of China during the Enlightenment.

Apparently inspired by the publication in du Halde's work, Voltaire wrote a successful play, *L'Orphelin de la Chine*, in 1755, and dedicated it to the great soldier "Monseigneur le Maréchal Duc de Richelieu," apologizing for not having Italian marble statues to offer him, only "some Chinese figures," none of whom had "supported a republic on the verge of crumbling, nor could think of overturning an English column with four cannon." He described the play as "an example of the natural superiority derived from reason and genius over blind and brute force. The action lasts over twenty-five years as in the monstrous farces of Shakespeare and Lope de Vega which are called tragedies. It's a mass of incredible events." Voltaire's version is also quite an incredible distance from the original. He makes the king of Jin into Genghis

Khan, raising the question of conquest rather than good government, and sets it in Beijing: "*La scène est dans un palais des mandarins qui tient au palais impérial, dans la ville de Cambaluc, aujourd'hui Pékin . . .*" ("The action is set in a mandarin's residence close to the imperial palace in Khanbalik, today known as Peking . . .") The last speeches, between Genghis Khan and his minister, reveal what Genghis Khan has learned over these twenty-five years. As he hands over the orphan of Zhao whom he has protected, he tells his minister (thereby revealing his submission to Confucian ideas of virtue, which held no place in the traditional Mongol scheme of things): "Make the ministers as noble as you are, teach them reason, justice, and morality. Let the vanquished govern the conquerors. May wisdom reign . . . overcome force and it will do you homage. I shall take the lead and submit my weapons to your laws." Apparently unable to believe his ears, his minister asks, "What inspired you?" and Genghis replies, "Your VIRTUE." Curtain.

In 1834 the great French sinologist Stanislas Julien published a full translation, *Tchao-chi-kou-eul* [a French transcription of *Zhao shi guer*], *ou l'Orphelin de la Chine: drame en prose et en vers*. In this closer version to the original, an early speech by General Tu'an Gu sets out his villainous plans. Julien explains that in a Chinese drama each character introduces himself, since many actors play several parts and the introduction lessens confusion. "I am Tu'an Gu, general of the kingdom of Jin. Since our king took the throne, there are only two officers he trusts: in civil matters it is Zhao Dun, in military matters it is me. I have a constant desire to kill Zhao Dun but so far I have not succeeded . . . I ordered a loyal soldier, Zhou Ni, to take a dagger and kill Zhao Dun . . ." However, the soldier, finding Zhao Dun asleep, could not go through with it and killed himself instead by running full tilt at a cinnamon tree. (Bashing one's head against a tree as a form of suicide or protest is not unknown in Chinese literature; for example, it also occurs in the Qing-era drama *The Peach Blossom Fan* [*Taohua shan*].)* Tu'an Gu's next attempt to kill Zhao Dun involved a huge dog, a golden mastiff offered to the king as a form of tribute. Tu'an Gu describes his plan: "I kept him locked up for four days with nothing to eat or drink. Then I hung a straw man in the garden behind my house, wearing clothes like Zhao Dun's, a purple robe, a jade belt, an ivory tablet, and black boots. I put sheep entrails and hearts inside. I brought the dog along who in the twinkling of an eye tore the purple robe apart and gorged itself." This vicious process of preparing the dog was then repeated for a hundred days.

Tu'an Gu then told the king there was a traitor at court and that the mastiff had the unusual gift of sniffing out traitors. The king was interested, having heard of such precedents in the past, and when the dog was unleashed, it tore at Zhao Dun. He escaped, with the help of the cook whom he had once saved from starvation. Nevertheless, Tu'an Gu managed to kill him eventually and to destroy the Zhao family, with the exception of the baby boy who would one day avenge his family.

The last speech in Julien's 1834 translation is by the grown-up orphan, emphasizing the Confucian aspect of benevolent and just rule: "Thanks, O King, for your good deeds which descend bounteously over the whole realm of Jin. You have exterminated that infamous brigand and all his family. You allowed an orphan to change his name and take up his chances once more, to inherit the dignity of his forefathers and become a minister of state. Men who sacrifice themselves for honor and justice receive encouragement. Military officers keep to their appointed functions. Those who suffered are supported by your munificence. You construct funerary monuments to the dead and give great and noble recompense to their survivors. Who would dare skimp in praising your benefaction which stretches to the sky? I will risk my life on the battlefield and force all the other kings to place themselves at your service. The historians will keep your name in the annals to be transmitted from age to age in an aura of glory that will never fade . . ."

Three-Character Classic

Sanzi jing

(thirteenth century)

ATTRIBUTED TO WANG YINGLIN (1223–1296)

～ ✐

Memorized by schoolboys in traditional schools throughout China for centuries, the *Three-Character Classic* (*Sanzi jing*) originally consisted of some two hundred lines of instruction, with three characters per line, stressing Confucian ideas of the veneration of education and ritual and correct behavior, ending with lists of philosophers and the dynastic history of China. (It is possible that some girls also learned the *Three-Character Classic*, but in premodern China very few girls had a thorough education, and what they learned would have been taught at home.)

The work is traditionally attributed to Wang Yinglin, a renowned Confucian official and scholar who compiled several important encyclopedias and historiographical works. Many present-day versions of the *Three-Character Classic* (still used in Hong Kong and Taiwan) are longer and take the historical sequence of dynasties into the twentieth century. The *Three-Character Classic* epitomizes the traditional Chinese educational format of rote learning and takes the child through age-old cosmological beliefs, through family and other relationships, and through Chinese history, all significant aspects of traditional Confucianism.

There is another text, somewhat similar but more complex, called the *Thousand-Word Essay* (*Qianzi wen*), in which a total of 1,000 characters are used, arranged in 250 rhyming lines of four characters each. The *Thousand-Word Essay* is thought to date to the sixth century CE and also formed part of the traditional curriculum in village schools throughout China. It has a richer, frequently poetic, vocabulary and is less moralistic than the *Three-Character Classic*, and it begins: "Sky and earth, black and yellow, the universe vast and chaotic / Sun and moon, waxing and waning, stars and planets in place / Cold arrives, heat turns, autumn harvest, winter store . . ."

The *Three-Character Classic*, on the other hand, begins with the following lines:

Ren zhi chu ("In their beginning" [humans at birth])
Xing ben shan ("Are naturally good")
Xing xiang jin ("Their natures are similar")
Xi xiang yuan. ("But their customs become different.")

It is not possible to reproduce the regular three-character rhythm of the monosyllabic Chinese in a translation into polysyllabic English. What follows are excerpts from the full text:

In their beginning [humans at birth] / Are naturally good
Their natures are similar / But their customs become different.
If you treat them badly by not instructing them / Their nature can change [for the worse]
The Way of teaching / Is with absolute respect [for teaching].
In the past, Mencius's mother / Selected a neighborhood
When her child would not study / She broke the shuttle on her loom. [She did this to show him it was a serious matter.]
Dou of Yanshan / Used righteous methods
He taught his five sons / And they all enhanced the family name. [This refers to a man in the tenth century CE whose five sons all passed the palace exams.]
To nourish without teaching / Is a father's transgression
Not to venerate learning / Is the result of a lazy teacher.
For a child not to study / Is not fitting
If he does not study when young / How will he act when old?
Unpolished jade / Cannot be made into a vessel
A man who has not studied / Does not know righteousness.
For a human child / There is so little time
Be close to teachers and friends / Practice ritual and righteousness.
At the age of nine, Xiang / Warmed his parents' bed
In filial piety toward parents / Be persistent. [Huang Xiang was one of the twenty-four exemplars of filial piety in the book of the same name.]
At the age of four, Rong / Let his brother have the largest pears

Submission to elders / Is the first way of understanding what is
  fitting. [Kong Rong was a descendant of Confucius.]
Begin with filial piety and love of brothers / Then look and listen
Learn to count / Learn to read.
One to ten / Ten to a hundred
A hundred to a thousand / A thousand to ten thousand.
The three forces / Are heaven, earth, and man
The three brightnesses / Are sun, moon, and stars.
The three principles / Are appropriate relations between ruler
  and subject
Love between father and child / Obedience of wife to husband.
  [These principles were based on traditional Confucian ethics.]
Speak of spring and summer / Speak of autumn and winter
The four seasons / Revolve eternally.
Speak of north and south / Speak of east and west
The four directions / Are dependent on the center.
Speak of fire, water / Wood, metal, earth
These five elements / Have their origin in numbers. [This is
  possibly a reference to their representation by hexagrams in
  the *Book of Changes* (*Yi jing*)].
We speak of benevolence, righteousness / Proper behavior,
  wisdom, and honesty
These are the five virtues / Not to be questioned.
Rice, fine millet, beans / Wheat, broomcorn millet,
  common millet
These six grains / Are the people's food.
Horse, ox, sheep / Chicken, dog, pig
These six animals / Are what the people eat.
Speak of happiness, anger / Speak of grief, fear
Love, hate, desire / The seven emotions.
Gourd, earthenware, skin / Wood, stone, metal
With silk, bamboo / Achieve the eight musical tones.
  [Musical instruments were made from these materials.]
Great-great-grandfather, great-grandfather, grandfather /
  Father and self

Self and child / Child and grandchild.
From child, grandchild / To distant . . . [great-great-grandchild]
To nine generations / Of human relations.
Benevolence of father to son / Obedience of wife to husband
Friendship from an elder brother / Respect from a younger brother.
Appropriate precedence between elders and young /
    Equality between friends
Respect from the ruler / Loyalty from subjects.
These ten obligations / Are the same for all.

The *Three-Character Classic* then turns to the Confucian texts to be studied:

In all teaching of the ignorant / There must be explanation
    and research
Teach the old texts with attention to detail / Parsing sentences
    and sections.
For would-be students / There must be a starting point
When primary school is finished / Then there are the Four Books.
The *Analects* / In twenty sections
All his disciples / Recorded his precious words.
The *Mencius* / In seven sections
Discusses the Way and virtue / Speaks of benevolence, right-
    eousness . . . [Here follow lines on "Doctrine of the Mean" and
    "Great Learning."]
Familiar with the *Book of Filial Piety* / Knowing the Four Books
Then the Six Classics [i.e., the Five Classics and the *Rites of Zhou*] /
    Can be started . . .

After describing the various Confucian texts in more detail, and listing five philosophers (including Laozi and Zhuangzi), China's history
from the mythic era of creation onward is set out:

Familiar with the classics and philosophers / Read all the histories
Study the connection between eras / Understand beginnings
    and ends.
From [Fu] Xi [creator of hunting, fishing, cooking] and

> [Shen] Nong [inventor of agriculture] / To the Yellow Emperor
> [inventor of medicine]
> The three sovereigns / Of ancient times . . .

The text continues through the legendary ancient rulers, good and bad, and increases in detail with the Qin and Han:

> Ying of the Qin [the First Emperor] / Started to unify
> After two generations / Chu and Han battled.
> Gaozu [founding emperor of the Han 206 BCE] triumphed /
> Established the Han . . .

Some versions of the *Three-Character Classic* continue and expand the history of China up to the modern period, and some versions also mention two women, the musician Cai Wenji and the poet Xie Daoyun.

There is an interesting translation of the *Three-Character Classic* made in 1873 by the eccentric sinologist Herbert Allen Giles (1845–1935). Giles started his career in the British consular service in China but eventually became professor of Chinese at the University of Cambridge (from 1897 to 1932). The last few lines in Giles's thundering rhyme sound much like a rousing Victorian hymn, but do convey the supremely didactic nature of the work:

> The dog is watchman of the night, the cock proclaims
> the day,
> Can man without instruction's aid his destiny obey?
> The silkworm spins, the busy bee toils on at nature's call,
> But man without instruction's aid falls far below
> them all . . .
> I give my sons this little book and give them nothing more.
> Waste not the flying moments in unprofitable play!
> Strive, O ye youths, with might and main, these precepts to obey!

Learned by heart, repeated by rote, the *Three-Character Classic* (as well as the *Thousand-Word Essay*) was the foundation of Chinese school education until the beginning of the twentieth century.

Twenty-Four Exemplars of Filial Piety
Ershisi xiao

(Yuan/1279–1368)

ATTRIBUTED TO GUO JUJING (1260–1368)

≈ ≈

Filial piety, respect for parents and gratitude for all they do for their children, goes back a long way in Chinese belief. Often associated with Confucian morality, it was—like many of the matters on which the sage pronounced—in his time already entrenched in Chinese family practice, along with respect for, and worship of, family ancestors. The *Book of Filial Piety* (*Xiao jing*) is another, much older standard work on the subject, but *Twenty-Four Exemplars of Filial Piety* (*Ershisi xiao*) became much more popular because of its stories and illustrations.

This book is thought to have appeared during the Yuan dynasty and is attributed to Guo Jujing, a scholar about whom little else is known, but many of the stories appeared in earlier works. Though the strongest association of filial piety is with Confucianism, one of the earliest surviving texts stressing the debt owed to parents is a Buddhist text from the Tang dynasty (618–907 CE), found among the thousands of documents from the fifth to eleventh centuries CE in the cave-temple complex near Dunhuang in Gansu province.

Twenty-Four Exemplars of Filial Piety contains twenty-four brief chapters, each introducing one of these remarkable individuals who, during various dynasties, served their parents in astounding (even miraculous) ways. Though the first two exemplars are emperors, the others are commoners, many of them poor and some of them women. Each tale is presented as the description of an actual person, but there is no way of verifying if they actually existed; they simply served as role models.

Often printed with charming illustrations and published in hundreds of editions throughout the centuries, *Twenty-Four Exemplars of Filial Piety* was studied by schoolchildren well into the twentieth century. It also provoked the compilation of similar uplifting texts, and one of these, consisting of twenty-four female exemplars intended to educate girls, was blamed by the lascivious main character in the novel *The Carnal Prayer Mat* (*Rou putuan*) (1657) for his wife's lack of interest in sex.

The first exemplar is the mythical Emperor Shun whose filial piety "moved heaven to sympathy." Emperor Shun was supposed to have been chosen by the (equally mythical and equally benevolent) Emperor Yao to succeed him because he was so honest and good and showed remarkable filial piety. According to the story, Shun's mother died when he was very young and his father, who was blind, remarried. Shun's stepmother had a son, and both of them were very cruel to Shun while his father remained oblivious to the harsh treatment, ragged clothing, and poor food given to Shun—who endured it all without complaint. One day he was driven out of the family home, but everywhere he went his abilities and hard work gained him support. Finally, heaven itself was moved to create him emperor, through the agency of Emperor Yao.*

The second exemplar is the historic emperor Wen of the Han (r. 180–157 BCE). His story, "Personally Tasting the Medicine," begins: "Emperor Wen, whose name was Heng, was the third son of Gaozu [founding emperor of the Han dynasty]. His mother, later known as Empress Dowager Bo, was secondary wife to Gaozu. Before his accession he was appointed Prince Dai and he cared for his mother without fail. During the three years of her illness, he never closed his eyes. He did not undress at bedtime (so as to be constantly ready to serve her) and she was never given any medicine unless he had personally tasted it [to make sure it was suitable]. Hence his benevolence and filial piety were known throughout the empire."

The third exemplar's story is entitled "Allowing Mosquitoes to Drink His Blood" and features the young boy Wu Meng who lived during the Jin dynasty (265–420 CE): "When he was eight years old, Wu Meng of the Jin dynasty served his parents with great filial piety.** As the family was poor, they had no bed-curtains. Every summer evening, mosquitoes crowded on his skin, keen to drink his blood, but he did not wave them away for fear that they might fly off and bite his parents instead. This was the pinnacle of his love for his parents."

The fourth story, "Catching Carp by Lying on the Ice," also features a boy during the Jin dynasty: "Wang Xiang of the Jin, whose courtesy name was Xiuzheng, suffered the death of his mother at an early age. His stepmother, whose surname was Zhu, was unkind to him and spoke badly of him in front of his father who lost all love for him. His [step-] mother always liked to eat fresh fish and so, on a cold day with much ice, Wang Xiang lay down on the frozen pond to try and catch some fish. [His warm body] melted the ice and two carp leapt up. He caught them and took them back home to his [step-] mother." (The text is imprecise: the stepmother [*jimu*] is directly described at first, but subsequent references are simply to "mother" [*mu*]. Presumably the stepmother is the one he is catching fish for, despite her attitude.)

The title of the fifth story is "Hearing Thunder and Weeping by the Grave," and it features Wang Pu, a filial son at the time of the Wei (there were several Wei dynasties between 386 CE and 556 CE, but it is not indicated which of them is meant here): "Wang Pu of the Wei was exceptionally filial. During her lifetime Wang Pu's mother was very frightened of thunder. On her death, she was buried in a mountain grove. Whenever a clap of thunder could be heard during a rainstorm, Wang Pu would rush at top speed to her tomb and kneel down, with his hands held together in obeisance and weep, saying, 'I'm here, mother, do not be afraid.'"

The next story involves the carving of ancestral images. Though portraiture of living persons was rare in China, it was commonly used to commemorate the dead. Portraits of the deceased (of at least three past generations) were produced to be placed on the family altar at festivals and on commemorative birthdays. Some families just used simple tablets with the names of the deceased, others had paintings or sculptures. "Carving Wood to Worship His Parents" tells us that "Ding Lan, during the Han dynasty, lost his parents when he was young. Unable to serve them, he decided to carve two wooden statues of them so that he could carry out worship as if they were alive. After a long period, his wife disrespectfully stabbed the finger of one of the images and blood flowed down from the wooden figure. When Ding Lan saw this he wept, and when he understood what was going on he got rid of his wife."

The other stories take place during various dynasties and include "Carrying Rice [over very long distances] to Feed the Parents"; "Fighting a Tiger to Save His Father"; "Selling Oneself [into servitude] to Cover Father's Funeral Costs"; "Playing Like a Child [as an older man] to Amuse

Elderly Parents"; "Picking up Mulberry Seeds to Feed His Mother"; "Fetching Deer's Milk" (a cure for eye problems but extremely difficult to procure); "Working as a Servant to Support His Mother"; "Renouncing an Official Post to Search for His Mother" (who had been abandoned by her husband years before); and "Tasting Feces Causes Despair." Here, a son was advised by the doctor to taste his sick father's feces. A bitter taste would mean his father was getting better, but sadly it tasted sweet.

Other remarkable examples of filial piety are "Hiding Oranges as a Pleasant Surprise for His Mother," where a son hides the oranges offered at a feast, putting them up his sleeve to bring home to his mother; "Breast-Feeding Her [toothless] Mother-In-Law"; and "Burying His Son Alive to Save His Mother," which tells of a couple unable to feed the whole family—fortunately, a crock of gold was discovered just in time. "Weeping by the Bamboo and Growing Shoots" is about an elderly mother craving bamboo shoots in winter, and her son's tears beside the bamboo provoke miraculous, unseasonal growth. "Cleaning the Chamber Pot in Person" tells about a high official washing his mother's chamber pot.

Then there is the boy Huang Hsiang who, after losing his mother, cared for his father by fanning his bed in summer to cool it and lying in the cold bedding in winter to warm it. Next, "Bubbling Spring and Leaping Carp" exemplifies the rewards of filial piety: Jiang Shi and his wife walked six miles a day for years to fetch pure spring water and fresh fish for his mother, until miraculously a spring bubbled up beside their house, with two carp leaping out of it day after day. "Finger-Biting" features such a close relationship between mother and son that when Zeng Xun was on the road, he felt a sudden pain and, returning home, discovered that his mother had summoned him by biting her own finger. Last but not least, "Obedient to His Stepmother Despite Thin Clothing" tells of a cruel stepmother (who would deny warm clothing to her stepson) being humiliated by his paradoxical piety: "Only I suffer from her cruelty," he tells his father who wants to send the mean woman away, "but if she was gone we would all suffer."

These extraordinary stories of concern, self-sacrifice, and miraculous responses underline the traditional closeness and mutual responsibility of family members which persist to this day in China.

The Water Margin

Shuihu zhuan

(fourteenth century)

ATTRIBUTED TO SHI NAIAN (c. 1296–c. 1372)

OR LUO GUANZHONG (c. 1330–c. 1400)

≈ ⁄

It is generally agreed that there are four outstanding novels in the Chinese literary canon, one of which is *The Water Margin* (*Shuihu zhuan*, literally "the story of the water margin," or "marsh"). These four famous novels represent four different genres: *The Water Margin* is a narrative about heroics; *The Story of the Three Kingdoms* (*Sanguo zhi*) epitomizes the historical novel; *Journey to the West* (*Xiyou ji*) is a tale of epic travel; and Cao Xueqin's *Dream of the Red Chamber* (*Hongloumeng*) is a family drama. They were all written in the vernacular, in a version of Chinese that was closer to the spoken language than the stilted and often obscure classical literary style. This increased their readership and their popularity.

The earliest printed editions of *The Water Margin* date back to the sixteenth century, but some of the stories, loosely based on real events and real people, were no doubt used by market storytellers and appear in Yuan (1279–1368) drama. *The Water Margin* is traditionally ascribed to either Shi Naian or Luo Guanzhong (or to both), although there is apparently no basis for either attribution; thus the authorship remains unknown. (Shi Naian, whose dates are very uncertain, is thought to have been a writer from Suzhou [Jiangsu province], active in the fourteenth century and possibly the teacher of Luo Guanzhong, whose dates vary and whose place of birth is disputed.) While the work most likely developed from oral tales, it became one of the most popular Chinese novels of all time.

The story, which describes the exploits of rebels and outlaws, takes place during the Xuanhe reign period (1119–25) of the Huizong emperor (1082–1135) of the Song.* *Xuanhe* means "Proclaiming peace" and indicates a desire for peace at a very unsettled time, toward the end of the Huizong emperor's reign, when the state was threatened by external enemies from the north as well as by internal rebellion.

The central character, Song Jiang, was the historic bandit leader of an uprising in 1119–21. That, and his subsequent submission to the Huizong emperor and acceptance of an amnesty, after which his bandit troops joined the imperial forces to put down other rebellions and to resist the Jurchen invasion, are part of official history. In the novel, he and thirty-six other men set themselves up at Liangshan Marsh (surrounding Liang Mountain in Shandong province), where they were joined by more rebel bandits to form a total band of a hundred and eight outlaws—including three women. (The number 108 exemplifies the 108 Daoist "stars of destiny," meaning the stars to which each person's destiny is tied, here represented by 108 demons who descended to earth to form the rebel band.)

Much of the first part of the text describes the antics and attributes of these outlaws. All are violent and strong. Lu Zhishen, for example, kills a bully in a fight and is strong enough to uproot a willow tree. Though he enters a Buddhist monastery, he finds the vegetarian diet and restricted life unbearable and thus joins the ranks of the rebels. Lin Chong is driven to violence by the persistent advances made by a corrupt official to Lin Chong's wife; he finds himself excluded from society and so he, too, joins the outlaw band. Hua Rong, less predisposed to violence, is a skilled archer driven to fury when Song Jiang is falsely accused by a local bureaucrat. Although characterized by violence, almost all of these outlaws are victims, or observers, of bullies or powerful, corrupt officials, which drives them to rebellion against unjust authority and the imperial regime.

The political fortunes of the Song dynasty (960–1279) form a background to the novel, which begins with a poem about the peace and harmony of the early days of the Song:

> After the tumult and confusion of the Five Dynasties
>
> One dawn the clouds parted to reveal the sun again
>
> Old grass and trees flourished after new rainfall

In the lanes, the common folk wore silk damask

And the sound of music was heard

The entire realm was at peace.

This vision of peace and tranquility is reinforced in the first chapter: "Grain harvests were plentiful, the working people were happy, no one kept things dropped by others on the road [meaning people were honest about lost property], and doors were left unlocked at night." This peace and tranquility was dependent upon the emperor ("the sun") who was no longer surrounded by unreliable advisors ("the clouds"), but it was clear that over a century later, things were not so secure any longer and imperial failure was marked by peasant uprisings. (The picture of mutual trust, with belongings safe on public roads, is also used by Sima Qian in *The Grand Scribe's Records* [*Shi ji*] to describe good government.)

Of the 108 outlaws, Wu Song is one of the favorites. Violent and often drunk, his exploits are listed in chapter headings such as "Wu Song Offers [chopped off] Heads as Memorial Sacrifices"; "Wu Song's Prestige Shakes the Stockade"; "Wu Song, Drunk, Beats Jiang the Gate Guard Giant"; and "Wu Song Gets Wild at Flying Cloud Ponds." Wu Song beheaded his adulterous sister-in-law after she poisoned his brother. He was punished by having his face tattooed (a common form of punishment in traditional China) and was imprisoned, but he soon escaped and talked of covering his incriminating tattoos with medicinal plasters.

One of the novel's most famous episodes is Wu Song's fight with a tiger. The tiger had been eating travelers on Jingyang Ridge, and local officials had put up warning notices and sent out hunters to capture it. At a nearby inn, the landlord has his own warning notice: "Three bowls of wine and you can't cross the ridge" because of the danger. Wu Song drinks eighteen bowls of wine and sets off, regardless. "Suddenly, from behind a tangled thicket there was a roar and out sprang a white-browed, slant-eyed tiger. Wu Song shouted, 'Aiya' . . . grabbed his stick and dodged behind a rock. The tiger was hungry and thirsty and scratched at the ground with its front claws. Wu Song had a shock and the wine dripped from him as cold sweat. Quick as a flash he dodged behind the tiger . . . the tiger twisted sideways and up and tried to knock Wu Song over . . . it roared a thunderous roar that shook the ridge and swung its tail, like an iron bar, at Wu Song, who dodged . . . The tiger roared and whirled round. When Wu Song saw the tiger coming back at him, he grasped his big stick in both hands and brought it crashing down with all his might. He heard a crack and a huge branch came down from a tree. He'd hoped to smash the tiger but hit an old tree and his stick was broken in two. In a fury the tiger leapt at him with its front paws in front of Wu Song's face. He seized its ruff and held it down. The tiger struggled furiously but Wu Song mustered all his strength. He kicked it wildly, in the eyes and in the face. The tiger howled and scrabbled at the yellow earth, digging a hole. Wu Song pushed the tiger's face into the earth until it lost the strength to resist. Clutching the striped fur with his left hand, he pummeled the tiger with his iron right fist. After fifty to seventy blows, blood poured out of the tiger's eyes, mouth, nose, and ears and it lay still, breathing shallowly. Wu Song let go, found his broken stick under the tree and beat the tiger to death. When he could see it was dead, he put his stick down. 'I'll take this dead tiger down the mountain.' But he could not lift it from the pool of blood in which it lay, for his hands and feet were weak after his exertions. 'It's getting dark. If another tiger attacked, could I fight it? I'll go down and come back for it early tomorrow morning.' He found his felt hat, walked round the thicket and down the mountainside." (The excitement of such fights entranced Mao Zedong when he was young, and one of the last political campaigns he launched, in 1975, was based upon *The Water Margin*. Mao exhorted people to attack Song Jiang's "capitulationism." Arguing that Song Jiang had betrayed his fellow outlaws and the peasant class by joining the imperial forces, Mao did not name any current capitulationist, but the attack was assumed to be directed against Deng Xiaoping, seen as more of a pragmatist than a communist, and, perhaps, against Zhou Enlai. In retrospect, it might also have been directed at Mao's wife, since she had publicly praised Song Jiang as a sort of Robin Hood figure.)**

In later chapters of *The Water Margin*, after Song Jiang's submission to the Huizong emperor who has granted the rebels an amnesty, the former outlaws join the imperial forces to fight the Jurchen invaders as well as other rebel leaders, including Fang La, who was also a historical figure. The Fang La rebellion was partly the result of popular resentment of the "Flower and Rock Network," the name given to special taxes raised by a government agency in charge of collecting rare plants and strange rocks. The Huizong emperor was creating a massive pleasure park to be filled with these flowers and rocks brought at great expense from all over China. (One of Song Jiang's 108 rebels in *The Water Margin* is "blue-faced" Yang Zhi. He started out as a minor official in charge of one of the cargoes of rare plants and rocks seized from the common people for the Huizong emperor's pleasure park. The cargo goes down in a storm on the Yellow River, which means disgrace and dismissal, thus turning Yang Zhi's loyalty to the rebels.)

In the case of Fang La, his family's lacquer grove (a plantation of lacquer trees whose sap was used to create lacquer vessels) was expropriated by the government. Fang La and others wrapped their heads in red scarves and took up resistance. The "Flower and Rock Network" was discontinued as a result of the unrest, but Fang La was captured and sentenced to death by slicing in 1121. In the novel, tragically, 59 of the 108 heroes of Liangshan Marsh are killed as they fight Fang La's men on behalf of the emperor.

The Huizong emperor, admired to this day for his skill at painting and his distinctive spiky calligraphy, was a younger son of the previous emperor and not expected to rule.*** He appears in *The Water Margin* under one of his childhood names, Prince Duan, "the ninth [actually the eleventh] royal prince, good at lute-playing, chess, calligraphy, painting, and football."

The Jurchen, who were originally from Manchuria, had founded the Jin dynasty in 1115. They captured the Huizong emperor in 1127 and drove the Song dynasty south from its capital, Kaifeng, to establish a new capital in Hangzhou (among those who had to flee southward were the poet Li Qingzhao and her husband, Zhao Mingcheng, leaving behind their burnt library), but the Huizong emperor was forced to spend the rest of his life in captivity in Manchuria.

The Story of the Three Kingdoms
Sanguo zhi
(fourteenth century)
ATTRIBUTED TO LUO GUANZHONG (c. 1330–c. 1400)

≫ ≪

One of the "four great novels" of China, *The Story of the Three Kingdoms* (*Sanguo zhi*) is similar in some ways to *The Water Margin* (*Shuihu zhuan*), with battles and political struggles and questions about loyalty and legitimacy. Both are based on history, but where *The Water Margin*, with its 108 heroes (exemplifying the Daoist "stars of destiny") and its bawdy humor, is largely fictional, the more straightforward *The Story of the Three Kingdoms* has been described as two thirds historical and one third fictional. Almost nothing is known of Luo Guanzhong, to whom the novel is tentatively attributed.

The historic context of *The Story of the Three Kingdoms*—the collapse of the Han dynasty in 220 CE and the decades-long struggle of three smaller states (the "Three Kingdoms") for supremacy—is hugely significant in traditional Chinese historiography. The statement with which the novel begins—"The empire long divided, must unite; long united, must divide"—reflects not only the time period that it describes but also the underlying fear that this "unity" could break down. This fear has been present in the Chinese psyche since the First Emperor of the Qin created the united empire of China in 221 BCE by conquering six rival states. Seen from the viewpoint of the late Ming dynasty (1368–1644) when *The Story of the Three Kingdoms* was first printed (in 1522), there had been two major periods of division in Chinese history—that of the "Three Kingdoms" (220–280 CE) and the succeeding centuries before the Sui dynasty reunited the empire in 581 CE; and the much shorter period of fragmentation between the downfall of the Tang in 907 CE and the founding of the Song in 960 CE. During the Ming, anxiety about the breakdown of central, imperial power was increased by the threat from outside, from the Mongols (whose Yuan dynasty had ruled China from 1279 to 1368) and the

Jurchen (who would eventually conquer China in 1644 and establish the Qing dynasty). In the face of the threat of disunion, the major themes of legitimacy and loyalty in *The Story of the Three Kingdoms* were much on the minds of Ming readers.

The written style of the novel is close to the long tradition of historical writing in China, beginning with works such as the *Spring and Autumn Annals* (*Chun qiu*) of the state of Lu for the years 722–481 BCE. The "dynastic" history book *History of the Han* (*Han shu*), completed in 111 CE and covering the period from 206 BCE to 23 CE, echoes *The Story of the Three Kingdoms* with its battles and shifting allegiances, and it provides very similar conclusions about loyalty and legitimacy. According to the *History of the Han*, the uprisings against the Second Emperor of the Qin were justified by the cruelty of his regime and the consequent righteousness of those who sought to overthrow him. Two leaders of rebel bands appeared, Liu Bang (who subsequently triumphed and founded the Han dynasty in 206 BCE) and Xiang Yu, who committed suicide in 202 BCE when surrounded by Liu Bang's troops. The *History of the Han*, as an official compilation, sought to emphasize Liu Bang's virtue and includes significant passages demonstrating Xiang Yu's unfitness to rule.

The legitimacy of a ruler (and dynasty) in the Chinese historical context is not simply a question of family and heritage, but also of celestial approval, expressed through the Mandate of Heaven. By the time *The Story of the Three Kingdoms* begins, in 168 CE, the ruling house of Han has effectively lost the approval of heaven. This is expressed in the appearance of natural disasters such as earthquakes, tidal waves, and sex changes in chickens, as well as the uprising of the Yellow Scarves (or Yellow Turbans). The apparent loss of heavenly favor calls loyalty into question, and the "Three Kingdoms" of the story emerge in the early third century CE from the power struggle of three great warlords: Cao Cao (155–220 CE), whose son, Cao Pi, founded the state of Wei in the north; Liu Bei (161–223 CE), founder of the state of Shu (or Shu Han), in the west; and Sun Quan (182–252 CE), who founded the state of Wu, in the south.

In the first chapter of the novel, Liu Bei, Guan Yu, and Zhang Fei, military figures and major characters in the novel, meet in the Peach

Garden to pledge an oath of loyalty to the Han. It is apparent that the Han is already in terminal decline and the empire is breaking up, but the situation is complicated by the aspirations of Cao Cao who—though apparently possessed of almost unbounded ambition—nevertheless stops short of proclaiming himself ruler of Wei, for he knows that that would be the ultimate disloyalty.

As the story unfolds, Cao Cao controls northern and central China. Though Liu Bei has made an oath of loyalty to the Han, he joins Cao Cao but then turns against him. Liu Bei takes Zhuge Liang as his strategic advisor and allies himself with Sun Quan. Their combined armies defeat Cao Cao at the Battle of the Red Cliff near Chibi (Hubei province) in the winter of 208/209. The alliance of Liu Bei and Sun Quan breaks down and Sun Quan, for a limited time, joins Cao Cao. Sun Quan executes Liu Bei's general Guan Yu and Liu Bei attacks Sun Quan, seeking revenge. Zhuge Liang leads a series of unsuccessful attacks on Cao Cao's son, Cao Pi, and the state of Shu is eventually defeated by the forces of Wei. Finally, Wei and Wu are conquered by the newly established state of Jin.

Considered to be the bloodiest period in China's imperial history, the story is driven forward by the ambitions of the rival warlords and enriched by the exploits of Zhuge Liang (181–234 CE), the chief advisor to Liu Bei, whose cunning stratagems never cease to amaze; they are repeated in schoolbooks and language textbooks to this day. (It is hardly surprising that Mao Zedong, champion of guerrilla warfare, enjoyed the novel as a boy.)

One of Zhuge Liang's famous ruses (in chapter 46) is how he "collects" much-needed arrows from the enemy. Desperately short of arrows and with no time to make thousands of them, Zhuge Liang orders twenty ships to be padded with bundles of straw covered in black cloth and fixed to the outsides of the vessels. On a (fortunately) foggy night, the ships are rowed past the enemy, Cao Cao's army, with their crews drumming and shouting as if about to attack. Protected by the straw, they row backward and forward as Cao Cao's soldiers blindly shoot countless arrows, "up to a hundred thousand," at their noisy but invisible foe.

Perhaps the most famous of Zhuge Liang's stratagems is that of the "empty city" (chapter 95). With the majority of his troops deployed elsewhere or moving grain supplies, Zhuge Liang was trapped in the city of Xicheng by the approach of Sima Yi, one of Cao Cao's generals. Zhuge Liang ordered all the banners and flags removed (to make it look as if the city was unoccupied) and instructed some twenty soldiers to act as commoners, sweeping the road before the city gates which were flung wide open. Then he climbed up on top of one of the city gates, put on his "crane-feather cloak" and took out his *guqin* (a long, flat, zither-like stringed instrument) and plucked it peacefully, with incense burning beside him and a servant holding a yak-tail fly-whisk (which was a symbol of authority). Sima Yi's soldiers, knowing Zhuge Liang's reputation for cunning, assumed that this peaceful setup was a bluff and that hidden inside the city were hundreds of soldiers ready to attack, and beat a hasty retreat.

From the chill opening statement through the endless stories of loyalty and betrayal, the novel exposes the problems of controlling the vast territory of China without strong central leadership. It informed readers while keeping them enthralled by heroic achievements.

The Story of the Lute
Pipa ji
(mid-fourteenth century)
GAO MING (c. 1305–c. 1370)

≈ ⁄≈

G ao Ming's *The Story of the Lute* (*Pipa ji*) is one of the most famous and popular dramas in Chinese history, as demonstrated by the fine illustrated editions that appeared in the late Ming dynasty (1368–1644). Gao Ming was born into an official family in Wenzhou (in Zhejiang province) but his father died when he was young. He eventually served as an official in the last years of the Mongol Yuan dynasty (1279–1368), benefiting from a late decision of the Mongol emperor to broaden access to the bureaucratic exams. He was well-known as a good local magistrate but did not enjoy his period of service, which included combating the pirate Fang Guozhen (who was ravaging the coast of Zhejiang province). Gao Ming retired from official work in 1356, in order to write.

The Story of the Lute is a *chuanqi* drama. This was a form of theater developed in the fourteenth century from a cruder, local form called *nanxi* ("southern drama"), which originated in the Wenzhou area.

Chinese dramas consisted of alternate passages that were sung or spoken (as in operas in the Western world). In the northern form of drama, the *zaju*, the songs were all performed by the main character only. (Famous examples of *zaju* are *Romance of the Western Chamber* [*Xi xiang ji*] and *The Orphan of Zhao* [*Zhao shi guer*]).

In the southern form of drama, on the other hand, many characters sang and there was a broad range of characters, including comics for light relief, and the more serious scenes alternated with entertaining ones. The comic roles included servants, monks, vagabonds, petty officials, and thieves. The language varied as well: since there was no scenery, descriptions of scenes and settings were in parallel prose (i.e., lines of equal length but not rhymed), while monologues and conversations were in verse. There were very limited stage directions included in the text, but the actors developed a huge repertoire of well-known gestures to indicate actions—like riding a horse (hands held together as if holding the bridle) or entering a room (raising one leg very high as if stepping over the high threshold)—and emotions such as worry, indicated by rippling fingers down through long stage beards. The musical accompaniment was provided by a small ensemble (consisting of not more than half a dozen players) with two-stringed violins, lutes, flute, clappers, drum, gong, and cymbals.

The southern form dramas were characteristically very long, with forty or fifty scenes, usually arranged alternating between tragedy and comedy, settings of wealth and poverty, and often performed over several days. Dramas were performed in theaters, in teahouses, and on open-air stages throughout China by professional (all-male) troupes of traveling players. They were enormously popular.

There are various predecessor tales to *The Story of the Lute*, which depicts struggles of loyalty to different higher authorities: parents, to whom filial care was owed according to Confucian beliefs; political masters, to whom full allegiance had to be shown; as well as marital commitment and devotion.

The main story line concerns a young man, Cai, and his wife, Wu, who live in a village. The play, in forty-two scenes, begins with Cai determining to stay at home and drink spring wine and, as a filial son, care for his parents, but his father presses him to go to the capital to take the top examinations and become an official to bring glory to the family. In the next scene, set in the capital, a steward describes the wealth and power of Prime Minister Niu and the beauty of his daughter, Miss Niu. He is joined by a maid and they joke together until interrupted by Madame Niu, the prime minister's wife. A further scene between Cai and his father sees the latter continuing to persuade his son to go to the capital and take the exam. Cai finally agrees to go and promises that he will not take a second wife. In a scene in the capital, a matchmaker goes to the Niu household but Prime Minister Niu makes clear that his daughter will only marry a top candidate in the palace exams.

On his way to the capital, Cai grieves over his separation from home and family but other travelers foresee wealth and good fortune for him. In the capital, there is a scene where the examiners entertain the winners of the exam with some slapstick performances. Back in Cai's village, the area is stricken by famine. Again, this serious and sad scene is followed by a comedy where the trade of the matchmaker in the Niu household is satirized. Because Cai came first in the exams, the prime minister would be proud to marry his daughter to the young man. But Cai refuses, to the fury of the matchmaker. Madame Niu is shocked at the marriage proposal since she does not approve of a marriage where one partner is unwilling (of course we know nothing of the feelings of Miss Niu). Cai petitions the emperor to be allowed to return home but this is refused as Cai's highest "filial" loyalty should be to his emperor (and ergo to the prime minister).

Even in the famine-stricken village, there is a comedy scene about a local headman who has been pilfering grain, which needs to be replaced before government officials arrive to distribute it as famine relief (a situation that recalls one of Yuan Mei's poems in the 1700s about the travails of a tax collector). The headman finds some grain but not enough, and he keeps reappearing in different disguises to beg for more. Cai's wife, Wu, has some grain but the village headman steals it from her. She attempts suicide but is found in time by Cai's father, who then tries to kill himself. Both are rescued by a neighbor.

Back in the capital, the matchmaker calls on Cai and there follows a scene of a magnificent wedding, at which Cai continues to protest. Back in the village, Wu is reduced to eating grain husks, which upsets her mother-in-law. Both ladies faint and Cai's mother dies. They are so poor by now that the neighbor has to pay for her burial. While Cai remains miserable in the capital with his new, second wife, Miss Niu, his father sickens (despite medicine administered by Wu) and dies. Wu cuts off her hair to pay for the funeral. A swindler delivers a fake letter to Cai, which tells him all is well back home, even though, at that very time, Wu is so poor she has to dig the grave of Cai's father herself. A messenger from the spirit world suggests she should go to the capital. She paints portraits of her dead parents-in-law to take to the capital. Meanwhile, Miss Niu suggests that she and her husband should go to his village, to cheer him up, but her father refuses as her departure would be unfilial to him.

Wu takes to the road to the capital, carrying her ancestral portraits and her lute (*pipa*). She loses the portraits (which are later, amazingly, discovered by Cai), but she carries on, playing her lute, the only way she can make a little money to support herself. Her performances in various places give rise to some small comic scenes. Eventually, disguised as a nun, she enters the Niu household in the capital where she discovers her portraits and writes an anonymous message on the back about lack of filiality.

Prime Minister Niu finally allows his daughter to go to Cai's village. He also petitions the emperor, asking him to commend Cai's filial devotion to his parents, thereby exonerating him from disloyal behavior to his emperor. Then the prime minister himself makes the long trip to Cai's village. This sequence is interrupted by comic scenes in which a messenger runs backward and forward between capital and village and is eventually stripped of his clothing. It all ends happily, with the two wives participating filially in mourning for Cai's parents, whereupon he returns to the capital with both wives to resume his brilliant career. (Given Cai's treatment of his first wife, Wu, it is not, perhaps, surprising that in a different, earlier version of the story, Cai is killed by lightning, perhaps fitting retribution for both his treatment of Wu and his rather dilatory filial piety.)

It is said that the founding emperor of the Ming, Zhu Yuanzhang (1328–1398), was so enthusiastic about *The Story of the Lute* that he wanted all the aristocratic families to purchase a copy and ordered that it be performed on a daily basis.

The Classic of Lu Ban

Lu Ban jing

(fifteenth century)

AUTHOR UNKNOWN

~≈ ⁄≈

The Classic of Lu Ban (*Lu Ban jing*) is described as a carpenter's manual. It was compiled in the fifteenth century on the basis of earlier material from the Song (960–1279) and Yuan (1279–1368) dynasties. The character *jing* in the Chinese book title is the character used to describe most of the Confucian classics (such as the *Book of Songs* [*Shi jing*] and the *Book of Documents* [*Shu jing*]), appropriated by carpenters to give respectability to their manual and trade.

Lu Ban is often described as the "patron saint of carpenters," a mythical figure said to have lived in the fifth century BCE, his divine future signified by a miraculous perfume and a flock of white cranes surrounding the house at the moment of his birth. Though they are not listed in *The Classic of Lu Ban*, according to folk legend he invented the carpenter's square and plane, drill and ink-box (a pot through which a string was drawn, picking up the ink, in order to mark straight lines), the siege ladder and grappling irons (hooks) for naval warfare, and he also created a wooden magpie that could fly. His wife is said to have invented the umbrella, to keep the rain off craftsmen as they worked. *The Classic of Lu Ban* tells us that he retired at the age of forty to live as a recluse, settling on Mount Li. There he met a Daoist immortal who taught him to fly on the clouds. Lu Ban then ascended into the skies, leaving behind his saw and axe in the Cave of the Immortal of the White Deer. In succeeding dynasties, he would appear magically when required. Many of the legends about the construction of the Forbidden City (*Zi jin cheng*) (early fifteenth century) in Beijing, and the surrounding city walls, refer to magical intervention by Lu Ban. Carpenters were baffled by the task of constructing the timber frame of the corner towers on the walls when suddenly an old man appeared carrying a complex birdcage. The cage had an upper part that provided a model for the corner towers. When they wanted to thank the old man, he had disappeared. Likewise, when stonemasons were puzzled how they could collect enough stones to pave the great gates of the city wall, an old man appeared leading a flock of sheep and goats. He had spoken to some stones in the river and changed them into a flock which he could easily drive into the city. There, the animals miraculously turned into perfectly cut blocks of stone and settled into place.

Lu Ban was worshipped by carpenters of all sorts, housebuilders, masons, tile makers, and furniture makers. During the Ming (1368–1644), and possibly earlier, craftsmen such as carpenters and stonemasons grouped themselves into guilds. These crafts were hereditary and it was generally compulsory for sons to follow their fathers in the same craft. The carpenters' and stonemasons' guild naturally took Lu Ban as its "patron saint." The guilds had little power but nevertheless operated to support guild members, to try to protect them from the abuse of officials, to provide welfare assistance if possible, and sometimes to set up institutions such as guild cemeteries. Probably their most important functions were the standardization of wages and the organization of rituals and celebrations of their members, marking such events as the legendary birthday of Lu Ban. At annual meetings, apprentices who had served their training period of three years and three months could apply to join, kowtowing three times and burning incense before an image of Lu Ban.

During the construction process of a simple Chinese house, much building magic was involved. When the foundations for the wooden framework of a house were prepared, it was customary to place coins where the main door, and the four corners of the main floor, were planned.

As the curtain walls (which were not load-bearing) were erected around the wooden framework, the prospective owner of the house might slip in a cinnamon leaf to ensure generations of high officials for his family, or a handful of rice to ensure prosperity—but the carpenters, if unhappy with their pay and conditions, could put in a fragment of pottery and a broken saw which could cause the death of the husband, remarriage of the wife, and dispersal of the family. If in their anger they inscribed the character for "prison" on a window joint, this was meant to bring lawsuits and imprisonment. Many such practices are listed in the *The Classic of Lu Ban*, most designed to bring happiness and prosperity to the household, but other sources list a number of methods of revenge for disgruntled builders.*

Other aspects of folklore relating to building included in *The Classic of Lu Ban* are auspicious days for construction and related activities such as felling trees in the mountains, good days for cutting bamboo to avoid it being worm-eaten, leveling the ground, erecting the columns, hoisting up the ridgepole (an occasion for celebration and a special meal for the housebuilders), plastering, making a door, repairing a stove, erecting a pigsty, and even suitable days for building a bed and hanging the bed-curtains. Determining the best time for certain activities reflects the traditional Chinese almanac, *Tongshu*, with its listings of auspicious and inauspicious days for setting out on journeys or embarking on other specific activities.

The Classic of Lu Ban is divided into three sections, and many editions contain useful illustrations. The first and second sections list many of the technical tasks carried out by builders. These include joinery for the main hall; joinery for an ancestral hall; the construction of a garden kiosk over water; building of a granary; construction of a cowshed and the "prescribed measurements of the timber parts of a cowshed"; putting together a stand for a horse saddle or a carrying case for chickens; making an official sedan chair; as well as making articles of furniture such as clothes stands (Chinese robes were often kept folded over on clothes stands), clothes chests, or chairs and tables and chessboards. It is thought that these instructions (which vary between precise measurements and rather vague poems) were largely symbolic and would not have been closely studied and followed, since carpenters would learn their trade from their master and their level of literacy might not have been high.

The physiognomy of a house and its surroundings were of great importance. Poor siting of the house itself, or of the approach to a house, could bring bad luck. The third section of *The Classic of Lu Ban* consists of little rhymes about good and bad aspects of construction and plan and their consequences:

If the door leaves are askew, Husband and wife will not get on,
The family property is squandered, The family members plan
to leave.

If there are many knots in the door timbers, The family will suffer
from boils and ulcers,
If the knots are in rows of two or three, Your sons will leave
home to become soldiers. [This would be a disgrace, since
traditionally in China, soldiers were regarded as low ruffians.]

If the road in front of the house resembles a goose's foot,
The family will argue endlessly.

Winding and tortuous like a worm, A winding path will bring a
bad atmosphere,
There is inevitable separation, Sons and wife will suffer and
bankruptcy ensue.

If there is a stone slab in front of the house as flat as a plate,
The family will be rich and renowned.

These beliefs could be ascribed to geomancy or *fengshui*, the art of
favorable siting of buildings and graves, and there are certainly similar-
ities—but the term *fengshui* does not occur in *The Classic of Lu Ban*,
since practitioners of geomancy were quite different from carpenters.
Geomancy is strongest in south China and is most closely associated
with burial, particularly secondary burial (in which bones that had
previously lain in a temporary grave were cleaned and removed to a
permanent grave-site selected by a geomancer)—which had nothing to
do with the practice of carpentry and building houses. Carpenters and
their associates might work within the same belief system, but their own
craft was quite separate and it was their pride in the craft that gave rise
to their own "classic" text.

Journey to the West
Xiyou ji
(sixteenth century)
ATTRIBUTED TO WU CHENG'EN (c. 1500–c. 1582)

≈ ≈

J ourney to the West (*Xiyou ji*), possibly the best-known of China's "four great novels" (the others being *The Water Margin*, *The Story of the Three Kingdoms*, and *Dream of the Red Chamber*), is a strange combination of history and legend, adventure and fantasy, and ranges through Buddhism and Daoism, Confucianism and the pantheon of heavenly rulers.

Journey to the West is loosely based on the famous pilgrimage of the seventh-century Chinese Buddhist monk Xuanzang, who—like Faxian some two hundred years earlier—traveled westward to India in search of Buddhist scriptures.* Born in Henan province around 602 CE, Xuanzang left Chang'an (today's Xi'an) in 629 (even though he had not received the Tang emperor's permission), visited major Buddhist sites in India, and, for several years, studied Buddhism at the great Nalanda Monastery. He returned to China in 645, bringing many Buddhist texts with him to be translated into Chinese, and was warmly welcomed by the emperor. Xuanzang spent the rest of his life translating a number of these texts in the Great Goose Pagoda in the capital city, and he also wrote an important account of his journey, *Great Tang Records of the Western Regions* (*Da Tang xiyu ji*).

However, in contrast with Xuanzang's historic travel account, in the fictional *Journey to the West* the pilgrim-monk Xuanzang (also called Tripitaka, meaning "Three Baskets," the Buddhist canon) is joined by four superhuman companions: a monkey who was King of the Monkeys until he disgraced himself; a pig; a sand monster; and a white horse who once was a dragon prince.

Whereas the sand monster (Mr. Sand) and the white horse are effectively servants, looking after Xuanzang/Tripitaka, the Monkey and the Pig are both characters who add depth to the story. They may be viewed as characterizations that enrich the Buddhist content, the Monkey serving as an exemplar of the complexity of mind and heart that must be subdued, and the Pig, always chasing food or pretty women, emblematic of the more animal side of human nature, which must also be overcome in the pursuit of Buddhahood.

Its status as one of the "four great novels" apart, the work has been immensely popular in China for hundreds of years, not just in its full form but through adaptations of all sorts. There are Peking opera versions (of the whole story and of parts), and the monkey character, in particular, appears in dance and acrobatic performance. Illustrated children's books, especially those that feature the Monkey King, have long been popular and continue to be published all over the Far East. Just as popular in Japan as in China, long series of television films and cartoon versions have been produced and shown around the world.

Journey to the West is attributed to the little-known Wu Cheng'en, although many authorities disagree on the attribution. Wu Cheng'en was a sixteenth-century scholar from Huai'an (in today's Jiangsu province) who served in the imperial university in Nanjing. Known for his classical poems, in later life he is said to have become interested in the folktales that form part of the legends around Xuanzang and his epic journey to India.

Early printed editions of *Journey to the West* survive from the 1590s. Comprised of one hundred lengthy chapters, the novel has two main parts (the first part setting up the story, the second part telling the journey itself), and it opens with several chapters describing the extraordinary birth and subsequent escapades of the Monkey King. Born from a stone, the Monkey King was endowed with magical powers that enabled him to lead the monkeys to defeat demons, but he was also cheeky and overconfident, challenging sages and rulers. His downfall came when he ate all the peaches in the garden of the Queen of Heaven, whereupon the Buddha had him imprisoned until he was set free by the compassionate Bodhisattva Guanshiyin (or Guanyin, famously described in the *Lotus Sutra*) and ordered to become one of Tripitaka's travel companions.

At the beginning of the novel, a rock that had been present since the beginning of the world suddenly split open and gave birth to a small rock egg. This rock egg, in turn, cracked to reveal a stone monkey. He could climb and run and his eyes flashed a brilliant light that shone as far as heaven where the Jade Emperor (one of the Daoist Three Great Ones, or major deities) sat in his cloud palace. The Jade Emperor noticed this flashing light and was informed of its origin. Meanwhile the stone monkey led all the other monkeys through a waterfall to a magical land, the Mountain of Fruit and Flowers, where they all lived happily together. The stone monkey became the Monkey King. One day he felt sad and told the monkeys that he had a premonition about the future, and determined to find out what dreadful things might happen. He set off to find the secret of immortality. He first sought answers from the Buddhist patriarch Subhuti (who appears in the *Diamond Sutra*) but did not like metaphysics, nor mental exercises, nor meditation—although he *was* grateful for instruction in the seventy-two transformations by which he could turn himself into anything he fancied and travel any way he wanted, soaring through the clouds or diving through water without harm. The Monkey King then organized his monkeys, expanded them into a huge army by plucking his own hairs and turning them into more monkeys, and collected armaments by magical means. Going up to heaven, he was entrusted with the care of the Peach Garden with its 3,200 peach trees. These trees ripened at different times, with the large peaches that could convey immortality ripening once every nine thousand years. When the Queen of Heaven with her ladies came to collect some of the large peaches for a banquet, she discovered that the Monkey King had eaten them. Furthermore, he had stolen the elixir of immortality belonging to the great sage Laozi. Having also acquired a magic iron cudgel that he could conceal behind his ear by turning it into a needle, he was finally brought down by the Buddha who imprisoned him under a rock. His kingship lost, the Monkey was rescued by Guanyin, who wanted him to atone for his sins by accompanying Tripitaka to India to collect Buddhist scriptures. (Tripitaka is obliged to control the Monkey by means of a metal cap on his head that tightens painfully whenever Tripitaka recites the "cap-tightening scripture.")

The other superhuman travel companions of Xuanzang/Tripitaka are also chosen by the Bodhisattva Guanyin. Encountering an old man whose daughter has been imprisoned by the Pig, who has an appetite for food to match his appetite for women, they free her and take the Pig along with them. It transpires that he had formerly served as the Admiral of the Navy of Heaven but had been banished to earth for flirting with Chang E, the Moon goddess. Like the Monkey, it seems that Guanyin sent the Pig on this difficult journey in order for him to atone for his previous transgressions. A further companion is added to the group, Mr. Sand, who had previously served as a guard to the Queen Mother of the West, a Daoist divinity who presides over paradise. He, too, was banished, because he broke one of her crystal goblets. The travelers also acquire a white horse, who had been the third son of the Dragon King, sentenced to death for burning his father's huge pearl but saved by Guanyin.

They journey on, endlessly meeting apparently impossible obstacles such as a river 8,000 miles wide without a boat in sight (they cross it by tying together a set of skulls seized from a demon and adding a gourd to create a boat), or an apparently frozen lake that is not as safe as they had assumed (they are saved by a giant white turtle). Demons with massive armies, whirlwinds, and a variety of fish monsters appear at all times, and the Monkey frequently has to use his seventy-two transformations (and the Pig his thirty-six, and Mr. Sand his eighteen, transformations) to master all these challenges.

Eventually they meet the Buddha himself in India and receive the scriptures, although two of the Buddha's disciples, angered at not receiving bribes, first present them with blank pages. Even on the way home, though the demons and other evil forces have receded, there are still moments of drama, as when they are shipwrecked and have to rescue the precious scriptures. They are welcomed back to the capital, Chang'an, and Tripitaka settles down to translate. He and the Monkey are rewarded with Buddhahood, Mr. Sand becomes an Arhat (an enlightened being), the white horse is turned into a Naga (a wise being, half human and half snake, presumably intended as an improvement in lifestyle), and the Pig is made an altar cleaner. He is upset and jealous but the Buddha points out that he can eat all the spare food offerings.

The main attraction of the novel lies in its lively descriptions of armies of demons and of the physical difficulties that face the pilgrims. Their cunning, supernatural weapons and heroic feats, derived from endless folktales about evil spirits and their destruction as well as the more prosaic but real difficulties faced by Chinese Buddhist pilgrims on their way to India, create a narrative of constant excitement and surprise.

Plum in a Golden Vase
Jinpingmei
(c. 1582–96)
AUTHOR UNKNOWN

The Carnal Prayer Mat
Rou putuan
(1657)
ATTRIBUTED TO LI YU (1610–1680)

～ ✍

These are two famous erotic novels, nearly contemporary but different in content and approach and, indeed, attribution. Separate research by two major scholars, Wu Han and Patrick Hanan, suggests that *Plum in a Golden Vase* (*Jinpingmei*) was circulating in manuscript form from about 1582, during the reign of the Wanli emperor of the Ming (r. 1572–1620), and that it includes an underlying criticism of the emperor—who by this time was seriously neglecting affairs of state and refusing to attend court or to organize proper resistance to the growing threats from the north. Reinforcing this criticism is the setting of the novel, in the last years of the Northern Song (which deliberately echoes the background of *The Water Margin* [*Shuihu zhuan*]), during the reign of the equally disastrous Huizong emperor (r. 1100–1126)—who, as mentioned, was forced to flee his capital, Kaifeng, as it was overrun by the Jurchen Jin troops from the north.

The author of *Plum in a Golden Vase* is unknown, although there is a preface written by the "Laughing Scholar of Lanling." The Confucian philosopher Xunzi was appointed magistrate of Lanling (in southern Shandong province) in 255 BCE, and the reference is presumably intended to draw attention to the theme of the novel, the destructive nature of self-indulgence and fixation on status and wealth. Chinese readers would have been aware that Xunzi believed that human nature was essentially bad and needed the constraint of morality and ritual to lead it to goodness (in direct opposition to Mencius, who held that human beings were fundamentally good). The story of the decline of the parvenu hero, Ximen Qing, in *Plum in a Golden Vase* would seem to follow Xunzi's view.

The novel is written in the vernacular and, bizarrely, begins by repeating the famous episode in *The Water Margin* where the rebel Wu Song kills a tiger. In *The Water Margin*, Wu Song avenges the murder of his brother by killing the brother's murderous wife, Golden Lotus (Pan Jinlian). In *Plum in a Golden Vase*, on the other hand, Wu Song stays with his brother and his shrewish sister-in-law, Pan Jinlian, who makes every effort to seduce him. She fails but soon after meets Ximen Qing, a newly rich merchant, who kills her husband and takes her as one of his wives.

It is not only in the overlap of characters that *Plum in a Golden Vase* incorporates elements of *The Water Margin*. The storytelling format is similar, and *Plum in a Golden Vase*, like the earlier novel, is divided into a hundred chapters, each containing two or more situations or stories, and each chapter ends with the same narratorial exhortation, "And if you don't know what happened next, listen to the next chapter."

Though borrowing from *The Water Margin*, *Plum in a Golden Vase* differs from it (and from other historically based novels such as *The Story of the Three Kingdoms* [*Sanguo zhi*]) because most of the text concentrates on one completely fictitious character and the women in his household. The unusual stress on domestic affairs and the lives of women is reflected in the novel's Chinese title, *Jinpingmei*, which is composed of characters from the names of the three major female figures: Pan Jinlian, or "Golden Lotus" Pan; Li Ping'er, or "Little Vase" Li; and Pang Chunmei, or "Spring Plum Blossom" Pang.

The first sixty chapters record the rise and success of Ximen Qing and the many sexual encounters he enjoys, both with his six wives and with the many other women in his household. There are detailed descriptions of various types of sexual congress, and though the language may seem flowery, involving "jade flutes," "tortoise heads," "cinnabar fields," and "flower hearts," there are also more sexually explicit descriptions. One illustration used in many editions of the novel bears the intriguing title "Golden Lotus Plays the Jade Flute and Hits the Cat," but it turns out that only the first part refers to sex because Golden Lotus does indeed hit out at an angora cat that has foolishly leapt onto the lovers' bed.

In the second half of the novel Ximen Qing dies, exhausted by sex but also poisoned by a powerful aphrodisiac that he obtained from a mysterious monk "from the West." The novel suggests that human capacity for sex is limited, and Ximen Qing has gone well over the limit, even before taking the poisonous aphrodisiac. His favorite son dies, his favorite wife dies, and after his own death his household gradually collapses. His only surviving son by his first, legitimate wife enters a monastery (he is also encouraged by a mysterious monk) to lead a celibate life—which means the end of Ximen Qing's family line and that his ancestral spirits will no longer be fed and cared for.

The novel is, however, much more than just a series of seduction scenes (which in fact make up only a small part of the entire text) and the underlying Confucian moral lesson. It contains an enormous amount of detail about daily life in the Ming era, such as clothing, food and its serving, festivals with lanterns and fireworks, and formal visits and how they are conducted. In chapter 15, the women of Ximen Qing's household watch the bobbing red globes of the lanterns seen everywhere on the evening of the Lantern Festival (i.e., the fifteenth day of the first month), which closes the festivities of the Chinese New Year. They notice their neighbor's children and their smaller lanterns in the shape of fish, shrimps, and crabs, and they go out onto the streets where bamboo scaffolds have been put up to hang more lanterns. In a procession of lanterns, the women see lanterns shaped like snowflakes, monkeys, elephants, and more crabs.

Some of Ximen Qing's wives and female servants take birthday gifts to an older lady, "two plates of longevity peaches, a jar of wine, and a plate of long-life noodles." (In China, peaches are symbols of longevity; similarly, extra-long noodles signify long life and are still often served on birthdays.) The old lady wears a long-sleeved, silk padded jacket with flowers on a red ground, a pale-green skirt, and a sable coat. Three young women wear white damask padded jackets and blue satin skirts. One of them also has a sleeveless over-jacket in dark green with a gold border, and they all have pearls and jade on their piled-up hair, which is held in place by phoenix-shaped hairpins.

The second erotic novel, *The Carnal Prayer Mat* (*Rou putuan*; it can also be translated as "Prayer Mat of Flesh"), is very different from *Plum in a Golden Vase*: shorter, wittier, and with a fairly preposterous act of surgery at its center. There is also less detail of clothing and furnishings in *The Carnal Prayer Mat*, which was probably written by the versatile Li Yu (1610–1680). Born in Rugao (in present-day Jiangsu province), Li Yu was a novelist and short-story writer, an actor and playwright, as well as a publisher (he was involved with the *Mustard Seed Garden Manual of Painting* [*Jieziyuan huazhuan*]).

The Carnal Prayer Mat tells of a young scholar whose sobriquet is Weiyangsheng (meaning "Before Midnight Scholar") and who is very keen on sex, particularly sex in the evening. Early in the novel, Weiyangsheng meets a Buddhist monk who is devoted to the ascetic life, to meditation on his prayer mat, and avoiding all temptation. He cautions Weiyangsheng against carnal pleasures, pointing out that these can multiply disastrously, bringing catastrophe on a family. Ignoring this warning, Weiyangsheng, who is married to the daughter of a very strict man, is keen to introduce his wife to erotic delights though he finds her prudish (and blames her reading of books about virginal female exemplars of filial piety). He also suffers from self-doubt. Questioning his friend about aspects of sex, he exaggerates his stamina only to be told, "that's not a superior performance," and that his equipment is lacking in size. Through a chance meeting with a bandit, Weiyangsheng is introduced to a Daoist magician who carries out an improbable implantation on him. Weiyangsheng enjoys affairs with many married women. The husband of one of these avenges the insult by having an affair with Weiyangsheng's wife and eventually selling her to a brothel, where she is so ashamed she kills herself.

Though *The Carnal Prayer Mat* is less moralistic than *Plum in a Golden Vase*, it also reflects the end of a family line, for Weiyangsheng finally enters a Buddhist monastery.

Travels of Xu Xiake
Xu Xiake youji
(seventeenth century)

XU XIAKE (1587–1641)

Tracks of a Wild Goose in the Snow
Hongxuan yinyuan tuji
(1847–50)

LINQING (1791–1846)

≈ ⁄

Travel as a literary subject has a complicated history in China. For Buddhists such as Faxian and Xuanzang, travel as pilgrimage was a major subject. Most government officials were obliged to travel widely, both to reach the cities that they had been appointed to govern, and to understand the area over which they had control. Thus many poems and essays written by officials such as Du Fu and Li Shangyin contain reference to travel, and they sometimes include descriptions of particular places. Some scholars describe travel writing of the Song dynasty as a specific genre, although examples are generally culled from poems.

Both *Travels of Xu Xiake* (*Xu Xiake youji*) and *Tracks of a Wild Goose in the Snow* (*Hongxuan yinyuan tuji*) are accounts of travels in China. Xu Xiake's work is extremely well-known and taken seriously (but quite hard to read), while Linqing's writings are less-known but more lively accounts of journeys taken for cultural interest.

Toward the end of the Ming period (1368–1644), Xu Xiake spent over thirty years traveling around China and recording his travels in an account that was published posthumously. He was born in what is now Jianyin in Jiangsu province, and unlike officials who traveled on government business, he seems to have traveled out of personal interest. He crossed China accompanied by a servant, traveling on foot and on muleback, frequently relying on the hospitality of Buddhist temples to stay overnight. His work is meticulous, with detailed measurements of distance, and he is credited with locating the source of the West River (Xi jiang), near the border of Guizhou and Guangxi, and establishing the source of the headwaters of the Yangtse River (thus correcting long-held beliefs about the magical flood-control works of the mythical Emperor Yu, as recorded in the Confucian classic *Book of Documents* [*Shu jing*]). Xu Xiake's descriptions are indeed precise, but very much concerned with the physical aspects of the countryside through which he traveled. In 1633, for example, he visited the famous Buddhist Mount Wutai (Wutai shan) (meaning "Five Platforms Mountain") in Shanxi province, one of the four sacred Buddhist mountains of China (the others being Mount Emei, Mount Putuo, and Mount Jiuhua). The highest of Mount Wutai's five peaks is about three thousand meters above sea level. The scenery is majestic, but even more interesting to most travelers from the ninth century CE onward (when a Japanese monk, Ennin, came to visit) have been the more than fifty wonderful temples there, including the two oldest surviving timber-frame buildings in China, which were new when Ennin saw them.* (In addition to the four sacred Buddhist mountains in China, there are four sacred Daoist mountains—Wudang, Longhu, Qiyun, and Qingcheng—as well as the older classification of the Five Great Mountains, which represent the four directions and the center in traditional Chinese cosmology.)

Xu Xiake, however, does not describe any of the temple buildings of Mount Wutai, and his descriptions are strictly those of a geographer. "I left the capital [Beijing] on the twenty-eighth day of the seventh month . . . in order to travel to Wutai. On the fourth day of the eighth month I reached the southern pass of Fuping. The mountains rise from Tang county and grow more massive at the Tang River. When you get to Huangkui, they flatten out and are not so tortured. From Fuping, going southwest, I crossed a stone bridge and to the northwest all the peaks rose in sequence. I traveled eight *li* [a *li* is a Chinese mile, about three quarters of a kilometer] northward along the left bank of a stream to where a small stream joins it from the west. Leaving the large stream, I followed the one from the west, turning north as the mountain gorge narrowed. After seven more *li*, I ate at the post station [the place where horses used by couriers were changed] at Taizipu. After going north for fifteen *li*, I heard the sound of a stream. Turning my head, the rock walls were very high and dropped straight down like slices of melon. Above was a waterfall but because of the current drought, the waterfall was dry."

Only occasionally does Xu Xiake write in a more personal manner, for example when visiting the Wuyi mountains of Fujian province, describing the ascent of Bright Cliff where a perpendicular rock face had an iron chain and notches cut into the cliff for footholds and he found himself "clinging to the chain." In a narrow cleft, "I went on my knees and wriggled like a snake through a gap . . ." that was not even half a meter wide.

Some two hundred years later, a far more accessible series of travel descriptions can be found in *Tracks of a Wild Goose in the Snow*, the memoirs of Linqing, a Manchu who served as a high official, as had his father. (The image of footprints in the snow in the book title suggests the ephemeral nature of human life.) Linqing passed the highest palace exams in 1809 and was appointed to the Grand Secretariat (the imperial secretariat at the highest level) and the Hanlin Academy (the imperial academy); he served as a local official, provincial judge, and provincial governor, and supervised the strengthening of the flood defenses of the north bank of the Yangtse in 1840–41, during the First Opium War. His mother was a descendant of the famous painter Yun Shouping (1633–1690), and it was said that Linqing's broad cultural interests were due to her. Late in life he acquired a famous garden in Beijing, the Banmu yuan (Half-Acre Garden), believed to have been created by the famous seventeenth-century garden designer and writer Li Yu (who wrote the preface to the *Mustard Seed Garden Manual of Painting* [*Jieziyuan huazhuan*]).

Throughout his life, Linqing visited as many famous landmarks as he could (traveling by various methods including on muleback, by boat, and carried up mountains on bamboo litters) and enjoyed the life of an intensely cultured man—which was depicted in the many illustrations to *Tracks of a Wild Goose in the Snow*. Illustrations show him with his children "reading the classics in the Preservation of Calm Studio" located in his garden, with a fine bonsai and a pot (with a cracked-ice glaze) in which a small rock stands like a miniature mountain. He describes the Hangzhou bore, or tidal flood (when a great wave rushes up the Qiantang River); and how he, his mother, and grandmother, on a visit to the beautiful city of Hangzhou, fed the colored carp in the Jade Spring pool at the Jinglian monastery. On Hangzhou's famous West Lake, near the six bridges, Linqing "questioned the willows" (meaning he studied the calligraphic pattern of willow leaves). Also in Zhejiang province, he records his pride at visiting, near Shaoxing, the "tomb" of the mythical Emperor Yu (an earlier "tamer of the floods") as a young man of seventeen. (Linqing was three years younger than the great Han historian Sima Qian had been when he visited the site in the second century BCE.) Linqing describes the Orchid Pavilion near Shaoxing, where the greatest of all calligraphers, Wang Xizhi (c. 303–c. 361 CE), enjoyed a famous poetry-writing party beside a "cup-floating stream" (an artificial stream along which cups of wine were floated); and he comments on the most famous private library in China, the Tianyige at Ningbo, which held 70,000 volumes in its heyday—and served as the inspiration for the Qianlong emperor's (r. 1735–1796) imperial library, called Wenyuange, in the Forbidden City.

Linqing climbed the sacred Mount Tai (Tai shan), one of the Five Great Mountains (which was climbed by many emperors seeking to commune with heaven); and he watched the autumn ceremony of worship in honor of Confucius in the Confucian temple in the sage's hometown of Qufu: "We saw the solemn ritual performed by the last descendant of Confucius accompanied by other officials and followers." Dressed in official uniforms, they bowed and turned and waved long pheasant feathers in a slow and solemn dance as music was played on ancient jade chimes, bronze bells, and flat sounding boards: "I will boast about having been to the sage's hall." In the nearby Grove of Confucius, the family's graveyard, Linqing was told that the very different trees there had been brought from all over China, and he was surprised to see no birds' nests or brambles in them.

Scenes from Linqing's own life are depicted between descriptions of sightseeing tours. In the chapter "Receiving Bounty in the Hall of History" he wrote that "in 1821, I was appointed to be the Chief Editor of the *History of the Han* [*Han shu*], and I had the honor to receive gifts from the emperor: two pieces of fine silk, eight pieces of porcelain, a box of dried fruit, a pair of perch, and a deer." He also described his seven-year-old daughter gathering magnolia petals as he wrote in his studio, while a servant boy fanned a little brazier heating a kettle. (The image of a servant boy using a bamboo fan at a little stove is one that is included as a set type in the *Mustard Seed Garden Manual of Painting*. Used in many landscape paintings, it evokes the pleasure of welcoming friends to a rustic hut for tea or warm Shaoxing wine.)

When he was governor of Guizhou, "the provincial governor's *yamen* [office] was on Jiuping Hill. One evening, a long-horned cow came in and lay down in the main hall and looked as if it had grievances to recount. [Part of Linqing's job as governor consisted in deciding upon the grievances brought before him.] I ordered it to be brought in and it shook its tail as if in supplication. I learned that it belonged to a local man named Cai, a butcher, who had planned to slaughter it that day but it had escaped. I paid Cai the price for the cow, telling him not to kill it. It was set free on Jiuping Hill."

Linqing's account of his life illustrates the mixture of Confucian institutionalism and Buddhist and Daoist sensitivities adopted, or felt, by Chinese gentlemen during the Ming and Qing dynasties.

The Craft of Gardens
Yuan ye
(1631–34)
JI CHENG (1582–c. 1642)

≈ ≋

In the seventeenth century, during the final years of the Ming dynasty (1368–1644), there was a demand, among the merchant class in particular, for handbooks of style and connoisseurship to enable individuals to emulate the sophisticated lifestyle of the literati. What antiquities should they buy? How should they furnish the different rooms in their houses and what should their gardens look like? Ji Cheng's *The Craft of Gardens* (*Yuan ye*) falls somewhere between a handbook and a poetic treatise on gardens, containing technical instructions and illustrations as well as lyrical descriptive passages.

"Literati" is a vague term, loosely indicating the cultural aspirations and interests of the social class that achieved government office through passing the series of examinations (which allowed entry into the bureaucracy). While in office and then, particularly, in retirement, government officials aspired to write poetry, create gardens, and to achieve a certain skill in calligraphy and painting or connoisseurship of these arts. Merchants, too, aspired to this lifestyle, but in order to acquire respectability and then educate their sons for the examinations, they first had to acquire land. Being a merchant was despised, but land equaled wealth and respectability. Their wealth also often allowed them to create gardens.

Apart from Ji Cheng's date of birth and his place of origin (Tongling in Jiangsu province), almost nothing is known about him. The fortunes of *The Craft of Gardens*, considered one of the great works of garden writing, suffered due to the fact that it had a preface written by Ruan Dacheng (c. 1587–1646). Ruan is known for his poems and plays but he was also a politician from a "family of influence, but of corrupt and unsavory reputation," and his disreputable career meant that *The Craft of Gardens*, with which he had associated himself closely, was lost and forgotten for many decades.

Though imperial and aristocratic gardens and hunting grounds had been created in China for millennia, it was mainly from the Song dynasty (960–1279) onward that it became fashionable to create small garden retreats, either on plots within a city or on land outside. These gardens became very much part of the literati tradition, a self-conscious, partially Daoist-inspired setting for literati pastimes such as poetry gatherings (where wine was drunk as a forfeit if someone could not provide an appropriate line of verse), for playing the (zither-like) *guqin*, for sitting in a specially constructed pavilion to admire the moon or listen to raindrops pattering on banana leaves, and to appreciate plants in their season. Gardens also often contained special library buildings and rooms for overwintering plants.

China's favored region for garden construction was Jiangnan (in the Yangtse delta area), in and around towns such as Suzhou and Yangzhou, where many famous gardens still survive. These two towns—favored by retired bureaucrats, famous for their luxury products, and with a relatively mild climate and plenty of water—were ideal for garden construction. Twelve major gardens can be visited in Suzhou and at least four in Yangzhou, with others in Shanghai and Nanjing. (There are many gardens in the north of China, too, which differ slightly from the Jiangnan gardens described by Ji Cheng.)

Some of the Suzhou gardens are very early: the Canglang ting (Pavilion of the Dark Blue Waves) was constructed in 1044, the Shizi lin (Grove of Stone Lions) in about 1336, and the Wang shi yuan (Garden of the Master of the Fishing Nets) in 1140 (although it was remodeled in the late eighteenth century). The other gardens in Suzhou are mainly late Ming or Qing constructions. As these gardens have survived within the city walls, it is often assumed that private gardens were mostly urban constructions and attached to family residences. However, as indicated in Ji Cheng's list of different types of garden sites, many more gardens were created in the outskirts or at some distance from the city and were not necessarily connected to residences. These extramural gardens have simply not survived anywhere in China. And though the Suzhou gardens are often described as "private," some were temple gardens (accessible to temple visitors), and even private gardens were thrown open to the public on occasion. Another assumption is that gardens were strictly beautiful places of retreat, but in the fifteenth and early sixteenth centuries many garden owners prided themselves on the productivity of their plots and pools and offered presents of fish and fruit to their friends. While today's visitors may think that what they see is what was always there, it is more likely that gardens changed during the Ming and after, although there is little evidence to demonstrate changes in fashion.*

As *The Craft of Gardens* demonstrates, Chinese gardens contained much more than plants. Water, rocks of all sorts, and garden buildings were just as important (if not more so), and editions of *The Craft of Gardens* contain many pages of illustrations of window lattices, balustrades, and decorative openings—from simple circular moon gates to doorways in the form of leaves, vases, and plum blossom—all intended to create ever-new and surprising views in a small space. Though Ji Cheng mentions many different types of planting, from flowers to trees, there is no section in *The Craft of Gardens* devoted solely to plants. The first two (out of six) sections are "Situation" and "Layout." In "Situation," Ji Cheng lists mountain forest settings and river or lakeside sites; urban and village settings; settings within a dwelling; and sites in the distant, uninhabited countryside. The section on "Layout" includes major structures in the garden such as halls, towers, pavilions, and covered walkways, as well as artificial mountains (which were major structural elements in themselves). Smaller garden buildings and architectural features are listed next, followed by two sections on architectural details such as screen doors, windows, shutters, doorways, walls, and paving. There is a final section on how to erect artificial mountains in the garden, how to select special rocks, and the art of the "borrowed view"— which meant constructing a building in the garden, such as a belvedere or tall pavilion, that overlooked the garden's surroundings and could make a viewpoint of a hill or other natural setting that lay outside the garden itself.

Rocks were an important structural and decorative element of many gardens. The Shizi lin (Grove of Stone Lions) in Suzhou centers on a courtyard filled with strangely shaped rocks from Lake Tai (near Wuxi in Jiangsu province) that are said to resemble lions. Garden rocks were used architecturally but also to form viewpoints for contemplation, and artificially weathered rocks from Lake Tai were favored above all others.

(As mentioned, the Song emperor Huizong was famously fond of garden rocks and almost bankrupted the state in order to acquire the finest specimens from all over the country.)

The most heavily illustrated sections of *The Craft of Gardens* are those describing architectural details, and there are no depictions of overall plans or of artificial mountains and rocks; and its writing style is complex. It moves quickly from lyrical description to practical advice, leading one garden historian to assume that Ji Cheng, uncertain of his literary skills, may have employed someone else to write the more poetic parts.

In the book's first section, Ji Cheng sets out a series of desirable aspects, constructions, and plants for the garden, before dealing with more specific sites such as urban or rural settings. He begins by stating that a secluded location is the best. "Cut and clear undergrowth and follow the natural scenery. In a gully, grow orchids and angelica . . . the outer wall should be concealed in creepers and the roofs of the buildings meander above the treetops . . . nothing but nature will be seen. Seeking a secluded place among bamboos, your heart will be intoxicated. The verandah, tall pillars, and the windows offer a view. Your view should be a vast expanse of water, containing the brilliance of the four seasons. Phoenix trees shade the ground and Scholar trees cast shadows on the wall. Willows on the dykes; plum trees beside the house, white grass in the bamboo. A long trench dug for the stream . . . If you raise deer, they can roam and fish can be caught . . . In cool pavilions the breeze rises from the trees and bamboos; in warm, heated rooms, make tea from [melted] snow and forget your cares. The night rain patters on banana leaves like a mermaid's tears. The morning breeze whispers through the willows . . . Plant bamboos by the windows and select pear trees for the courtyard. Moonlight, a lute, the sound of wind, and a semicircle [semicircular pool] of autumn water . . . There are no rules for the size of windows, make them as they suit you. See railings as in a painting . . . Make things fresh, eschew the old. It may not be monumental but it will be small and just right."

Exploitation of the Works of Nature
Tiangong kaiwu
(1637)
SONG YINGXING (1587–c. 1666)

≋ ⁄⁄

From the Song dynasty (960–1279) onward, a number of Chinese works on technology and science are known. They vary from architectural manuals (stipulating standard sizes and building types) to short essays (called *biji*, literally "brush notes") on scientific subjects, related to the more common *biji* essays that refer to aspects of social life and aesthetic views. They were created by a variety of writers and usually published as collections.

One of the most striking technical manuals and a rare survival is the *Treatise on Architectural Methods* (*Yingzao fashi*) by Li Jie (c. 1065–1110), first printed in 1103. Setting out the plans and construction of a wide range of buildings, it is illustrated throughout with fine and accurate depictions of joints, brackets, and complex roof constructions. The near-contemporary *Notes from the Dream Pool* (*Mengxi bitan*) by Shen Guo (1031–1095) is not illustrated but contains brief notes on technical subjects, from Bi Sheng's famous experiments with ceramic movable type (in the eleventh century) to architecture and sword manufacture.

Less wide-ranging than *Notes from the Dream Pool* but fully illustrated like the *Treatise on Architectural Methods*, Song Yingxing's *Exploitation of the Works of Nature* (*Tiangong kaiwu*) explores and explains a wide range of human activities and inventions. Song Yingxing was born in Yichun, in Jiangsu province, during the late Ming era. Though he passed the provincial exams, he was unsuccessful in his repeated attempts to pass the palace exams and only served in lowly provincial official posts. His great achievement was this one book for which he is known.

It contains essays on agricultural works: irrigation, plowing, sowing, harvesting, the treatment of crops and the implements used, as well as the production of oils from sesame seeds and the manufacture of sugar. Textile technology is also described: the production of cloth from cotton, hemp, and silk—in the latter case from raising silk cocoons—to reeling, spinning, weaving, and dyeing. The extraction of minerals, from salt to cinnabar, and the production of vermilion and ink are examined, as well as the manufacture of paper, ceramics, ships and carts, weapons and cast bronze bells. The last two sections discuss the making of alcoholic beverages and the harvesting of pearls with special diving equipment.

The production of paper is described under the heading "The Essence of Things" and provides a justification for the production of books themselves. "Master Sun asks what it is that transmits the mysteries of the universe and nature's wonders from ancient times to the present and from the central plains to the border regions? How are these things recorded? The gentleman and the commoner communicate; the teacher transmits knowledge to his pupil. If these things are dependent on endless oral transmission, how many problems can they solve? If there is a document or a textbook, which through words and pictures makes the matter clear, not only can the content be transmitted throughout the realm but the differences of opinion and the misunderstandings of pupils will disappear as easily as the breeze or melting snow. Fortunately there is Sir Mulberry [paper] and both the wise and the foolish all depend upon his profound benefit." Song Yingxing continues: "Paper is made from the raw materials of bamboo and tree bark [paper mulberry, silk mulberry, and hibiscus]. With the transformation of green bamboo into white paper, the essays of a hundred experts become ten thousand volumes, the foundation of manuscripts and of printing. Fine paper can be used [for manuscripts and printed books]; coarse paper for burnt offerings [at home, in temples, at funerals, etc.], for windows to keep out drafts, and as protective wrapping paper [for fruit, medicines, books, parcels, and much else]. The manufacture of paper goes back to high antiquity and there are very rare records of named persons [associated with its production] in the Han and Jin."

Here, Song Yingxing is presumably referring to the reference in the *History of the Later Han* (*Hou Han shu*) (compiled in the mid-fifth century) that describes how in 105 CE, Cai Lun, the court eunuch in charge of manufacturing, reported on the successful production of paper from bark, cloth rags, and fishing nets to Emperor He. The invention of paper in China is traditionally dated to this moment, although recent archaeological finds of paper, dated to some two hundred years prior to 105 CE, probably mean that Cai Lun was not reporting on the invention but on the perfection of papermaking—to a point where it could impress the emperor.*

Paper-related technical terms used by Song Yongxing, such as "killing the green" and "sweating the green" (glossed as "cutting down the bamboo" and "cooking and straining the bamboo"), do refer to papermaking processes, but they become a little confused because Song Yingxing and his contemporaries were not familiar with ancient formats—slips made of wood or bamboo—used for writing. These ancient formats are now familiar through the excavations made near Dunhuang by Sir Aurel Stein in 1907 and subsequent discoveries in southern China. Stein discovered thousands of wooden slips used for communication and writing in northwestern China during the Han dynasty (206 BCE–220 CE), while bamboo slips were traditionally used in the south. Before the invention of paper, these long, thin slips (or strips) were inscribed, joined together by threads, and rolled up for storage—but they were not known in the Ming dynasty except through textual references; thus Song Yingxing (wrongly) interprets the ancient term *jian*, used for these wooden or bamboo slips, as "sheet" or "sheet of paper." He ridicules the idea that joining such slips and rolling them up could create a "book," and he states that "before the Qin dynasty [221–206 BCE] 'burning of the books' there were already many books in existence; could so many books have been written on bamboo strips?" With the benefit of modern archaeological discoveries we now know that there were indeed many pre-paper books, written on slips of bamboo and wood.

Song Yingxing describes the contemporary manufacture of bamboo paper, a specialty of Fujian province in the southeast where young plants, just about to leaf, were cut down in early summer. A pit was dug on the mountainside where the bamboo grew and the stems were soaked in water for a hundred days, the pits kept filled with water by a system of bamboo pipes. The bamboo pulp was pounded, mixed with lime, and boiled in a covered pot (similar to those used to make salt) for eight days and eight nights. It was then cooled for a day and washed in a pit lined with wooden planks to keep mud out (though for coarse paper this precaution was unnecessary). After washing, the fibers were mixed with wood ash, put into another (covered) vat, covered with rice-straw ash, boiled, and then strained. "After ten days the pulp is rotten and stinking. It is then pounded [with a water-powered tilt hammer in mountainous areas] until it is the consistency of noodle dough and then placed in a tank whose dimensions are determined by the size of the papermaking screen." "Paper medicine" (paper was one of many medicinal ingredients used at the time), usually made from "peach bamboo leaves" (though there are many variant local names), was added to produce a pure white paper when dried. "The papermaking screens are made from fine split bamboo and the thickness of the paper depends upon the worker's manipulation as a shallow immersion [of the screen into the pulp tank] produces thin paper, [and] a deeper immersion thicker paper. The water drains away from the screen and when it is turned upside down, the paper is dropped onto a board in piles of a thousand sheets. These are tied and pressed between boards [to squeeze out more water], and then each sheet is carefully picked up with copper tweezers and heat-dried" on a hollow brick double wall, inside which fires are lit.

Song Yingxing also describes paper recycling, where ink and colors are washed off before soaking in the pulp tank, but he notes that this is rare in southern China where bamboo grows so abundantly. He states that while fine writing paper is made from pure bamboo, and paper for red calling cards is dyed with safflower juice (calling cards were sheets of paper, used much like today's business cards, and traditionally dyed red), coarse wrapping paper is made from a mix of bamboo and rice stalks. Similarly, in his description of bark paper, he says that it is made from thirty percent rice stalks and seventy percent bark and bamboo (just as in the early days when Cai Lun used a mixture of bark, cloth rags, and fishing nets). Details of bark-paper manufacturing include Song Yingxing's note that window paper, traditionally used in China before the arrival of sheet glass in the nineteenth century, was made on a large screen handled by two or more men, and that different types of paper included paper to make fans, paper to be oiled for umbrellas, and paper used for painting.

While Song Yingxing's detailed description of papermaking is a product of its time, it remains enormously useful to historians today, and the same is true of his other commentaries on Chinese technology and science of the Ming period.

Mustard Seed Garden Manual of Painting
Jieziyuan huazhuan

(1679–1701)

AUTHOR UNKNOWN; PREFACE BY LI YU (1610–1680)

≈ ≈

It is a truism that Chinese painting requires long practice, particularly of stock elements such as mountains, rustic huts, trees, and clumps of bamboo, before a painter can channel the inspiration to create. Going back to at least the Song (960–1279), the existence and popularity of painting manuals, of which the *Mustard Seed Garden Manual of Painting* (*Jieziyuan huazhuan*) is the best-known, testify to the importance of mastery of such stock elements and their eventual combination into a finished work.

Chinese painting has a long history but the nature of the materials used, commonly silk or paper, means that early survivals are rare. Apart from mastering the fundamental component parts, it was also common to copy works by famous masters, both in order to understand their composition and methods and to preserve them through copying. Deciding whether a painting is original or a copy can be enormously difficult, although there is some compensation in the preservation of ancient works through diligent copying.

The appreciation of paintings in China was very much part of the literati tradition. The ability to paint, produce handsome calligraphy, to write poetry, and play the (zither-like) *guqin* were all regarded as the attributes of a gentleman-scholar, though not all of them could necessarily perform these arts so well. Within painting, there was also a traditional hierarchy, with monochrome ink paintings of soaring, mountainous landscapes regarded very highly from the Song dynasty onward, while colored depictions of animals, flowers, and fruit were rather looked down on—although a number of emperors, such as Song Huizong (1082–1135) and Ming Xuande (1399–1435), were accomplished painters of birds, flowers, and animals.

For those wishing to learn the art of painting without an individual tutor, introductions such as the *Mustard Seed Garden Manual of Painting* were useful guides to painting techniques. This manual, while by no means the earliest of such works, was first published in Nanjing between 1679 and 1701. The first part, printed in 1679, consisted of five *juan*, or sections, offering an introduction to fundamental concepts of painting; then instructions on how to paint trees; hills and stones; people and buildings; and, finally, a section on exemplary works of finished compositions. The manual was a woodblock-printed book with illustrations, many of them in color. As with printed texts, the blocks were carved from illustrations placed face down on the block. Multicolor prints were made from a series of separate blocks, usually one for each color.

The 1679 printing of the *Mustard Seed Garden Manual of Painting* had a preface by the polymathic Li Yu, usually described as the "publisher," although his death clearly intervened before the expanded version of 1701 was published. Rather, the manual is said to have been commissioned by Li Yu's son-in-law, Shen Xinyu, from four painters: the three brothers Wang Gai, Wang Shi, and Wang Nie, as well as Zhu Sheng, who made instructive drawings to be followed by aspiring painters.

The second printing, in 1701, incorporated the original five sections and added several new sections, with instructions on the painting of flora (including orchids, bamboo, plum blossom, and grasses) and fauna (insects, birds, and more) and further exemplary works. In China, the book has never been out of print.

As well as working as a publisher, Li Yu was an actor and playwright, garden designer, novelist, and short-story writer. He passed the first level of examinations but failed at the provincial level, and with the collapse of the Ming dynasty and the subsequent unrest and uncertainty, he abandoned all thought of a bureaucratic career. The famous erotic novel *The Carnal Prayer Mat* (*Rou putuan*) (1657) is attributed to him, and a couple of his short stories describe homosexual love affairs (in keeping with the theatrical traditions also seen in the life of the Qing period poet-scholar Yuan Mei, and in Wu Jingzi's eighteenth-century novel *Unofficial History of the Grove of Literati* [*Rulin waishi*]). Li Yu's humorous essays include mention of food and other pleasures.* Li Yu was also famous for his garden, near the South Gate of Nanjing, which was called Jiezi huayuan (Mustard Seed Garden) because, in his own words, "It occupies only a hillock, hence the name 'Mustard Seed' to designate its smallness. When visitors who come and go notice that it has hills and dales they remark that it brings to mind the [Buddhist] saying 'Mount Sumeru is contained in a grain of mustard seed.'"**

The name Mustard Seed Garden was also given to Li Yu's bookshop and publishing house in Nanjing. In his preface to the *Mustard Seed Garden Manual*, Li Yu writes of how he had always loved paintings, though he couldn't paint himself, and found looking at a painting as good as looking at scenery itself. In a painting, "a person can find himself beside spring waters, ready to set out to walk over hills and gullies, free to wander without having to wax his sandals or take up a bamboo staff." He mentions his son-in-law and his activities in commissioning albums about paintings, and how to create paintings, down to details such as "dotting leaves." The sections in the manual contain plenty of text referring to painting, including "the six essentials," "the twelve points to avoid," and "the fifteen basic brushstrokes"—from strokes that resemble "spread-out hemp fibers" and "horse's teeth" to combinations of "spread-out hemp fibers with dots like rainbows."

The "six essentials" to master are: powerful brushwork; basic design according to tradition; originality without abandoning the nature of things; color (if used) should enrich; the brush should be handled with spontaneity; and the artist should learn from the masters without repeating their (unspecified) faults. The "twelve points to avoid" include "trees with less than four branches," "water with no obvious source," "scenes without inaccessible places" (which seems to suggest the exaggerated, towering mountains so frequently seen), and "neglect of the atmospheric effects of mist." Though most of the sections are devoted to elements of monochrome brush paintings, there is one section on how to make colors, including white from oyster shells or lead; mineral blue and green; reds and yellows from safflower and sophora; as well as how to make gold leaf liquid by mixing it with soap beans.

There are instructions on how to paint birds: "Birds come from eggs, so their shape resembles an egg with head, tail, wings, and legs added." In painting birds, one should "begin with the beak, then the eyes above the upper part of the beak. Before completing the eyes, draw the head." In painting orchids with their calligraphic leaves, the brushstrokes known as "nail ends," "rats' tails," and "mantis belly" should be used.

The instructions apart (and it is often difficult to read about the complexities of how to paint), it is the illustrations to the text that inform and attract. In the section on how to paint plum blossoms, for instance, there are thirty different views of plum blossom—from the earliest bud to fully opened flowers seen from above, behind, below, and from both sides. These are followed by three pages of blossoms on twigs and branches, before the artist gets to consider a bit more of the whole tree.

The section on how to paint people is particularly charming because all the little sample figures—including gentlemen staring into space, sitting on rocks, or standing in space—are glossed. A man standing in the middle of nowhere is "reciting a poem," a man who seems to be looking down with a twig in his hand has actually "gathered chrysanthemums by the bamboo fence to the east, joyfully contemplating the southern mountain," and a gloomy-looking man lying on a rock is in fact feeling that his "heart is lifted as the clouds high above." There are also illustrations of stock figures such as fishermen in long, low boats; farmers in straw raincoats and hats; and servant boys, some carrying *guqin* instruments, some carrying flasks of wine, and some crouched beside low stoves and waving a bamboo fan as the kettle heats up.

The Peach Blossom Fan
Taohua shan
(1699)
KONG SHANGREN (1648–1718)

≈ ⁄≈

Perhaps the best-known drama of the Manchu Qing dynasty (1644–1911), the story of *The Peach Blossom Fan* (*Taohua shan*) is based on events that culminated in 1644, when the Ming dynasty fell and the Qing dynasty came to power, and includes many historical figures in its large cast of characters.

It was written by Kong Shangren, who was born into this time of upheaval. He was a direct descendant of Confucius in the sixty-fourth generation. He spent most of his life in the area near Qufu (in Shandong province), the home of Confucius, and devoted much of his time to the compilation of the family genealogy and a history of the locality. In 1684 the Kangxi emperor (r. 1661–1722) visited Qufu, and Kong Shangren lectured him on the Confucian classics. Impressed, the emperor made him a member of the imperial academy, and in 1686 he was appointed to assist in conservancy works on the Yellow River. Returning to Beijing in 1694, Kong Shangren was appointed to serve in the Board of Revenue, but he was dismissed in 1699. His dismissal may have been connected to the authorship of *The Peach Blossom Fan*, because the emperor was said to have been angered by its theme of loyalty to the fallen Ming dynasty, although the absence of further punishment of Kong Shangren leads some scholars to conclude that this was not the case.

There were a number of reasons for the fall of the Ming (1368–1644), including emperors with little interest in the affairs of state, the growth of corruption and economic problems, tension between the literati and the growing merchant class, natural disasters, and peasant rebellions that broke out in the first half of the seventeenth century. This state of chaos eventually allowed the Jurchen from Manchuria (who had begun to call themselves *Manchu*) to sweep down and conquer the country.

Toward the end of the Ming there were several groups of intellectuals who sought to revive the spirit of the nation, at a time when notorious characters, such as the corrupt court eunuch Wei Zhongxian (1568–1627) and the "corrupt and unsavory" official and playwright Ruan Dacheng (c. 1587–1646), rose to power. (As mentioned, Ruan Dacheng's connection to *The Craft of Gardens* [*Yuan ye*] was probably responsible for the book's relative failure at the time it appeared.) Ruan made use of the influence of Wei Zhongxian to advance his career, a ruse which failed, but he rose again to serve in a short-lived "Ming" regime in Nanjing that was set up as the Ming dynasty was collapsing under the peasant rebellions and the Manchu invasion.

When Li Zicheng (c. 1605–1645), the leader of a powerful rebel band, took Beijing in April 1644, the last Ming emperor, Chongzhen, hanged himself. But Ruan and others supported the prince of Fu (Zhu Yousong, a grandson of the Wanli emperor of the Ming), who set up a new "Ming" court in Nanjing that lasted from 1644 to 1645—when it was destroyed by the invading Manchus, who had taken advantage of the collapse of the Ming in Beijing and Li Zicheng's unsuccessful attempt to hold the city. Ever the turncoat, Ruan Dacheng surrendered to the Manchu invaders and died in Fujian province in 1646 while following the Manchu Qing army in their conquest of southern China.

The response of some prominent Chinese to the fall of the Ming and the establishment of the Qing dynasty was to retire from office. Ming "loyalists" included the famous painters Zhu Da (Bada Shanren) and Shitao—both descendants of the Ming imperial house—and Hongren, who all preferred to live as monks or away in the mountains rather than have any contact with the Qing.

The main characters in *The Peach Blossom Fan* are Hou Fangyu (1618–1655) and his consort Li Xiangjun, although the fate of the characters in the drama is different from their actual experiences. Hou Fangyu was a fine writer, famous for his essays, a lover of drama who kept a troupe of boy actors (like the great Qing poet Yuan Mei, and some characters in *Unofficial History of the Grove of Literati* [*Rulin waishi*]); but he fell foul of Ruan Dacheng. Hou's father and uncle had been members of the "politico-literary" party known as the Donglin ("Eastern Grove") Academy, which sought to combat corruption by the revival of Confucian morality, and Hou himself founded the Restoration Society with the same aims. In 1644, he escaped imprisonment by Ruan Dacheng, and died when he was only in his thirties. In the drama, however, at the fall of the Ming, Hou Fangyu retires to live as a Daoist recluse and Li Xiangjun becomes a Daoist nun.

The Peach Blossom Fan is a southern form drama in forty-four scenes that was usually performed, by all-male actors, over several days. Its broad range of characters includes the real-life characters Ruan Dacheng, General Zuo Liangyu, and the poet and painter Yang Wencong, as well as comic characters such as temple servants and yamen runners. It takes place in Nanjing and begins with Hou Fangyu falling in love with Li Xiangjun and giving her a fan to celebrate their union. However, the villain Ruan Dacheng tries to unite her with another man, and though she rejects him (to Hou's satisfaction), they are separated through Ruan Dacheng's machinations. Meanwhile, Li Zicheng and his rebels have captured Beijing and the Chongzhen emperor of the Ming has hanged himself.

In Nanjing, a new emperor is set up by Ruan and others. He is the prince of Fu (Zhu Yousong, a scion of the imperial house), but he gives way to debauchery in Nanjing, as well as persecuting reformers from the Restoration Society. When a local governor wants to take Li Xiangjun as his concubine, she dashes her head against a pillar (much like the would-be assassin in The Orphan of Zhao [Zhao shi guer]) and blood stains her fan. Yang Wencong draws a branch and leaves onto the fan to turn the blood spots into a painting of peach blossom. (Early flowering peach blossoms were, like plum blossoms, favorite subjects for painters, expressing hope since they herald spring.) The fan is sent to Hou Fangyu to show Li Xiangjun's determination to remain faithful. Ruan Dacheng and his gang want to make Li Xiangjun an imperial concubine but she refuses and is savagely beaten. Hou Fangyu is imprisoned by Ruan Dacheng.

Amid increasing chaos, the Qing march south and the Nanjing emperor is captured. The drama ends with a great Daoist mourning ceremony for the defeated Ming dynasty, and Hou and Li retire to their respective Daoist temples.

There is a passing reference in The Peach Blossom Fan to another, but earlier, famous Chinese drama, *The Peony Pavilion* (*Mudan ting*) by Tang Xianzu (1550–1616), when Li Xiangjun sings songs from the latter. While a similar mixture of songs, drama, and acrobatics, and with serious episodes interrupted by comic scenes, the story of *The Peony Pavilion* could not be more different. Though a love story (with a happy ending, unlike *The Peach Blossom Fan*) and one that involves several characters drawn from history, it refers to a very different period of history, the fall of the Song dynasty to the invading Jurchen.

Also, while the Peony Pavilion hardly appears in the drama that bears its name, the theme of "peach blossom" in all its varieties is somewhat overused in *The Peach Blossom Fan*. It appears in place names; in references to the *Peach Blossom Spring* (*Taohuan yuan*) by Tao Qian (or Tao Yuanming, 365–427 CE), a famous prose description of a hidden valley full of happy people which had come to represent "utopia" in Chinese literature; and in the arrival of spring: "the peaches are flowering again . . ." and "The beauty and her lover are separated but the peach flowers are as fine this year as last."

The symbolic fan itself (a common gift between men, friends, and men and women) is frequently mentioned: "my precious fan is stained with blood . . ."; "I will paint leaves and petals around the stains to make them into a painting of flowering peach blossom . . ."; "This is the finest painting of peach blossom I have seen—it is truly a peach blossom fan."

The Peach Blossom Fan, like other Chinese dramas, is not a continuous telling of the main story. It is interrupted by scenes of military action (reflecting the background of the time) and comic scenes, one of them about "sacred peas" (referring to the practice of Confucius as a child laying out peas in imitation of the solemn layout of ritual objects), which relieve the otherwise somewhat unrelenting tragedy.

Poems/Essays

(eighteenth century)

YUAN MEI (1716–1798)

≫ ⁄≈

Yuan Mei was highly acclaimed as a poet in his lifetime, but he was much more than just a poet. He wrote a collection of stories about the supernatural (not unlike some of those in Pu Songling's *Strange Stories from the Liao Studio* [*Liaozhai zhiyi*]) and gave it the witty title *What Confucius Did Not Say* (*Zi bu yu*), a hint that the contents were amusing and entertaining, rather than dry and uplifting. The stories told of ghosts who appeared in three forms—one form to scare people away, one to block their path, and one to utterly terrify them—although Yuan Mei's heroes were able to outwit all three forms. (A student of strange behavior, he also collected court cases, based on his own experience as a magistrate.) One of his best-known works is *List of Food from the Garden of Harmony* (*Suiyuan shidan*). This has often been described as a "cookbook" but it is more of a guide to elegant eating than a collection of recipes.

One of Yuan Mei's great talents was the composition of funerary inscriptions, carefully composed essays full of reminiscence and praise of the departed, an art form greatly appreciated at the time. His memoir of his third sister is particularly moving: he recalled with great tenderness the games they shared as children, particularly their love of crickets and their careful burial of these little pets when they died of the cold.*

Though his career as an official mirrors that of thousands of his contemporaries, Yuan Mei is distinguished for his wide interests, fine poetry and wit, as well as his encouragement of other poets, particularly women. A number of his granddaughters became poets. For his encouragement of young people, especially women, he was criticized; and while he was one of the most successful poets of his time (he recorded that he was once paid 1,000 silver taels for a funerary inscription), he was criticized after his death for lacking seriousness.

Yuan Mei was born in Hangzhou, beside the West Lake, into a family of modest means. His father was often away, acting as a badly-paid secretary or tutor in different parts of the country, and Yuan Mei said of his mother that "she did not eat vegetarian food, was not a Buddha worshipper, did not believe in *yin-yang* or prayers, she simply sewed and embroidered and read Tang poetry." Taught by his aunt and private tutors, his examination career was up and down (reflecting some of the stories in Wu Jingzi's contemporary novel *Unofficial History of the Grove of Literati* [*Rulin waishi*]). When only eleven, he passed the "boy's examination" (which qualified him to take the next examination), and soon after, at a very young age, he passed the first official exam (which, during the Qing, was at county level). In 1736 a special examination, the *Boxue hongci* ("search for broad learning and extensive words"), was held in the capital, Beijing (the previous *Boxue hongci* had taken place in 1679). It was intended to select men of high literary capability who would compile important documents such as official histories. Yuan Mei was the youngest of the two hundred candidates, the oldest being Wan Jing, in his seventies, who had been one of the compilers of the famous *Kangxi Dictionary* (*Kangxi zidian*) (1716). Apart from the standard essays on Confucian themes, candidates had to write a poem of twenty-four lines, with seven syllables to each line and alternate lines rhyming with characters pronounced "shan." The theme of the poem was "The Golden Pheasant Dancing in Front of a Mirror," telling the story of a famous pheasant that was so entranced with its reflection in a mirror that it danced until it died.

Fifteen candidates passed the examination, but both Yuan Mei and Wan Jing failed. However, in 1739, in his early twenties, Yuan Mei passed the palace exams; and instead of being sent off as a district official, he was appointed to the prestigious Hanlin Academy (in the capital), where scholars worked on the Confucian classics and prepared whatever literary works the imperial court required. Unfortunately for Yuan Mei, the Manchu rulers of the Qing dynasty had recently instituted a requirement that Hanlin scholars pass an exam in Manchu. (Yuan Mei recorded that his Manchu tutor was a great cat lover and at banquets used to feed tidbits to both his grandchild and the cat, taking care to treat them equally "to prevent snatching.") Finding it hard to make head or tail of what he called "tadpole" script, Yuan Mei failed this Manchu exam, coming right at the bottom of the list, and left the Hanlin Academy in 1742. He subsequently served very successfully as district magistrate in four districts in Jiangsu province, the last in the outskirts of Nanjing, but asked for early retirement in 1748 after his appointment to a more significant post was not ratified by the Ministry of Civil Office.

According to his grandson, he published accounts of some of the cases he encountered as a magistrate, including "The Decision about the Centipede," "The Decision about the Donkey," and "The Decision about the Basket," and they became popular folktales in Nanjing. One of his cases involved a complaint about a daughter-in-law. A man named Li wanted a divorce for his son because his daughter-in-law had disappeared, presumably to join a lover, but then reappeared. The daughter-in-law denied that she had gone to see a lover, claiming that she had been swept into the air by a typhoon and carried thirty miles away. Yuan Mei found a precedent in the collected works of Hao Jing, a minister of the Mongol emperor Khubilai Khan (1215–1294), and declared her innocent. Yuan Mei's patron, the governor-general of the province, was impressed and said that it showed the importance of wide reading in the work of a magistrate.

When Yuan Mei retired, he acquired a piece of land in Nanjing that had once been part of an estate belonging to the influential Sui family. First named Sui yuan (Sui Garden) after the Sui family, Yuan Mei retained the pronunciation but changed the character to another *sui* meaning "content." Even earlier, this garden was thought to have been created by the Cao family, who for three generations (from 1663 to about 1722) had served as imperial textile commissioners in Nanjing. Cao Xueqin (c. 1715–1763), son of the last textile commissioner Cao, described a grand mansion and garden in his novel *Dream of the Red Chamber* (*Hongloumeng*), and Yuan Mei liked to think that his piece of land was the original Cao garden.

Yuan Mei wrote poems on a wide variety of themes, some of which were almost commonplace: the beauty of mountains, the pleasure of traveling to famous beauty spots, the joy of friendship, and the sorrow of parting. However, he also wrote about his life at home, about food and marvelous tea from the Wuyi mountains in Fujian province, about aging and illness and his own jade false tooth—and the difficulties of a local magistrate dealing with natural disasters. One poem is titled "The Lament of the Tax Collector." A district magistrate was supposed to exact taxes, even when "winter snow is followed by drought," when "fields and villages turned into swamps, house swallows nest in forest trees," and there were no fat pigs to be seen.

He addressed some of his poems to young male actors who played female roles, just like "Lucky Yu" and "Miss Xiao" in the *Unofficial History of the Grove of Literati*. After an excursion to Hangzhou with a young actor who had to leave early to return to his stage work, Yuan Mei wrote a brief poem of abandonment—a classical theme but not usually associated with abandonment by young male actors of female roles:

> In a life of meetings and partings, there is much sadness,
>
> A five-day entanglement and then what remains?
>
> The gardens of Nanjing are white as snow in the
> moonlight,
>
> I long to hear one note of the song the fair one is singing.

List of Food from the Garden of Harmony, Yuan Mei's pronouncements on food and how it should be prepared and enjoyed, included practical notes about the culinary staff involved. In his view a good meal owed sixty percent to the cook and forty percent to the steward (who did the shopping). The best cooking oil was "Suzhou old oil," but the best vinegar not necessarily from Zhenjiang (still famous for its vinegar); he preferred the sharper vinegar from Banpu or Pukou. He stressed the importance of washing ingredients so that there were no feathers in the birds' nests, no mud on the sea slugs, and no sand on the sharks' fins. He also railed against excess—"It is folly to put powdered crab with birds' nests or Lilium japonicum with chicken or pork"—and felt that to mix strong flavors in the same dish, and not treat meat with respect (for its varied flavors), was liable to provoke the souls of ducks, pigs, geese, and chickens to lodge a formal complaint with the god of the underworld.

According to Yuan Mei, guests should be invited three days in advance to allow for proper planning, although there were some foods that could be cooked in a hurry, such as fried chicken strips or bean curd with tiny shrimps. His love of food reflects a national passion in China that was often celebrated by poets. Even the ancient poetry of the *Songs of the South* (*Chu ci*) includes a lengthy lyric calling the soul of the departed back by listing an irresistibly mouthwatering series of dishes.

Unofficial History of the Grove of Literati
Rulin waishi

(1750)

WU JINGZI (1701–1754)

≈ ⁄

W u Jingzi's rambling satirical novel describes the social milieu of the literati, with which he was intimately associated. The literati were educated according to a very narrow curriculum and prepared, through the imperial examination system, to enter the government bureaucracy. Three emperors of the Qing dynasty (1644–1911) succeeded each other during Wu Jingzi's lifetime, but *Unofficial History of the Grove of Literati* (*Rulin waishi*) is set in the previous Ming dynasty (1368–1644), with regular references to Ming emperors and their attitudes to education and government.

Wu Jingzi was born in Anhui province into a family of officials. His grandfather achieved one of the highest honors in the entire country, being placed third in the palace examinations, although his father only managed to pass the prefectural exams. Wu himself declined to enter the most competitive exams, just like one of his characters in *Unofficial History of the Grove of Literati* named Du Shaojing (who is regarded by many as an autobiographical portrait).

The novel is composed of fifty-five chapters introducing a cast of over two hundred characters, many (but not all) of them participants in the examination process. There is no single narrative thread but the separate stories are linked by the underlying theme, which satirizes the corruption and inefficiency of the exam system and the bureaucracy it was designed to produce. There are successful candidates as well as those who fail, and most are motivated by greed for wealth, power, and status—rather than a desire to serve. There are characters such as Jing Lanjiang, "pseudo-scholar, hat shop manager"; Mu Niu, "highwayman, later soldier"; and Niu Bulong, a "peddler who passes himself off as a scholar and poet." Though the novel's characters are fictional, it opens with an account of the life of a real person,

Wang Mian (c. 1287–1359), who was famous both for his beautiful paintings of plum blossom and his refusal to serve in the government bureaucracy. Even when he was personally sought out by Zhu Yuan-zhang, later to become the first emperor of the Ming, he refused to take office and disappeared into the mountains to paint. By placing his story at the beginning of the novel, Wu Jingzi suggests that this refusal to participate in the exams and bureaucracy is, perhaps, the only honorable course.

The examination system that dominates the novel saw only minor changes from Ming to Qing. The main cycle of examinations consisted of three levels: provincial exams; metropolitan exams (held in the capital); and the highest-level exams, which were held in the imperial palace itself. Before taking the provincial-level exams, potential candidates had to take licensing, or qualifying, exams at both the county level and pre-fectural level. These were held every two or three years, but successful licentiates had to keep renewing their qualifications if they did not go straight on to take the triennial provincial exams. Competition in the examinations was fierce and complicated by political decisions over provincial quotas, set up to avoid graduates from any particular province dominating the government bureaucracy. The number of candidates who could pass was restricted to between about fifty to one hundred from a whole province with a population in the tens of thousands; it has been estimated that only 1.5 percent of eligible candidates passed the provincial-level exams during the Ming dynasty.* The stories of unsuccessful licentiates populate the pages of *Unofficial History of the Grove of Literati*.

While the examination system did not change much from Ming to Qing, it became increasingly dependent upon the exam essay called *ba gu wen*. This is usually translated as "eight-legged essay" but would be better rendered as "eight-section essay," since it consisted of eight carefully regulated sections (two of them in straightforward prose, the others in specified numbers of parallel sentences), all elaborating on a quotation from Confucius or one of his major disciples. Some of these quotations were fairly straightforward—such as a line from the *Analects* (*Lun yu*), "If the people have sufficient, how can the ruler suffer insufficiency?"—while others were less so: "Where the people rest." The format and style of the essay were strictly regulated, and ink blots alone could disqualify a candidate.

The examinations themselves could last from one to three days, during which time hundreds of candidates were locked into individual cells in large, specially constructed examination halls (some of which survived until fairly recently in Chinese cities). They carried their food and bedding rolls and, as described in *Unofficial History of the Grove of Literati*, often took illegal cribs in with them.** Even if they did not cheat, examination candidates could make use of cheap printed editions containing "model" *ba gu* ("eight-legged") essays, in order to prepare themselves. Such a compilation, by Ma Junshang, a stout defender of the system, is described in chapters 13 and 18 of the novel. However, not everyone could take the examinations. Merchants were forbidden and had to acquire wealth, particularly in the form of land, before their sons could be considered eligible—as landowners, rather than as merchants.

Almost all the two hundred and more characters in the novel are literati of one sort or another and demonstrate the privileges and difficulties of this social class, found throughout Ming and Qing China. There are characters who keep trying, and keep failing, to pass exams, still presenting themselves as candidates when white-haired and elderly. One of them is Fan Jin, who tells the examination commissioner that he first took the county-level exam when he was twenty and has taken it some twenty times since—and never passed. Now he is still trying, at the age of fifty-four. Some candidates paid others to take the examinations for them, including Kuang Zhaoren in chapter 19. The efforts, whether intellectual or financial (and for some whether legal or illegal) were all in order that high office might be achieved. As Cang Liaozhai explains in chapter 32, when he applied to Du Shaojing for a loan, in a complicated series of deals, he had tried to buy a licentiate title for someone else, which was frowned upon as strictly illegal. So he ended up putting his own name forward as a "salaried scholar," a title to which he was theoretically entitled. Not unnaturally, the unsuccessful licentiate wanted his money back. Cang explained how he had got into the difficulty: "A salaried scholar has a better chance of passing the next exam and then you become an official. Even if you don't pass, after a dozen years you become a senior licentiate, and when you pass the palace exam you'll be appointed a magistrate or a judge. Then I shall wear fine boots, hold court, pass sentence, and have people beaten."

Occasionally Wu Jingzi describes a magistrate's work in the same satirical vein. "There were three cases that day, the first involving the [alleged] murder of a man's father, the plaintiff being a [Buddhist] monk. The monk stated that he had been collecting firewood on the mountainside when he noticed a grazing cow staring at him. He went up to the cow and tears flowed from its eyes, and when he knelt in front of it, the cow licked his head and wept freely. The monk realized that this was his father who had entered the body of the cow. He pleaded with the cow's owner to give it to him so he could take it to live in the temple, but a neighbor came and took the cow away and killed it." The story continues: "The magistrate questioned the neighbor who told him that three or four days ago the monk had sold the cow to him and he had then killed it. But yesterday, the monk had come and said the cow was really his father and demanded more money and started to get abusive. The neighbor said that it wasn't the monk's father at all but that for years the monk had been putting salt on his shaven head and approaching cows, which licked his head for the salt and that made them shed tears freely. The monk would then announce that the cow was his father and beg its owner to sell it to him—and he would then sell it on." The magistrate said: "Transmigration has always been considered a mystery, but this is incredible. Furthermore, if he believed the cow was his father, he should not have sold it. The monk is a scoundrel!" With that, he sentenced the monk to twenty strokes.

Among the episodic stories of literati, both good and bad, Wu Jingzi's descriptions of everyday life in Qing (rather than Ming) China are very rich. There are endless descriptions of meals because for literati, social life revolved around hospitality. In chapter 29, Du Shenjing serves his guests orange wine, bamboo shoots, boiled meat dumplings, duck dumplings, cakes fried in goose fat, and the best Luan tea—prepared with pure rainwater. Another aspect of literati entertainment was the theater, with all-male actors; those who performed the female parts dressed as pretty women, answered to names such as "Lucky Yu" and "Miss Xiao," and were always ready to flirt with their gentleman admirers. There are also descriptions of weddings, with brides carried in red sedan chairs in a procession of carts carrying red-wrapped wedding presents; of the retinue of officials as they passed through the city streets, preceded by attendants carrying yellow umbrellas (symbolic of their office) and (bannerlike) placards announcing name and rank; and of rituals in a newly built temple in Nanjing with music, candles, lanterns, more placards, and sacrificial offerings of wine, silk, incense, and slaughtered animals.

Three Hundred Tang Poems
Tang shi sanbai shou
(c. 1763)
SUN ZHU (1722–1778)

≫ ⁄≈

This collection of poems written during the Tang dynasty (618–907 CE), which was compiled by Sun Zhu in the eighteenth century, is perhaps one of the best-known books in China, widely used as a textbook and for pleasure ever since it first appeared. Included are just over three hundred poems by seventy-nine poets. There is one poem by the Tang emperor Xuanzong and one anonymous verse, a lament. The Tang was considered to be the golden age of Chinese poetry (and of much else), and so the collection was widely welcomed.

Sun Zhu was a Qing dynasty (1644–1911) scholar. It is said that his compilation was the result of looking at Ming (1368–1644) compilations of Tang poetry and, finding them unsatisfactory, creating his own selection. It is difficult to know why this particular collection became so popular—but it was a useful and affordable introduction, and while broad in coverage not so huge that it would have become expensive to print.

The fact that there are slightly more than three hundred poems presented in *Three Hundred Tang Poems* (*Tang shi sanbai shou*) recalls the number of poems in the ancient classic *Book of Songs* (*Shi jing*), which was popularly known as the "three hundred poems," although it actually includes 305 poems. We do not know how many poems exactly Sun Zhu originally included in his collection, because the first edition of the work has not survived. It is possible that later printings by different publishers may have included verses not contained in the original.

In *Three Hundred Tang Poems*, Du Fu (712–770) and Li Bai (701–762), considered by many to be China's two greatest poets, are included with the largest number of poems per poet: there are thirty-nine poems by Du Fu, and thirty-four by Li Bai. The great painter-poet Wang Wei (c. 699–c. 761) is represented with twenty-nine poems, and Li Shangyin (c. 813–c. 858) with twenty-four poems. It is quite clear that this anthology is based on personal choice, because Sun Zhu included only five poems by the widely revered Bai Juyi (772–846) and none at all by Li He (790–816), who is generally considered to be one of the great poets of the period (although apparently Sun Zhu did not think so).*

Three Hundred Tang Poems is not arranged by poet or by subject but by type of poem, starting with poems in the *gu shi* style (as in the work *Gu shi shijiu shou* [*Nineteen Old Poems*]), with five characters per line, and ending with *yuefu* ("ballad" style) verses.

Perhaps length was a factor in the small selection of poems by Bai Juyi, because one of those included is his long "Song of Everlasting Regret," which records the devastating end of the legendary love affair of the Xuanzong emperor (r. 712–756 CE) and his favorite concubine, Yang Guifei, who was killed in 756 at Mawei (by the emperor's own troops) during the An Lushan rebellion. The story, and Bai Juyi's poem, were immensely popular throughout the Far East. (As mentioned, Li Shangyin also wrote a poem about her death.)

Yang Guifei had originally been one of the concubines of a Tang prince, the future Suzong emperor, son of the Xuanzong emperor, who wanted to take Yang Guifei as his own concubine. After a brief period in which she took shelter in a Daoist nunnery, Xuanzong achieved his end. Known as the "fat concubine" for her full figure, Yang Guifei favored the loose robes of Central Asia.

The poem begins with the beauty of Yang Guifei, described as she bathed in the hot springs near the capital, and how the emperor became besotted by her and neglected his responsibilities:

> One day she was selected to accompany the emperor.
>
> Turning her head with a smile, beautiful in all ways,
>
> The painted ladies of the six palaces were colorless.
>
> In the cool spring she bathed in the Pool of Elegant Purity
>
> The hot spring water nourished . . .
>
> This was when she began to enjoy imperial favor.

Cloudlike hair, a beautiful face, gold hairpins,
    a swaying walk

Within lotus screens, warm, she passed spring nights.

Spring nights were cruelly short, the sun rose high

But now the emperor did not attend morning court.

She accompanied him to banquets . . .

In spring she accompanied him on his spring tours,

She filled his nights.

In the rear palace there were three thousand concubines

But the love for those three thousand, he gave to
    just one . . .

And after Mawei, the emperor sent Daoist priests to search for her and she appeared from beyond the Yellow Springs (the Chinese equivalent of the underworld) while the palace (and government) suffered:

In the western palace and the southern inner palace

Autumn grass grew thickly,

Leaves covered the red steps but no one swept them.

In the Pear Garden, the pupils' hair was turning gray

In the Pepper Hall, the maids and eunuchs were
    growing old . . .

Less well-known poems in the anthology include an anonymous lament by an exile. The theme of exile or separation from home, whether for reasons of work or political disfavor, is a very common one in Chinese poetry. Here, the poet regrets his absence from home at the Cold Food Festival, which overlaps with the Qingming Festival (in early April) when families get together to remember their ancestors, sweep family graves, and, most importantly, make offerings of food at the graves to feed the hungry souls:

The Cold Food time is near, rain makes the grass grow lush

The wheat shoots blow in the wind, willows are mirrored
    by the dyke

We have families but we cannot go home

The cuckoo endlessly calls in our ears . . .

Chinese readers of this lament know that the call of the cuckoo
sounds like "*bu ru gui qu*," or "nothing is as good as returning home,"
thus wordlessly expressing the sorrow of the exile.

One of the poems by Meng Haoran (c. 691–740)—one of the best-
known Tang poets, famous for his descriptions of landscape—expresses
with irony his distaste for office (and he was a government servant only
for a short time):

Going home to Southern Mountain at the end of the year

I will not submit any more memorials at the gate of the
    Northern Palace.

I'm going home to my poor cottage on the Southern
    Mountain,

A man of no talent is cast aside by a wise ruler.

A sick man is shunned.

White hair drives my aging,

Spring follows the end of the year.

Eternal regrets and sorrow prevent sleep

The moon in the pines by my empty window.

Meng Haoran contrasts the joys of the simple life and uncomplicated
friendship in a poem entitled "Visiting an Old Friend in His Village":

My old friend has prepared chicken and millet

And invited me to his home among the fields.

Green trees enfold the village

Blue mountains slant away from the outskirts

From the verandah we overlook his plot

And drink wine and talk about mulberries and hemp.

I'll wait for the Double Ninth and come back for
chrysanthemums . . .

At the Double Ninth Festival (on the ninth day of the ninth month of the Chinese calendar), people traditionally climb mountains or hills and drink chrysanthemum wine, to ward off the excessive *yang* energy of the date (since the number nine is a very *yang* number). Interestingly, the word *qing* used in the fourth line for the color of the mountains can mean either "green" or "blue." It sometimes seems unnecessarily "poetic" to translate it as "blue," but here it contrasts with the word *lu*, the color "green," of the trees in the previous line. *Lu* is indisputably the "green" of leaves and so the use of *qing* in the next line must be deliberate.

Another poem by Meng Haoran sets a scene that could be taken from a Chinese landscape painting where a scholar with his *guqin* sits in a lonely hut in the mountains. (Studying the *guqin* was one of the classical accomplishments of the scholar.) The only other figures in such painterly landscapes, dominated by towering mountains and expanses of water, are fishermen or woodcutters, the "natural" inhabitants of such scenes. The poem has the title "Staying the Night in My Teacher's Mountain Cottage, Waiting for Old Ding Who Never Turned Up":

The evening sun passes over the western peak,

All the valleys are now dark.

The moon in the pines brings forth the cool of evening

Wind on the spring water, everywhere a clear sound

The woodcutters will soon be home

In the mist the birds have perched in the trees.

He had arranged to come

Alone with my *guqin*, I wait by the path covered
in creepers.

Strange Stories from the Liao Studio
Liaozhai zhiyi
(1766)
PU SONGLING (1640–1715)

~~ ~~

Some five hundred stories, tales, and anecdotes, many with super-natural or fantastical aspects (such as encounters of humans with ghosts, fox spirits, and talking snakes), were collected and rewritten by Pu Songling over several decades. The collection was not published until 1766, long after his death, and remains a favorite with readers of all ages to this day.

Pu Songling was born to a rich merchant family in Shandong prov-ince and, contrary to family expectations, spent all his life there. At a young age, he did extremely well at the first level of the examinations, but despite this early success (and repeated attempts throughout much of his life), he was never able to pass the second-level exam and thus remained in Shandong, working as a secretary and as a tutor in the homes of the rich. While it might seem that the content of his stories and tales would be best expressed in the vernacular—inspired by the long tradition of *chuanqi* ("strange tales," or "tales of the unexpected"), which were first written down in the Tang dynasty (618–907 CE), and by anecdotes and stories told to him by friends—Pu Songling wrote *Strange Stories from the Liao Studio* (*Liaozhai zhiyi*) in quite complex classical Chinese.

The stories include some fairly straightforward accounts of events that read almost like newspaper reports, such as the one about an earthquake, said to have occurred in 1667. It caused such panic that people ran out into the streets wearing only their nightclothes—or less. Pu Songling recounts with some amusement how, in the aftermath, neighbors stood around in the streets talking excitedly about their experience of the quake, until they realized with horror and embarrass-ment that they were nearly naked. Another story tells of a wealthy man from Yangzhou who was tricked when he purchased a concubine. He discovered that the apparently pretty girl was, in fact, a boy. A friend of his took a fancy to the boy and paid the same price for him, so all ended well for the gentleman from Yangzhou. Two short pieces present a description of a box of frogs which croaked out tunes when tapped, and an account of a traveling entertainer with a charming troupe of trained mice that enacted scenes from famous dramas, dressed up in tiny costumes. There is the tale of the mynah bird, which could not only imitate speech but actually converse. When his master was traveling and found himself short of money, the bird suggested that the master sell him to the local prince. The transaction was successfully concluded but the mynah bird, after a meal and a bath in a golden bowl, fluffed out his feathers and flew away to rejoin his master.

Some other accounts are more sensational and contain descriptions of strange phenomena or odd behavior, such as the description of the hairy man who ate only pine nuts and stones for months at a time; the man who liked to eat snakes and possessed an uncanny skill of finding them; or the man with a strange hairy birthmark on his back who dreamt that in a previous incarnation, he had been condemned to be reborn as a sheep—but halfway through the process, Yama, ruler of the underworld, had relented. And then there was the man whose throat was cut by bandits but who, remarkably, survived—until he heard a particularly funny joke and laughed until the wound reopened and he died.

A particular group of people often referred to in Pu Songling's stories are Daoist adepts. As mentioned, since the Han (206 BCE–220 CE), Daoism had developed two major strands, philosophical and religious, and the Daoist belief system had been transformed to incorporate all sorts of folk beliefs and practices. Supernatural powers were attributed to some Daoists, and many Daoists carried out spells, often involving the ingestion of magical characters written down on paper. In one of Pu Songling's stories of a Daoist exorcism, the fox spirits that were haunting the Dong household, causing roof tiles and bricks to fly about, were exorcised by a Daoist who placed charms written out in red ink on the walls. The exorcism was not without its dangers and a maid fell dead after hitting one of the foxes, but she was miraculously restored to life.

A mysterious Daoist in Ji'nan, the capital city of Shandong province, is described as being able to conjure up a banquet as well as a lake filled with lotuses, but this man also demonstrated another aspect of his supernatural powers when his yellow sash was stolen while he bathed in the river: he immediately turned into a fierce yellow snake until the sash was returned.

A large number of the tales in *Strange Stories from the Liao Studio* involve fox spirits. While in the Western world ghosts are usually thought of as the spirits of the dead haunting houses, or poltergeists causing pots to fly around the room, in China such phenomena are often ascribed to fox spirits. A creature of dusk and night, the fox in Western literature and folklore is commonly presented as a cunning and sly hunter—but in Chinese popular belief, foxes also have (usually malevolent) magical powers. A common theme is that of a beautiful young woman who lures a young scholar away from his studies and weakens his health, only to reveal that she is, in fact, a female fox spirit. Male fox spirits could cause similar harm to young women, and in Chinese literature the image of a deserted house and garden where foxes lurk is always one of mystery, decline, and danger.

One of Pu Songling's characteristic tales of the danger of enchantment by a fox spirit is that of the young scholar Dong Xiasi from Qingzhou in Shandong. Though his exact status is not specified, we can assume that Dong Xiasi was somewhere in the process of the series of examinations that could lead, eventually, to high office. One evening he went out with a friend, Wang Jiusi, and they both had their fortunes read, with rather depressing results. When Dong Xiasi returned home, he found a ravishingly beautiful young woman sleeping in the bed in his study. Caressing her, he was horrified to feel a long bushy tail. She woke up and reassured him and, sure enough, the foxy appendage had disappeared. Spending the succeeding months with the fox spirit, his health and strength declined until, despite having sent her away at last and returned to his wife, he died, spitting blood. His friend Wang Jiusi subsequently received a visit from an exceptionally beautiful and irresistible young woman and took her as his lover, with the same inevitable impact on his health. Perhaps a little more aware than Dong Xiasi, he resolved to exorcise her and lit more and more incense sticks until she lay down and died and turned into a small, dead fox. Wang Jiusi, his health and energy drained by the fox spirit, was ill for months but eventually recovered.

The strength of belief in the supernatural and the fascination with strange phenomena can be found in earlier Chinese literature, but some surprising descendants of *Strange Stories from the Liao Studio* appeared in illustrated weekly journals such as the *Dianshizhai* pictorial supplement to the *Shen Bao* newspaper, published in Shanghai in the second half of the nineteenth century. It included illustrations of hauntings and hysterics among depictions of fires, balloon flights, and shipwrecks. Even during the Cultural Revolution (1966–1976), when most traditional literature was condemned as feudal and irrelevant, a few of Pu Songling's tales were still studied and included in the school curriculum.

Dream of the Red Chamber
Hongloumeng
(late eighteenth century)
CAO XUEQIN (c. 1715–1763)

≈ ⁄

Without dispute the greatest of Chinese traditional novels, *Dream of the Red Chamber* (*Hongloumeng*), also called *Dream of Red Mansions*, appears to have been left unfinished by its creator, Cao Xueqin. Manuscript versions of the first 80 chapters were circulating in Beijing soon after his death; in 1791, Cheng Weiyuan and Gao E published a version in 120 chapters, claiming that the last 40 chapters were created from Cao Xueqin's own papers. Many scholars still doubt the authorship of these last 40 chapters.

The title of the novel is likewise complex. While Cao Xueqin's title was *Shitou ji* (*The Story of the Stone*), the work eventually became known as *Hongloumeng*. In translation, the two characters *hong* (meaning "red") and *meng* (meaning "dream") present no problems. However, the middle character, *lou*, has been interpreted either as "mansion," with great, red-walled mansions standing for the houses of the rich, which form the background of the novel; or it is understood as "room" or "chamber," which, when associated with the color red, is seen to mean women's chambers—and indeed, while the novel's hero is male, the majority of its characters are women.

A very complex and detailed novel featuring dozens of main characters and numerous minor characters, it takes place in Nanjing, mainly in two sprawling private residences and their gardens, and follows the fortunes of the Jia family from the height of wealth, prosperity, and pleasure to the depths of ruin and despair as the family falls from imperial favor—with a tiny upturn at the end.

Cao Xueqin was descended from a family which had enjoyed imperial favor for generations. Han in origin, rather than Manchu, one of his ancestors had been a settler in the northeastern area of Manchuria. He was captured by the Manchus in the early seventeenth century and made a bond servant of the Plain White Banner, one of the military groupings of the Manchus. When the Manchus conquered China and established the Qing dynasty in 1644, many of their trusted bond servants were given important roles in government. The Cao family held positions as imperial textile commissioners in Suzhou, Nanjing, and Hangzhou (the centers of silk production), responsible for overseeing the textile factories and producing massive quantities of silk of all sorts for the imperial household. Cao Xueqin's great-grandmother nursed the Kangxi emperor (r. 1661–1722) as a child, and her husband served as textile commissioner in Nanjing. Cao Xueqin's grandfather Cao Yin (1658–1712) likewise served as textile commissioner, and the emperor also entrusted him with the compilation of a massive volume of some 50,000 Tang poems titled *Complete Tang Poems* (*Quan Tang shi*). Another of his duties was to act as host in Nanjing to the Kangxi emperor during four of his "tours of inspection of the south." This involved creating a "traveling palace," a construction of dwellings and gardens for the emperor and his vast retinue—a task which is reflected in fictional form in chapters 16 and 17 of the novel, where a new garden is laid out for an imperial concubine, a member of the Jia family.*

The Cao family was already in decline and financial difficulties when the Kangxi emperor died in 1722. The Yongzheng emperor (r. 1722–1735), who, in effect, seized the throne to succeed the Kangxi emperor, was suspicious of the bond servants and, as part of a massive political purge, in 1728 stripped the Cao family of their posts and estates in Nanjing. They moved to Beijing, where Cao Xueqin probably spent much of his life and died in poverty.

Scholars have been preoccupied for decades with the question, how autobiographical is *Dream of the Red Chamber*? By the time Cao Xueqin was born, the Cao family's wealth and glory were exhausted, so he would have been describing the past—a past that may still have seemed very present to the family, which was effectively in exile in Beijing. There is also the question of whether the great mansions described in the novel were inspired by buildings in Nanjing or in Beijing; some have identified the grand Gongwang fu (Mansion of Prince Gong) in Beijing, with its large garden separated from the mansion by a narrow lane, as the inspiration for the Rong mansion in the novel.** However, detailed searching for autobiographical cues downplays aspects of imagination and creativity, and it should be concluded that Cao Xueqin, while describing a social milieu with which he was familiar and using his own family history, created an extraordinary, many-layered, and highly imaginative novel. It may be summed up in the couplet quoted at the beginning of the novel: "Truth becomes fiction when the fiction's true; Real becomes not-real when the unreal's real."***

As in so many other Chinese novels, there is a brief introductory section; here a goddess, a Daoist priest, and a Buddhist monk are magically involved in the creation of the hero, Jia Baoyu. The novel proceeds to tell the story of the hero and his cousins, their relatives, and their many servants in two great mansions in Nanjing.

Jia Baoyu, born with a magical jade stone in his mouth (his name means "Precious Jade"), is first encountered as a young boy, living with his grandmother in the western wing of the great Rong mansion. His main companions are two of his female cousins, Lin Daiyu ("Dark Jade") and Xue Baochai ("Precious Hairpin"). Daiyu is prone to illness, quick to take offence, and quite sharp-tongued, while Baochai is straightforward, sensible, and unusual in her taste for plain furnishings and ornaments. Baoyu's parents intend him to marry Baochai, and she possesses a gold locket that bears an inscription very similar to that on Baoyu's jade, which states that as long as the wearer keeps the jade or locket, they will be certain of a long life.

Baoyu, throughout the novel, fails to demonstrate any common masculine traits, always preferring female company and proclaiming that girls are better than dirty, nasty boys. Apart from his grandmother and his cousins, he is surrounded by a flock of maids with wonderful names such as Amber, Avocet, Caltrop, Citronella, Crimson, Emerald, Kingfisher, Mackerel, Melilot, Nightingale, Oriole, Silver, Snowgoose, and Sunset. The complexities of family life in the mansions include the complexities of managing a vast retinue of servants who live in close proximity with their masters and mistresses, and the servants' fortunes (some tragic, some happy) are intertwined with the fortunes of the great family.

One of the delights of the novel is the detailed description of buildings, gardens, furnishings, clothing, and jewelry, which offer a rich source of information about the lives of the rich in eighteenth-century

China, whether in Beijing or Nanjing. Another indulgence is the entertainment. The Crab-Apple Flower Club has been formed by the women of the family specifically to enjoy the flowering of the crab-apple trees, to eat crabs, drink wine, and compose poetry. The use of poetry is also invoked in the chapters describing the construction of the wonderful new garden for the imperial visitation, whose buildings and views are incomplete until embellished with quotations from poetry, making the garden something of a verdant literary puzzle as guests strain to catch the allusions and recognize the poems used.

Ever since its first publication, the novel has been very popular in China, inspiring the creation of various operatic versions and, in more recent years, film versions. Such is the complexity of the creation, the breadth and depth of possible investigation and interpretation, that a whole branch of literary criticism, known as "Redology," grew up in China in the twentieth century. Even during the Cultural Revolution (1966–1976), when such lyrical descriptions of wealth were anathema, parts of *Dream of the Red Chamber* were still studied.

Six Records of a Floating Life
Fusheng liu ji

(late eighteenth century/early nineteenth century)

SHEN FU (1763–after 1807)

~ ⁄⁄

Shen Fu, the struggling son of a literati family from Suzhou, tried to make a living as a secretary to a magistrate and also worked as teacher, painter, and merchant. He is famous for his charming, deeply affecting, and intimate memoirs, *Six Records of a Floating Life* (*Fusheng liu ji*). The title of the book suggests an insubstantial, insignificant life, and its written style is simple and straightforward. This humble self-description is characteristic of Confucian modesty, but it does not convey the depth of emotions recorded in Shen Fu's autobiographical pieces.

Shen Fu's father was a low-grade official, serving as a magistrate's secretary, and he arranged for Shen Fu to follow him in this profession. Shen Fu began work as a secretary in the early 1780s, and in 1787 he obtained a post in Anhui province but soon left this position due to disagreements with his colleagues. He joined a relative in a brewing business which, sadly, soon failed. For many years he tried to provide for his family as a secretary, teacher, and trader. An attempt to live from his paintings, sold from a studio in Suzhou, failed, and from 1792 to 1793 he went to Guangzhou (Canton) to try and sell Suzhou products. After his father's death, in 1804, a brother cheated Shen Fu out of his inheritance. In 1805, he obtained a position as secretary to a friend, the prefect of Chongqing in Sichuan, and they traveled together to Dongguan in Shaanxi province and Ji'nan in Shandong. In 1807 he served as secretary to an embassy to the Ryukyu Islands, a string of islands that run from the southern tip of Japan to the north of Taiwan. Under Japanese control, they had a formal relationship with China, hence the official visit. The embassy probably lasted two years since much time was spent waiting in Fujian province for favorable winds. There is no record of Shen Fu's life after the trip to the Ryukyu Islands (although some say that he at last achieved some success with his painting), and his date of death is unknown.

Shen Fu was devoted to his wife of twenty-three years, Chen Yun (1763–1803)—though they were compelled, by such work as he had, to spend time apart. Owing to various misunderstandings, she did not get on very well with Shen Fu's parents, and despite their poverty they had to leave the family home in 1801 and scrape by in Yangzhou.

The title *Six Records of a Floating Life* comes from the six "records," or chapters, of Shen Fu's account of his life. He was happy at times, things were difficult at times, sometimes through his fault, sometimes not. The chapters are organized around major themes, rather than chronological events. However, by the time the text was first printed, in 1877, the last two sections had been lost, so the book should really be entitled "Four Records." (It is thought that his narrative of the embassy visit to the Ryukyu Islands formed the last two, missing, chapters. A version produced in 1935 included two final chapters, but they have been shown to be compilations from other sources.)

The first "record" describes Shen's married life, while the second "record" relates the pleasures of gardening, flower arrangement, and other aesthetic pastimes. The third "record," or chapter, details the problems with his family and the death of his wife, and the fourth (and last surviving) "record" presents his travels to Guangzhou, Dongguan, and Ji'nan.

In the first chapter, titled "The Record of the Lady's Chamber," Shen Fu begins, "I was born during the winter of the twenty-seventh year of the Qianlong emperor [r. 1735–1796]. It was a time of peace and prosperity and I was born into a family of officials that lived beside the Canglang ting in Suzhou." The Canglang ting (Pavilion of the Dark Blue Waves) is one of the earliest of the famous gardens of Suzhou, first constructed in the eleventh century. Entered over a broad stream, the garden rises through rocks, bamboos, and trees to quite a height. It is famous for its stone-carved landscape pictures set into the walls. Shen Fu continues, "You could say that I was blessed. As the poet Su Dongbo wrote, 'All things are like spring dreams, leaving no trace.' If I didn't write down what happened then, I could not avoid ingratitude . . . When I was young, I was engaged to a Miss Jin Shayu but she died when she was seven years old, so I was engaged to a daughter of the Chen family. Her name was Yun [Rue (plant)] but her literary name was Shuzhen

[Beautiful Treasure]. She was born intelligent. When she was learning to talk she learnt the 'Pipa Song' poem and could repeat it again and again. She lost her father when she was three." As a result her family was very poor but the young Chen Yun was a skilled embroiderer and her handwork supported them.

Shen Fu and Chen Yun married in 1780, when they were both seventeen, and he recounts their happy life together in remarkable detail, including conversations about literature and their different tastes in food. "Every day she soaked her rice with tea and she liked to eat bean curd cured with mustard and salt, which was popularly known in Suzhou as 'stinking bean curd.' She also liked pickled and salted cucumbers. All my life I'd hated both of these." Chen Yun defended these dishes—because they were affordable—and teased Shen Fu until he pinched his nose with his fingers and dared to taste a pickled cucumber—and "found it good." Their pleasure in food was simple but inventive.

In the second chapter, "Record of Pleasurable Pastimes," Shen Fu describes how they created miniature landscapes in pots, arranged Buddha's Hand citrons (used to scent clothes and rooms) and quinces in bowls, and various flowers in pots. Just like the Jia family in Cao Xueqin's *Dream of the Red Chamber* (*Hongloumeng*), they enjoyed poetry parties and crab-eating parties and improved their picnics by taking along a little brazier to make tea.

Shen Fu often had to travel to find work, despite the fact that Chen Yun was sickly, and he recorded his travels in detail. On a trip to Guangzhou he visited a temple where he admired the fine *pencai* (bonsai) in pots set all around the main courtyard, which "hadn't been clipped but were naturally beautiful in their strange shapes. Most were Huang shan pines." His peaceful enjoyment of the plants was interrupted by a performance in the courtyard that attracted "a tidal wave of people."

After a New Year's Eve when the mosquitoes buzzed like thunder, Shen Fu went with friends to another Guangzhou tourist attraction, the "flower boats" with their sing-song girls. Regretting the absence of his wife (whose presence might have restrained him), he meets a madam who has reserved the uppermost part of one of the houseboats for him. Grateful to her ("You really are a fairy under a lotus leaf!"), he climbs up the steep steps with Xi'er, a sing-song girl, and exclaims, "You can see the moon from up here! A bright round moon hung over a broad expanse of sky and water, [and] randomly scattered, like floating leaves, were the wine boats, their lanterns twinkling like stars spread across the sky. Smaller boats plied to and fro with sounds of music and song. My emotions stirred, I said, 'Young men should not visit Guangzhou . . . It's a pity my wife could not come.' I looked at Xi'er. Under the moonlight she looked a little like Chen Yun, so I helped her down and we put out the candles and lay down in bed."

A few days later, together with friends, he visited the Sea Pearl Temple, also in Guangzhou. "It was in the middle of the water, surrounded by a wall like a city wall. On all four sides, about five feet above the water, were holes where large cannon were placed to defend against pirates. As the water rose and fell, the holes always seemed to be in place without any logical explanation." Further up the Pearl River, he described the buildings of the foreign traders: "The Thirteen Foreign Hongs were west of the Yulan Gate." These were the Western-style complexes (part warehouse, part residence) used by foreign traders, including those working for the British East India Company—who, from about 1700, made regular annual trips to Guangzhou to buy tea for the English market, as well as some silks, porcelain, and other luxury goods. They were not allowed to reside in Guangzhou at this time but spent the brief trading season in their unique dwellings. The lower part of these foreign structures was comprised of warehouses and offices (known locally as "godowns"); above were rooms with long, shady verandahs against the oppressive heat of Guangzhou. According to Shen Fu, "They looked just like structures in a foreign painting. Just opposite them was an area called The Flower Ground. This was Guangzhou's flower market [and a great attraction to the plant collectors sent by the British East India Company]. I thought I knew a lot about flowers, but I could only recognize some six or seven out of ten and had to ask their names. Some of them were not even registered in the *Register of Beautiful Flowers* (*Qunfang pusuo*), or perhaps it was something to do with the local pronunciation of their names."

Following his descriptions of literati homelife characteristic of Ming and Qing China, Shen Fu's reference to the "Thirteen Foreign Hongs" reflects the dramatic changes presaged by the arrival of brash Western traders in southern China.

Poems

(late nineteenth to early twentieth centuries)

Qiu Jin (c. 1875–1907)

≈ ⁄≈

Qiu Jin was born in Fujian to a family from Shaoxing (Lu Xun's hometown, in Zhejiang province), and executed in Shaoxing by government order in 1907. Her father served as secretary to various high officials, and she seems to have been educated at home. After an early marriage, which left her unhappy and shocked, Qiu Jin left her family behind in 1904 and went to study in Japan. (She was possibly politically inspired by the chaos of the Boxer Rebellion in 1900.) She studied in Tokyo and joined Chinese women's discussion groups. One of her fellow students described her as "a beautiful woman" in "Western male clothing . . . a blue hunting cap sitting sideways on her head. A dark blue secondhand business suit did not fit her at all . . . from the cuffs one could just see her white, delicate hands. She carried a slender walking stick. Beneath her baggy trousers, worn-out brown shoes peeped out. A green necktie hung loosely over her chest." Qiu Jin explained that she wanted a mind as strong as a man's, and that if she first "take on the form of a man, then I think my mind, too, will eventually become that of a man." There is a poignant photograph of Qiu Jin in her suit and cane, and another of her in a fur-trimmed kimono brandishing a short Japanese sword.

She was preoccupied with the position of women in China in the late Qing, the oppression caused by traditional marriage and the practice of foot-binding. In Tokyo in 1905, she joined the revolutionary Chinese organization Tongmenghui (Revolutionary Alliance) when it was founded by Sun Yat-sen (1866–1925) and others. (Sun Yat-sen was the leader of a series of revolutionary movements mainly directed against the failing imperial system, who came to be seen as the "father" of republican China after 1911.) The Qing government asked the Japanese government to control Chinese students there, since they were increasingly anti-Manchu and rebellious. Rather than submit, Qiu Jin attended a meeting in Tokyo of Chinese students and took out her short sword, stabbing the podium and declaring, "If on return to the motherland I surrender to the Manchu barbarians . . . stab me with this!"

She returned to China in 1906 and took up a post as a teacher in a school for girls in Zhejiang. Among her writings, which she wrote in vernacular Chinese (thus anticipating the ideas of the May Fourth Movement of 1919, which stressed the need to use the vernacular style), was an address to Chinese women: "The most unfairly treated people in the world are the two hundred million Chinese women. Once born, it is best to have a good father; for if he is the hotheaded, obstinate sort, he'll want to kill you for your opposition." She exhorted them not to bind their feet, and if they had children to send them away to school. "The revolution must begin within the family. This means equal rights for men and women." Her forcefully expressed ideas were dangerously ahead of their time, very much in tune with May Fourth sentiments but expressed a dozen or so years earlier.

Qiu Jin's anti-imperial activities included founding a newspaper for women in Shanghai, acting as head of various girls' schools, and participating in planning military activities directed against the government. Her school in Shaoxing was used as a meeting place and a military training ground where a revolutionary army was organized, with plans for revolt against Manchu rule, but the authorities uncovered the plot. Qiu Jin was captured in the school and beheaded on July 15, 1907.

Her poetry, often filled with classical reference, is dark. An example is "Sighing for China," which laments Western encroachment and the Chinese inability to react:

> Alas, my country is not as good as Western countries,
>
> Alas, it flourished in ancient times but is now desolate.
>
> How can the predominant grayness not reflect me?
>
> In the past, this poisonous mist filled the empty sky,
>
> The nature of my fellow countrymen was formerly entirely
>   beautiful,
>
> Why can't they surpass the white races?
>
> It is only because they are imprisoned in this dark dungeon,
>
> They are ground down by sacred inheritance.

She wrote several *Man jiang hong* poems. *Man jiang hong*, literally "the river is entirely red" (presumably with blood), refers to a series of poems, most notably one poem traditionally attributed to Yue Fei (1103–1142), the great Song dynasty general who was the epitome of martial prowess and loyalty.

One of Qiu Jin's *Man jiang hong* poems mentions Qin Liangyu (c. 1574–1648) and Shen Yunying (1624–c. 1660), female generals of the Ming dynasty famous for their battles against the Manchus:

> In this filthy world,
>
> How many men are generals?
>
> The only exemplars I have heard of are battalions of
> women like [Qin] Liangyu,
>
> [Shen] Yunying's life fills me with envy,
>
> Fills my heart with blood.
>
> Drunk, I stroke my sword and sing like a dragon, tragically.
>
> I've long wished to ignite the flame of my independence,
>
> Our nation's humiliation,
>
> When will it be erased?

A few of her poems are less dramatic and angry:

> Let us arouse ourselves from today,
>
> Exert ourselves in the cause of peace for us all,
>
> Prosperity beyond outward display.
>
> Think how impossible to act
>
> In three-inch slippers.
>
> They must be abolished!

Qiu Jin's "Song of the Sword of the Red Hairs" ("Red Hairs" meaning Western foreigners) refers to the superior military technology of the West, which had been seen in the suppression of the Boxer Rebellion and, earlier, in the Opium Wars, and which was a matter of grave concern to modernizers and reformers in China (however, attempts at reform in the late Qing, whether political or technological, were opposed by conservatives at court):

> Pure, clean, autumn water.
>
> From afar I did not know the gleam was a shining sword.
>
> It frightens jade dragons back into their boxes, waiting to soar skyward on a clap of thunder,
>
> They say this treasure comes from the Red Hairs,
>
> Beats Japanese, humiliates all others,
>
> Cuts through bones and joints, barely shedding blood,
>
> Cuts heads off before the victims know it.
>
> Unsheathe it, shake heaven,
>
> Sun, moon, and stars hurriedly dim.
>
> A swish stops the sea, a dark wind howls,
>
> On land it kills rhinos and elephants,
>
> In the sea it cuts the dragon.
>
> Spirits and sea and mountains flee.
>
> How many victims?
>
> Skulls from mountains, blood pours in waves,
>
> Hundreds of thousands of ghosts weep.
>
> Even when hung gently on a wall, a single stroke endangers all on earth.
>
> At night it seems to hiss and hoot like an owl,
>
> A martial spirit thirsty for the blood of war, a ghost thirsting for wine,
>
> Red hairs, red hairs, cease your arrogance.
>
> Despite its effectiveness, I don't want your weapon.
>
> Self-strengthening derives from people, not from weapons,
>
> How can you be so arrogant on the strength of one sword?

The Travels of Lao Can

Lao Can youji

(c. 1903)

LIU E (1857–1909)

≈ ⁄≈

The Travels of Lao Can by Liu E is a strange and oddly appealing novel, firmly based in the past yet with hints of the present and, indeed, mention of the future. It presents an interesting depiction of China in the dying days of the Qing dynasty (1644–1911) and mixes lyrical descriptions of landscapes and scenic spots with detective subplots and some wit.

There is an autobiographical aspect to the novel because its hero, Lao Can, resembles Liu E in his interests and skills (although Lao Can outperforms his creator). The name, Lao Can, literally means "old broken-down" or "old falling to bits," with the word "old" intended as a familiar, friendly epithet, rather than necessarily suggesting that Lao Can is elderly. (An early translator of the novel, Yang Xianyi, translated the name as "Mr. Decadent," which is not entirely appropriate to the character, who is idealistic and positive, but it encompasses the state of China at the turn of the nineteenth century that frames the whole novel.)*

Liu E (whose zi, or courtesy name, was Liu Tianyun) is considered one of China's most important writers during the late Qing. He was born in Jiangsu province in 1857 to a father who had achieved the highest level in the bureaucratic exams and served as a compiler in the imperial Hanlin Academy, as well as serving as a local official in Henan province. In his retirement, Liu E's father collected books, including works on Western scientific subjects such as mathematics and geography, which helped to form Liu E's education in a mixture of tradition and modernity. Liu E's career, however, was unusual. Instead of following his father into the bureaucracy, he embarked on a series of (mostly ill-fated) ventures such as opening a tobacco shop and a modern (lithographic) printing press and traveling around as a medical practitioner. Liu E's early interest in Western science, as well as his reading of

Chinese scientific classics, provided an opportunity when, in 1888, the Yellow River burst its banks near Zhengzhou and he offered his services to the director of the Yellow River Conservancy, a friend of his father's. (As mentioned, Kong Shangren, author of *The Peach Blossom Fan*, had also assisted with conservancy work on the Yellow River.) Working alongside the laborers, Liu E opposed the general opinion, which was to follow the advice of Jia Rang (of the Western Han dynasty) to broaden the riverbed to allow a greater flow of water—and proposed instead to follow the opinion of Wang Jing (of the Eastern Han dynasty) and dredge and narrow the riverbed to increase the flow and prevent the deposition of silt. His success was such that he was sent to Beijing in about 1894 to prepare for an official post. There he revealed his interest in new Western technologies, promoting the idea of a railway between Tianjin (on the northern coast) and Zhenjiang in Jiangsu province (which was shelved) as well as the opening of modern iron mines in Shanxi province. Liu E was in Shanghai when the Boxer Rebellion came to a climax in the Boxers' siege of the foreign legations in Beijing in 1900; but after the siege had been ended and the city occupied by the allied troops of eight nations, he went to Beijing and succeeded in feeding some of the starving population by buying rice from the imperial granaries which had been seized by Russian troops. (The Boxers were a fanatical group—first anti-dynastic, then anti-foreign—who had been murdering foreign missionaries and tearing up railways before advancing on Beijing.)

Liu E then devoted himself to the collection of books and antiquities and created a pioneering collection of oracle bones from the Shang dynasty (c. 1600–1046 BCE)—he recognized them as highly significant in the study of early Chinese history. These inscribed shoulder blades of oxen and turtle shells, used for divination by the Shang kings, were found in the ruins of one of the Shang capitals and ground up for medicine (they were locally known as "dragon bones"), until scholars such as Liu E realized that they bore the earliest writing surviving in China and provided details of the lives of the Shang kings.

Liu E never lost his interest in modern technology (nor his tendency to fail with it), promoting unsuccessful enterprises such as a steam-powered cotton mill in Shanghai, a mechanized silk mill in

Hangzhou, a steel refinery in Henan province, and a waterworks and tramline in Beijing. As foreigners began to occupy more and more of China, Liu E, seeing the prospects of Pukou (near Nanjing) as a port likely to be exploited by foreigners, bought up much land there.

A forthright character, Liu E incurred the enmity of high officials such as Yuan Shikai (1859–1916), a general under the Qing who became the first president of the Republic of China in 1912 and a few years later self-proclaimed emperor. In 1908 Liu E was accused of "stealing and selling imperial rice" in the aftermath of the Boxer Rebellion in 1900 and of being in foreign pay, and was exiled to Ili in the Kazakh region of distant Xinjiang, where he died in 1909.

His only novel, *The Travels of Lao Can* touches on many aspects of his life, particularly on his work on the Yellow River. Though written in the vernacular, it incorporates many aspects of the traditional novel including a mysterious and allegorical prefatory chapter, which introduces Lao Can as well as his cure for a sick man called Huang (Yellow)—who personifies the Yellow River, and whose bursting ulcers represent the bursting riverbanks. Lao Can dreams of an enormous sinking ship that represents China, whose passengers (i.e., the people) are being killed by the sailors (meaning those in charge) and he fails to rescue them. Sailing in a small boat with a (foreign) compass, he is accused of being a traitor and his rescue attempts are repelled.

As Lao Can travels through Shandong, he is shocked by the cruelty of the provincial governor, easily identified as the Qing official Yuxian (d. 1901). In the novel, the governor thinks nothing of sacrificing whole families as his corrupt police pretend to search out robbers, while the historic Yuxian was removed from the office of governor of Shandong (with some pressure from foreigners) as he had demonstrated a lack of enthusiasm in his suppression of the Boxers. The description in the novel of how an area should be governed by a wise official, of how possessions can be left on the road and not stolen once the bandits have been suppressed, harks back to descriptions in Sima Qian's *The Grand Scribe's Records* (*Shi ji*).

During his journey Lao Can criticizes the local governor and pursues robbers; cures the sick and rescues the local population from floods, fires, and thugs; discusses China's disturbing weakness; saves two women who had been sold into prostitution by their families; and investigates the poisoning of a family and the unjust imprisonment of innocent relatives. He also enjoys the tourist sights, describing the wonderful natural springs in Ji'nan, the capital city of Shandong, which bubble up in the lake and in temple grounds—where pavilions are inscribed with poetic couplets such as those that accurately described Ji'nan: "Lotus on four sides, willows on three, mountains within the city, lake over half the city." This response to natural beauty contrasts with Lao Can's interests in modern technology and references to contemporary history, creating a popular novel significant for its mixture of the old and the modern.

"My Old Home" (in *Call to Arms*)
"*Gu xiang*" (in *Nahan*)

(1923)

Old Tales Retold
Gushi xinbian

(1936)

LU XUN (1881–1936)

≈ ≈

L
u Xun, whose real name was Zhou Shuren, was born in the pretty southern town of Shaoxing (in Zhejiang province) where his family had been landowners, officials, and pawnbrokers for generations. He became the best-known writer of twentieth-century China, famous for his essays and short stories, the latter notably alternating between nostalgia and satire. However, his engagement with contemporary politics and with China's traditions were as strong as his dedication to his own writing.

Lu Xun's grandfather had passed the highest bureaucratic exams and became a Hanlin scholar, a member of the elite body that prepared and edited imperial scripts and decrees and set examinations. He was, however, caught trying to bribe an examination official and therefore sentenced to death; the sentence was later commuted but he was stripped of office. Lu Xun's father sank into an opium addiction and consequent ill-health, and some of Lu Xun's stories about his childhood recall times when he was sent to buy medicine for his father made from "monogamous crickets," sugar cane that had weathered three frosts, ink, and other unlikely ingredients.

Lu Xun's education began in the traditional style, in a schoolhouse called Sanwei shuwu (Three Flavor Studio), a charming little whitewashed building that still stands near Lu Xun's fine ancestral home with its many courtyards. His political education began then, too, as he witnessed poverty and its exploitation in Shaoxing.

After the death of his father in 1896, and in defiance of his mother's wishes, Lu Xun embarked on a more Western, modern education, yet many of his stories depend upon recollections of the past. In retrospect, his choices of the Naval Academy and the School of Mines and Railways, both in Nanjing, seem inappropriate, since it is hard to imagine the diminutive, frail, and tubercular young rebel against unreasonable or unjust authority submitting to the military discipline of these schools. More appropriately, and perhaps partly inspired by his father's decline into illness and the failure of traditional herbalists to save him, in 1902 Lu Xun chose to study medicine in Japan, where he attended several medical schools but was always hampered by his poor Japanese.

While in Japan, he saw some lantern slides of scenes from the Russo-Japanese War of 1904–5, which was fought over Chinese territory. A scene of passive Chinese spectators watching Japanese soldiers execute a Chinese accused of spying for the Russians moved him to change direction and "reinvent" himself as a crusader for cultural reform. "I no longer believed in the overwhelming importance of medical science. However strong a nation was in physical health, if its people were intellectually feeble, they would never become anything other than cannon fodder or gawping spectators . . . The first task was to change their spirit . . ."

Returning to China in 1909 (and after his mother had forced him to accept marriage to an illiterate woman with bound feet, the antithesis of all he now aspired to), Lu Xun embarked on a career of teaching and writing. His first major story to be published, in 1918, was "A Madman's Diary" ("*Fengren riji*"), which he had written in the vernacular. Though his style remained quite complex, he had made the decision to write in *baihua* ("plain language"), in line with the May Fourth Movement (1919), which sought to reinvigorate and modernize China after the terrible treatment of the country at the Versailles Peace Conference (where, despite China having joined the Allies in the hope of regaining lost territory, all of the old German "possessions" in China were handed to its threatening neighbor, Japan).

In "A Madman's Diary," the narrator is given a diary written by an old friend who must have suffered from severe mental illness: this friend, dwelling on Chinese legends and folk beliefs and practices such as that of eating an enemy's heart and liver to gain strength, had arrived at the conclusion that all the people around were man-eaters and ready to eat him. This was a view of a society trapped in its past, unable to escape from superstition, where collective goodwill had been lost and the fight for ideals and reform abandoned. The story ends with a quavering hope, "Perhaps there are children who haven't eaten men. Save the children . . ."

Not long after, Lu Xun published the novella "The True Story of Ah-Q" ("*A-Q zhenzhuan*"), which referred directly to his view of the "intellectually feeble." Ah-Q is a base "everyman" (the "Q" in his name standing for a round head with a pigtail), a fool convinced of his own intelligence, constantly beaten and thwarted but ever confident until— a "ridiculous culprit" punished for a crime he did not do—he is executed. It is uncomfortable to read.

The background to Lu Xun's writing was a terrible period in China's modern history. The country's new republican government was beset by warlords (former leaders of the imperial regional armies fighting among themselves), by rebellion from those who felt the government was too weak, and by the humiliating decisions at the Versailles Peace Conference. From 1919 to 1926 Lu Xun was living in Beijing, working for the Ministry of Education and also teaching part-time at various institutions (Peking University, Capital Normal University, and Beijing Women's College). In 1926 a peaceful student demonstration against the local warlord, Feng Yuxiang—protesting against his collaboration with the Japanese—was countered with violence, and two of Lu Xun's students at the Women's College were killed. Having written a fierce condemnation of the minister of education, Lu Xun left Beijing for the south. Accompanied by one of his students, Xu Guangping, who later gave birth to his only son, he taught for brief periods at Xiamen University and Zhongshan University (in Guangzhou) before settling in Shanghai. Life there was not entirely safe, either: Lu Xun continued to protest and to write and—though associated with left-wing writers and artists and a founder member, in 1930, of the League of Left-Wing Writers—he frequently quarreled with the Communist literary leadership in Shanghai. In 1931, the Guomindang (Kuomintang) executed twenty-five left-wing writers in Shanghai, five of them members of the League of Left-Wing Writers—one was a close friend of Lu Xun.

Politics, or a sympathy for those who suffer under appalling regimes, must have had an influence on another of Lu Xun's activities—the promotion of modern woodblock illustration and the introduction of contemporary European woodblock artists, including Käthe Kollwitz (1867–1945), to China. (The medium of woodblock was widely exploited in early twentieth-century Europe by left-wing artists and used to depict the sufferings of the poor and oppressed.) Lu Xun organized several exhibitions of woodblock prints, but it was not only modern woodblock printing that interested him: in the 1930s he collaborated with the bibliophile Zheng Zhenduo (1898–1958) to publish a facsimile of one of the greatest collections of Chinese color woodblock printing, Hu Zhengyan's 1644 production of the *Collection of Letter-Papers from the Ten Bamboo Studio* (*Shizhuzhai jianhua pu*). Lu Xun also wrote a scholarly study (the first of its kind), *A Brief History of Chinese Fiction* (*Zhongguo xiaoshuo shilue*).

Despite Lu Xun's adoption of the vernacular and his absorption with contemporary politics, he was also deeply influenced by the traditional past, as can be seen in his nostalgic stories such as "My Old Home" ("*Gu xiang*"), published in the collection *Call to Arms* (*Nahan*) in 1923. (The term *gu xiang*, translated as "old home," has greater resonance in China because it can incorporate "ancestral home" and refer to a place of distant origin with which a person has no current ties, but which is still of significance.) The narrator tells of returning to his ancestral family home after an absence of twenty years. His mother reminds him that his childhood friend, Runtu, will be coming. At the mention of Runtu, the narrator "suddenly saw a magical picture . . . a huge golden moon hanging in a dark blue sky. Below, on a sandy sea shore, an endless field, planted with watermelons. In the middle of the field is a boy of ten or eleven with a silver chain around his neck. In his hand he holds an iron pitchfork which he stabs fiercely at a 'zha' [an imaginary animal]. The 'zha' dodges from side to side and escapes between the boy's legs. The boy was Runtu." Because he was born in a leap month (*run*) and his horoscope was lacking the element "earth" (*tu*), his father had named him Runtu.

Despite the differences between the peasant boy and the wellborn narrator, as children they were great friends because Runtu had a wonderful imagination. "'In the evening I keep watch over the watermelons. You could come, too.' 'Do you watch out for thieves?' 'No! If a passerby wants a bite of juicy melon, we don't call that stealing. You have to watch out for badgers, hedgehogs, and "zha." Under the moonlight, if you hear a hooting sound, it's a "zha" eating watermelons. You have to take a pitchfork and creep up quietly . . .'"

When the middle-aged, weather-beaten, and poverty-stricken Runtu arrives, he addresses his childhood friend as "Sir" and instructs his little boy to do the same and to kowtow. His inventive imagination, from jumping fish and "ghost-frightener shells" to his description of the hunt for the hooting "zha," has been erased by the hardship of his peasant life. And yet, Runtu's son was later to become custodian of the Lu Xun Museum in Shaoxing, his name and the memories of his father confirming the strong autobiographical nature of the story.

Lu Xun's collection *Old Tales Retold* (*Gushi xinbian*), published toward the end of his life, is, as the title suggests, a collection of rewritings of legends. One story tells of Nuwa, in Chinese folklore the original female, the creator and progenitor who makes nice little human figures when she feels fresh—but when she is tired, they turn out as rats. There is the story of the mythical Emperor Yu, "tamer of the floods"; and a tale that explains why, in Chinese folklore, the moon is inhabited by a hare and a beautiful woman called Chang' E, who mixes an elixir of immortality. In one of the finest stories in *Old Tales Retold*, the eccentric philosopher Laozi endures visits from boring Confucius (who, Laozi knows, will speak ill of him behind his back). Such is the strength of his feelings for Confucius that Laozi decides to leave the country and go off to the northwest, passing through the Hangu Pass. There are comic scenes at the pass, where he undergoes complicated games to get past the Customs House, which is stuffed with confiscated bags of beans, salt, and sesame seeds.

Lu Xun's portrait of Laozi—toothless, difficult to understand, but, in his quiet way, astute—is affectionate, while Confucius, the eternally venerated sage, is described as ambitious and untrustworthy—which is an extremely provocative and amusing view.

Miss Sophie's Diary
Shafei nüshi riji
(c. 1927)

DING LING (c. 1904–1986)

≋ ⤳

D ing Ling was the most prominent woman writer of twentieth-century China, best known for two remarkably different works, *Miss Sophie's Diary* (*Shafei nüshi riji*) and *The Sun Shines over the Sanggan River* (*Taiyang zhao zai Sanggan he shang*) (1948).

Jiang Bingzhi, who took the pen name of Ding Ling (Ding being a common surname, and *ling* meaning "bell"), was born into a gentry family in Linli in Hunan province. Her father died while she was very young, and she was much influenced by her independent, progressive mother who worked as a teacher. Ding Ling refused to accept an arranged marriage with a cousin and left home in about 1920 to study in Shanghai, first at a progressive girls' school, then at Shanghai University for a year. Between 1924 and 1927 she attended classes at Peking University where she met the poet and novelist Hu Yepin (1903–1931); they married in 1925 and two years later moved to Shanghai. There, together with a close friend, the writer Shen Congwen (1902–1988), and in very difficult circumstances—with strict Guomindang government repression and censorship and intensifying arguments between left-wing and Communist groups over the purpose of literature—they started a literary magazine, which eventually failed. Hu Yepin and Ding Ling moved to Ji'nan in Shandong province, where he taught in a high school. The Guomindang government wanted to arrest him for his Communist views and the couple fled back to Shanghai. In 1930, Hu Yepin joined the newly formed League of Left-Wing Writers (one of the League's founders was Lu Xun), which was suppressed in the same year. Having joined the Communist Party, Hu Yepin was arrested at a clandestine meeting in January 1931 (possibly betrayed by rival Communist writers), and, together with four other members of the League and twenty other "Communists," he was executed on February 7, 1931.

Ding Ling joined the Communist Party in 1932, was imprisoned by the Nationalists, and in 1936 went to the Communist stronghold of Yan'an in Shaanxi province (which had been established after the Long March of 1934–35). There she held various posts, including that of director of the Chinese Literature and Art Association. Always combative, she criticized the atmosphere in Yan'an where women were ignored, belittled, and denied equality, and attacked the Communist leaders (including Mao Zedong) for discarding their wives with impunity. She was ordered to make a self-criticism, but her outspoken views led to further problems during the Anti-Rightist Campaign of 1957, when she was expelled from the Communist Party, and five years' imprisonment during the Cultural Revolution (1966–1976). It was only in the late 1970s that she was rehabilitated.

Ding Ling said that her early writing was influenced by Western literary realism, and *Miss Sophie's Diary* is quite unlike previous Chinese fiction in its self-absorbed stream of consciousness. Written in the first person, as diary entries dating from December to March, little happens to Sophie, who is confined to bed in Beijing suffering from tuberculosis, but her mind races and her thoughts twist and turn in self-contradictory turmoil. She is reactive and negative. She longs for visitors yet treats them badly; she longs for attention, particularly from an attractive Overseas Chinese acquaintance, Ling, yet rejects his physical advances. Aside from her illness, she reflects the dilemma of young, educated women in the early decades of the twentieth century faced with the dangerous possibilities of emancipation and the traditional demands of chastity.

She thinks of her friend Yun, who committed suicide to escape an unhappy marriage. "I can't bear to think of lying on the grass in the French Park [in Shanghai] listening to her sing 'The Peony Pavilion.' If she hadn't been tricked by God into loving that pasty-faced man, she'd never have died so early and I'd never have drifted to Beijing by myself." In her diary entry for January 3, she muses on her own death. "I'm always dreaming of things that would enable me to have no regrets when I die. I imagine myself lying on a bed in an extremely luxurious bedroom, my sisters kneeling on a bearskin beside the bed, my father sighing quietly by the open window, while I read lots of long letters from the people who love me, and my friends weep sincerely as they remember me . . ."—but her reality is rather different, infinitely less luxurious and considerably more lonely.

Even when she has an indication that people care for her, it is not enough. "Actually I do have a letter but it has only added to my unhappiness. It was sent to me by a rough man from Anhui who pestered me a year ago. All that 'love, love, love' in it made my flesh creep." Ling, the Overseas Chinese with whom she is obsessed, is attractive, well-dressed, and rich, and wants a rich wife who would entertain guests skillfully. "Ling hasn't come for several days. What would he want to come for? I'm badly dressed, no good at household things, I've got TB and no money . . ." She sends him a note saying she is ill and telling him not to come and see her, but wonders: "Could he have believed I meant it?" In March, in her last diary entry, she writes, "He came at ten last night to tell me in his clumsy way how he longed for me. My heart was touched but when I saw his eyes burning with sexual desire, I was frightened. 'Hey, be sensible and clear off to a brothel' is what I should have said but, although I was secretly mocking him, I forgot everything when he suddenly and boldly put his arms around me . . . If I'd had any self-control, I'd have thought of the other things beside his beauty and thrown him out . . . I've won! I've won! It was because when he kissed me, I knew the taste of what it was that bewitched me and at the same time I despised myself . . . I pushed him away and started to cry . . . perhaps he thought that his lips had given me such warmth, softness, and tenderness that my heart was too overcome to know what it was doing . . . why did I let a man I despise so much kiss me? I don't love him and was jeering at him but why did I let him embrace me? I'm my own worst enemy." After many such tortuous entries, *Miss Sophie's Diary* ends with the words "Quietly go on living and quietly die. I'm sorry for you, Sophie."

Sophie's narcissistic self-expression is completely different from the tone of *The Sun Shines over the Sanggan River*, written about twenty years later and based on several visits Ding Ling made to villages in the throes of land reform. Through these visits she hoped "to make good the deficiencies in my experience of life and in the novel by taking part in the mass struggle." (During land reform, from the 1940s to the early

1950s, land was seized from landlords; peasants were classified according to their background into "poor," "middle," and "rich," and the local land was reallocated accordingly.) Her black-and-white cast of characters, which she described as giving "a fairly accurate picture of a village with its crowd of living people," includes Old Ku, "a well-off middle peasant who has been carelessly classed as a rich peasant"; Landlord Jiang, surrounded by cardplayers and opium-smoking utensils; and the local despot Chen Wu, a "notorious scoundrel who beat up anyone who crossed his fields, who thought nothing of abusing people and raping women. It was common knowledge that he sold opium and concealed weapons . . ." With such a dedicated bad hat in the neighborhood, the question asked at a village meeting, "Whom should we struggle against this time?" seems almost rhetorical. The novel concentrates on the activities and final fates of these varied characters in an imaginary village in Inner Mongolia during this turbulent time when old scores were settled, often cruelly.

The striking contrast between these two works by the same author dramatically illustrates the dilemmas faced by a twentieth-century Chinese writer attempting to create literary texts while living through the different revolutions in thought and behavior and ideology that took place between the 1920s and 1950s and beyond.

Mr. Ma and Son
Er Ma
(1929)

Camel Xiangzi
Luotuo xiangzi
(1936)

Beneath the Red Banner
Zheng hongqi xia
(1966)

LAO SHE (1899–1966)

≫ ⁄≪

Lao She was born into a poor Manchu family in Beijing. His real name was Shu Qingchun and he was a Manchu of the Sumuru Plain Red Banner. The eight Manchu Banners formed a military and administrative system into which all Manchus were incorporated. True to the tradition of heredity, Lao She's father was a Banner soldier, killed in 1901 during the suppression of the Boxer Rebellion, which had involved the siege of the legation quarters in Beijing in 1900 and the occupation of the city by allied foreign forces until the end of 1901.

The death of Lao She's father, caused by the explosion of gunpowder that he was carrying, is described by Lao She's widow, Hu Jieqing, in the afterword she wrote for an English translation of Lao She's unfinished "autobiographical novel," *Beneath the Red Banner* (*Zheng hongqi xia*). This text is a wonderful evocation of the little-known lives of the Manchus in China at the beginning of the twentieth century.

Growing up in a fatherless family, supported by his mother (who worked as a laundress and seamstress) and his extended family and by the tiny stipend received by all Manchu Bannermen (soldiers) and their families, Lao She was educated in fits and starts. He did eventually graduate from Beijing Normal University in 1918. He then spent some years teaching in Beijing and Tianjin before setting off for London in 1924 for a five-year term teaching Chinese at the School of Oriental Studies (now the School of Oriental and African Studies, University of London) in Finsbury Square. He taught a mixed group of students who were preparing to go to China, most of them as missionaries, some as businessmen.* Lao She is said to have converted to Christianity, which would have helped him get the post in London, because most "sinologists" in Britain at the time were either former colonial servants or former missionaries. It was in London that Lao She wrote his first novels, including *Cat Country* (*Mao cheng ji*) (1933)—described as China's first work of science fiction—and *Mr. Ma and Son* (*Er Ma*), in which he portrayed his depressing impressions of life in London.

The two main characters, Mr. Ma and his son, Ma Wei, come to London to take over an antique and curio shop near St. Paul's Cathedral bequeathed to Mr. Ma by his brother, who had died in London. Their main contacts are two British families, the Elys and the Wedderburns. The Reverend Ely, a retired missionary, arranges for Mr. Ma and his son to lodge in Bloomsbury with a widow, Mrs. Wedderburn, her daughter, Mary, and their dog, Napoleon. Even the first transaction between the Reverend Ely and Mrs. Wedderburn is thick with anti-Chinese prejudice: Mrs. Wedderburn is horrified at the thought of Chinese lodgers who would eat dogs and cook rats and smoke opium, but the Reverend Ely suggests she could charge them more than her usual rate. She agrees but insists, "I can't allow them to use my bath."

The Reverend Ely is confident of his Chinese expertise, as we read in the novel: "Leaving aside the fact that he spoke Chinese very poorly, he was a walking Chinese encyclopedia and he truly loved the Chinese. In the middle of the night, if unable to sleep, he prayed to God to hurry up and make China a British dominion. His eyes filling with tears, he pointed out to God that if the Chinese were not taken in hand by the British, that vast mass of yellow-faced, black-haired creatures would never achieve their rightful ascent to the pearly gates." Later in the narrative, he tries to persuade Mr. Ma to write a book about China, and though he promises that he will translate it into English and it will do well for both of them, he admits that his motive is a desire to become a professor of Chinese—for which goal he needs to produce a book, and it is clear that he would exploit any text to his own ends. (This was a common practice, and even as late as the 1950s foreign academics were often reliant upon native Chinese speakers to help them with books, and they frequently "forgot" to acknowledge this essential assistance. Lao She's own experience in this area was to assist the former British officer Clement Egerton with his translation of the erotic novel *Plum in a Golden Vase* [*Jinpingmei*], called *The Golden Lotus* by Egerton and published in 1939. Lao She lodged with the Egertons in Holland Park and, though not acknowledged as a translator, the English-language edition was dedicated to him.) Unwilling to assist the Reverend Ely, Mr. Ma, a slightly bumbling figure and quite at sea in England, is happier planting chrysanthemums and dahlias in Mrs. Wedderburn's neglected garden and taking Napoleon for walks.

Subthemes in *Mr. Ma and Son* include the making of a film in London about China, supposedly set in Shanghai, for which extras are sought, and Mr. Ma is asked to consider playing "a rich Chinese businessman." Lao She's text reflects the prevailing view that Western people at the time had of China, seen through films and novels such as Sax Rohmer's Fu Manchu series (begun in 1913), which popularized the idea of the "Yellow Peril," and together with the smug condescension of missionaries and "old China hands," created the unpleasant atmosphere in which Lao She found himself in London in the 1920s.

One interesting character in the novel is Li Zirong (in Wade-Giles, Tzu-jung), a part-time student who had been running the antique shop. Unlike the vacillating Ma Wei and the bumbling Mr. Ma, who drops pieces of porcelain every time he comes near the shop, Li is practical, sensible, and—though ready to criticize as he sees necessary—loyal to both the Ma family and his own family back in China.

His practicality is evident in his acceptance of a marriage his mother has arranged for him in China (in contrast with Ma Wei's hopeless pursuit of Mary Wedderburn), in his ability to organize his time between work and study, and in his ability to enjoy himself in London: going to plays, the circus, and taking Ma Wei on a long, healthy fourteen-mile walk from suburban Barnet (where Lao She at one point had lodgings with disagreeable spinsters) to the fresh air of Welwyn Garden City.

188 ~ GREAT BOOKS OF CHINA

Overall, the novel is a bitter indictment of the racist treatment of, and ignorant attitudes to, Chinese in London in the 1920s.

Returning to China in 1930 (after teaching for a year in Singapore), Lao She became one of the major literary figures in China, producing novels such as *Four Generations Under One Roof* (*Si shi tong tang*) (1944) and several highly successful plays, including *Dragon Beard Ditch* (*Longxu gou*) (1951) and *Teahouse* (*Cha guan*) (1957). *Teahouse* was performed for decades throughout China. He was never prominently involved in literary politics, but he was, like so many writers, attacked during the Cultural Revolution and almost certainly committed suicide in 1966 after savage beatings by young Red Guards.

Camel Xiangzi (*Luotuo xiangzi*) is perhaps the best-known novel by Lao She. (It was translated as *Rickshaw Boy* in an American edition of 1945, with, apparently, a bowdlerized happy ending.) It is set in Beijing in the 1920s and describes the unhappy life of a rickshaw puller. The hero, Xiangzi, acquired his nickname, "Camel Xiangzi," because he escaped from a band of marauding soldiers outside one of the city gates of Beijing by hiding himself with three camels. A country boy who was orphaned at a young age, Xiangzi came to the city in search of work and became a rickshaw puller. Rickshaws, invented in Japan, were first used in China in the mid-1870s. They were two-wheeled vehicles intended to carry usually one passenger, and were pulled by a single runner holding on to long shafts. Even in a flat city like Beijing, the strain on the rickshaw puller was often evident, especially if he was old or in poor health. The British travel writer Robert Byron, who lived in Beijing in 1934, disliked rickshaw travel, as did Sir Harold Acton (one of the translators of *The Peach Blossom Fan* [*Taohua shan*]): "I think it is humiliating to feel one is humiliating someone else every time one goes out. But there is no other way of going about." But Lady O'Malley, the wife of the acting counsellor of the British Legation in Beijing from 1925 to 1927, who wrote some impressively evocative novels with Chinese settings under the pseudonym Ann Bridge, loved the Beijing rickshaw: "A rickshaw is the most delightfully civilised form of locomotion. Seated in a well-sprung bath-chair, the passenger bowls along on pneumatic tyres at a surprising speed: he is alone, for it holds only one; his view is unimpeded by anything but the lowered head and shoulders of the trotting coolie . . ."

Lao She's Camel Xiangzi is one of the "trotting" coolies, and in contrast with the carefree life of a passenger like Lady O'Malley, he encounters the complex world of rickshaw hire and rickshaw purchase and maintenance. The comfortable "pneumatic tyres" would often spring punctures at inconvenient moments, and unlit roads at night could easily lead to accidents that broke the long shafts, or worse. At the beginning of the novel, Xiangzi—young, healthy, and strong—is the owner of his rickshaw. Saving up to buy it had taken four years, "tens of thousands of drops of sweat," "gritting his teeth in the wind and the rain, skimping on food and drink." After he had only owned his rickshaw for six months, he unwisely took a fare far outside the city gates, at a time when bands of undisciplined soldiers were ravaging the countryside, a common threat throughout China in the 1920s as central control had given way to various warlords battling each other. Captured by bandit soldiers, he lost his rickshaw, although he gained three camels when the soldiers vanished overnight. Xiangzi was fond of the camels: "they were just as scruffy as he was . . . it was the molting season, and patches of their dark skin showed through the great tufts of limp, dangling hair ready to drop from their sides at any moment. They were like huge beggars of the animal kingdom. Most touching were their hairless necks, so long, bent, and clumsy, craning forward like scraggy, disconcerted dragons."

Camel Xiangzi could only sell the camels for a total of twenty dollars—while a replacement rickshaw would cost a hundred dollars—so he was reduced to living in squalid "Harmony Courtyard" (a courtyard house, shared with other families) with Mr. Liu, from whom he had to rent a rickshaw and whose daughter, Tigress Liu, as ugly as she was fierce, eventually tricked him into a marriage that ended in tragedy.

As Camel Xiangzi grows older, he is also beset by health problems and can see himself in the category of those rickshaw pullers with "the growing awareness that sooner or later they will topple over between the shafts and die on the road . . ."

Lao She's acute observations of the lives of the poor in Beijing is expressed partly through the changing seasons, as seen in the courtyard house that Camel Xiangzi and his Tigress wife had to share with several families for a while. Beijing's traditional houses were built on a courtyard plan and, ideally, one courtyard or more would be occupied by a single family. The poor were compelled to share, taking a room in one of the side wings surrounding the small central courtyard. Camel Xiangzi and his wife moved in during the winter, and "There were seven or eight families living in their courtyard, most of them crowded seven to eight [people], old and young, into one room. Among them were rickshaw pullers, peddlers, policemen, and servants . . . the children went off with small baskets to fetch rice gruel in the morning and to scrounge for cinders in the afternoon . . . Ashes, dust, and slops were all tipped into the yard, which no one bothered to sweep. The middle of it was a sheet of ice, which the older children used as a skating rink . . . hungry and thinly-clothed, the old people lay on icy brick beds . . ."

Spring melted the ice, but the "spring wind blew stinking odors from the dirty earth and swirled rubbish and scraps of paper against the walls . . ." In summer, "there was some cool breeze in the yard shaded by walls . . . everyone sat outside . . . tempers were short after the long hot day and hunger didn't improve them. One word out of turn and the men would hit their children or beat their wives . . . this din lasted till after supper."

The overcrowding, dirt, and squalor described here probably reflected the sort of household Lao She lived in during his childhood, when his widowed mother struggled to provide for her family.

Family
Jia
(1931)
BA JIN (1904–2005)

~ ⁄

L i Yaotang wrote under the pen name Ba Jin and is one of the best-
known Chinese writers of the twentieth century. He was born into
a wealthy family in Chengdu, the capital of the western province of
Sichuan, and his autocratic grandfather prided himself on having "five
generations under one roof" in their grand family complex of linked
courtyards. Ba Jin was educated at home in the traditional way by a
series of family tutors until the death of his grandfather in 1917; then
he was finally able to leave the family home and, from 1920, attended
the Chengdu Foreign Languages School. He studied English, although
his major trip abroad, in 1927–28, was to France where he lived, rather
unhappily, in Paris. His most distinguished novel, *Jia*, translated as
either *Family* or *The Family* (which makes it sound more or less universal), was published in 1931. *Family* was part of a trilogy of novels
called *Torrents* (*Jiliu san bu qu*), together with *Spring (Chun)* (1938)
and *Autumn (Qiu)* (1940). He also wrote more than twenty novellas.

Influenced by anarchist writings in his youth, particularly *An Appeal
to Youth* by the Russian anarchist Pyotr Kropotkin, Ba Jin's pen name
was taken from the transliterations into Chinese of the first syllables
of the names Kropotkin and Bakunin (Mikhail Bakunin was another
Russian anarchist). Ba Jin continued to write about the anarchist movement and became fluent in Esperanto, the "universal language." He
worked with his fellow Chinese writer Mao Dun (1896–1981) against
the Japanese invasion of China. Sadly, like Qian Zhongshu (1910–
1998), Ba Jin abandoned the writing of fiction in 1949, presumably
for fear of censorship and control, concentrating thereafter on essays.
He was savagely criticized during the Cultural Revolution (1966–1976)
but later rehabilitated. He was made chairman of the Chinese Writers'
Association in 1984.

There is much that is autobiographical in *Family*. Set during the early years of the Chinese Republic, not long after the May Fourth Movement of 1919 which galvanized China's youth after the betrayal of the country at the Versailles Peace Conference, it describes the life of the wealthy Gao family in Chengdu. The family consists of four generations, living in an extensive compound with a very large garden complete with lake and island pavilions. The main characters are three brothers: the oldest, Juexin, is married to Ruijue and very much under the thumb of his autocratic grandfather, the Venerable Gao, the head of the family. The middle brother is Juemin, a radical student interested in politics who gradually falls in love with a cousin, Jin, a student in a public girls' school; and the youngest brother, Juehui, also a radical student, interested in the ideals of the May Fourth Movement and anarchy. He is attracted to a female servant, Mingfeng. The three brothers, sons of Venerable Gao's eldest son, are orphans, although they have a sympathetic (but powerless) stepmother. The family, which also includes several uncles and their families, are all controlled by the grandfather, who has taken a rather fierce, plump concubine.

The novel is concerned with the dramatic changes in China in the first decades of the twentieth century. Though Juemin and Juehui have been allowed to study at the local Foreign Languages School, their grandfather is not keen on the new ideas that they absorb there (although Juemin actually spends much time preparing to take part in a dramatization of the harmless classic *Treasure Island*). Their grandfather would prefer them to follow the traditional Confucian precepts of *On Filial Piety and the Avoidance of Lewdness*, a text he gives to Juehui. Both younger brothers are shocked by their grandfather's hypocrisy, his concubine being hardly representative of avoidance of lewdness. They are further appalled by the random cruelty of the traditional feudal family system, particularly to women and the lower classes. The oldest brother, Juexin, is something of a victim of tradition, because he had been in love with a cousin, Mei (meaning "plum blossom"), but both he and Mei were forced into arranged marriages by their families. Mei was particularly badly treated by her husband's family and, after her husband's death, returned to Chengdu, condemned by tradition to live out her life as a "virtuous widow." Juexin's marriage has been happy because Ruijue turned out to be a sympathetic and kind wife and a loving mother to their little son, but Mei's unhappy return to Chengdu is upsetting to Juexin and the family. Faced with this, and with his grandfather's domination, Juexin deliberately chooses a very passive attitude to life within the family.

Juehui used to play with the servant girl Mingfeng when they were children, and now that they are grown up, he flirts with her. She loves him but suffers from knowing that their situation is impossible. She is totally at the mercy of the family, ordered about and insulted even by the brothers' teenage sister, and faced with the possibility that the family will dismiss her, or worse, send her off to be a concubine. This fate, indeed, awaits her when Venerable Gao decides to give her to one of his elderly and dissipated friends in yet another gesture of hypocrisy. The Venerable Gao is not only a controlling patriarch and cruel to his family servants, but also launches dangerous fireworks directly at dancers invited into the house on the ninth day of the New Year.

Historically, at the time the novel takes place, warlord battles over Chengdu were continuing, for the city was first attacked in 1916 by troops from the neighboring province of Yunnan and later by troops from Guizhou. These never-ending battles form a background to the novel, which includes an episode when artillery shells fall into the garden of the Gao family. But local political battles are also fought by the radical student body (including Juemin and Juehui) over military interference in their theater activities. The two are also keenly interested in events in Beijing and Shanghai and seek out copies of the latest journals, especially radical publications from Shanghai.

The battle between the generations, between tradition and modernity, continues, with Venerable Gao shocking his grandsons even further by the three-day opera performances put on for his sixty-sixth birthday, with particularly erotic scenes performed by his "favorite female impersonator," a far cry from the plays of Ibsen preferred by Juemin and Juehui. (This fascination with the male performers of female roles in Chinese opera recalls Wu Jingzi's descriptions in *Unofficial History of the Grove of Literati* [*Rulin waishi*] and has a long and ambivalent history in China, though it is here seen in its dying days in the early twentieth century.)

Much of the interest of *Family* lies in the novel's description and atmosphere. It encapsulates the struggle between old and new that is also seen in the works of Mao Dun and Qian Zhongshu. There is a long description of the festive activities around the Chinese New Year, with feasts and family rituals of kowtowing to ancestors and elders, and one of the most surprising events is when the women of the family enjoy their "annual comedy" of "going abroad," i.e., stepping out into the street to look around. It seems that in Chengdu, even in the early twentieth century, upper-class women normally never set foot outside their family homes except in a sedan chair. The ending of the novel sees much tragedy with the deaths of Mingfeng, Mei, and Ruijue and her second child; and only Juemin and Juehui escape from the oppression of the old system—the latter literally, since he leaves Chengdu.

Midnight
Ziye
(1933)
MAO DUN (1896–1981)

≫ ≪

M ao Dun was the pen name of Shen Dehong, one of the major
novelists of modern China; later he also served as the first minister of culture of the People's Republic, from 1949 to 1965. Disgraced,
like so many of his generation, during the Cultural Revolution (1966–
1976), he was subsequently rehabilitated. The pen name he chose
for himself was originally composed of the characters for "spear" and
"shield," used together to mean "contradiction," an expression of the
turbulent decades in which he grew up. It is said that the novelist
Ye Shengtao (1894–1988), a close colleague in the 1930s, worried that
"contradiction" was too political and possibly dangerous; so he changed
the first character by adding the radical for "grass," so that it came to
mean "straw" or "thatch"—a "straw shield" being a very different image.

Born into a well-educated family in northern Zhejiang province, the
young Mao Dun studied classical works such as the sixth-century CE
Selections of Refined Literature (*Wen xuan*; included in it are the *Nineteen
Old Poems* [*Gu shi shijiu shou*]); but in 1913 he went to Peking University where he studied Chinese and foreign literature. Due to family poverty (his father had died in 1906) he was unable to finish his studies and
moved to Shanghai, where he found a job as editor and translator in the
English section of the Commercial Press, a major publishing company.
He worked on the magazine *Fiction Monthly* (*Xiaoshuo yuebao*), creating
translations of works by Tolstoy, Chekhov, Balzac, Flaubert, Zola, Shaw,
Byron, and Keats.

Inspired by the radicalism of the May Fourth Movement of 1919,
Mao Dun joined the Communist Party. In Shanghai he continued to
write and edit journals with friends (one of whom was Ye Shengtao),
and he published a series of novels, including *Midnight* (*Ziye*). He also
became a member of the League of Left-Wing Writers.

A long and complex novel, *Midnight* is set mainly in Shanghai and is considered by many to represent the best picture of the city during the 1920s and 1930s. It has been compared to Zola's *Germinal*, although Mao Dun himself said he was influenced by Tolstoy's depictions of individual characters caught up in historical periods of turmoil. In a lecture in Xinjiang in 1939, Mao Dun described *Midnight* as being set at a time when Shanghai was beginning to feel the repercussions of world economic depression. He described three groups, or influences—Chinese industrialists, "feudal forces," and "comprador-capitalists"—in the novel: Chinese industrialists, "groaning under foreign economic repression," were hindered by "feudal forces" (meaning traditionalists) and threatened by the control of the money market by "comprador-capitalists" (glossed as "foreign imperialists"; "comprador" was originally the name given to Chinese agents employed by foreign companies doing business in China). The Chinese industrialists' response was to increase brutality and intensify "their exploitation of the working class." The response of the working class to increased brutality and deteriorating working conditions was to "put up a fierce resistance," an aspect of the story that Mao Dun said he could not explore and expose to his satisfaction because of contemporary censorship by the Guomindang. "Comprador-capitalists" represented a threat to the survival of Chinese industrialists (meaning the "national capitalists") in their manipulation of loans and capital and the stock markets.

A historic example is the silk industry in Shanghai in the 1930s, which was certainly under various types of pressure as the traditional methods of production were threatened by the Japanese, who set up superefficient modern filatures (silk-reeling facilities) in China, and world prices for silk dropped. Conditions in such filatures were horrific. Writing in 1939, Christopher Isherwood described ". . . silk-winding mills so full of steam that the fingers of the mill girls are white with fungus growths. If the children slacken in their work, the overseers often plunge their elbows into the boiling water as punishment . . ."*

A further hazard to workers' lives and the development of industry was the increasing unrest around Shanghai as the Japanese, having seized Manchuria in 1931, intensified attacks in China proper—which was already harrowed by combative warlords controlling different parts of the country, a Communist Soviet established in Jiangxi, and the failure of Chiang Kai-shek's government and forces to take overall control. *Midnight* begins with the arrival of old Mr. Wu in Shanghai, brought by his son, Wu Sunfu, a wealthy industrialist who owns several factories and a big mansion. Mr. Wu is moved from the ancestral family home in the unstable countryside (which is "stirred up by Reds") to the comparative safety of the city. A true representative of traditional China, Mr. Wu comes to Shanghai accompanied by a fleet of slick black Citroëns while clutching the *Book of Rewards and Punishments* (*Ganying pian*), a popular traditional Daoist text that emphasizes filial piety. Old Mr. Wu's faith in filial piety is shattered by the sight of his elder daughter, "half naked with bare legs and arms," and in a room "filled with countless swelling bosoms and bloodred mouths" he collapses and dies.

Mourners gather in Wu Sunfu's mansion. As they wait for the coffin, the funeral refreshments of lemonade, ice cream, and cream layer cakes arrive; a girl dances on the billiard table with all the men looking up her skirt as she twirls; and Colonel Lei, a staff officer in the Guomindang army, remarks that the fall in government bonds is "even more alarming than the news from the front." There is a nice little twist to Colonel Lei's presence. Wu Sunfu's wife has been dreaming of a student rebel who flashed through her life like a comet but suddenly disappeared, leaving her heartbroken. Colonel Lei presents her with a copy of Goethe's *The Sorrows of Young Werther*, with a rose squashed between the pages—it was him! They kiss. "My dear!" squawks the parrot in the room.

Wu Sunfu needs money to pay the workers in his filature but his first priority is to pay for materials. He is sufficiently desperate to consider destroying his daughter's reputation. The women workers are "conspiring" and he needs to "squeeze" the factories to compensate for losses on the stock exchange. When his women workers strike, he appeals to them. "It's a hard life being a factory owner"—but they are soon joined by the workers of his match factory, and Wu complains that the Swedish Match Trust takes advantage of light import duties and bribes. He determines to "get to work on the factories tomorrow. If we get rid of three hundred to five hundred workers from five factories, abandon overtime on Sundays, extend the working day by an hour . . . and cut wages by nine percent . . . And if the workers riot? We'll close the facto-ries for a fortnight and then see!"

Throughout the novel the complexities of stock-market dealing and the uncertainty of money supply beset Wu Sunfu and his major competitor, Zhao Boli, who plays the stock market and represents the "comprador-capitalist" class. But all suffer: "It was midnight. Most of Shanghai's workers and financiers were groaning with terrifying night-mares of cut-throat competition, though the nightclubs still echoed with the sounds of knives and forks and popping corks . . ."

A major aspect of the book is its portrait of Shanghai, parts of which are still familiar, beginning with the opening passages: "The sun had just sunk below the horizon. A slight breeze blew gently on people's faces. The muddy water of Suzhou Creek was transformed to a golden green as it flowed quietly west. The evening tide of the Huangpu had risen imperceptibly and the assorted boats that lined the banks of the Suzhou Creek floated high on the water, decks half a foot above the level of the landing stage. The wind carried the sound of music from the park on the Bund with the popcorn-like patter of drums.

"The towering steel frame of Garden Bridge was covered by evening mist. As trams passed over the bridge, the overhead cable shot out bright green sparks. Looking east from the bridge, you could see the foreign warehouses on Pudong, crouched like monsters with lights twinkling like hundreds and thousands of tiny eyes. Looking west, suspended high on the roof of a foreign-style building was a huge neon sign flash-ing flaming-red and phosphorescent-green: LIGHT HEAT POWER!"

Autobiography of a Girl Soldier
Yige nübing de zizhuan
(1936)
XIE BINGYING (1906–2000)

≈ ⁄≈

Born in Hunan province, Xie Bingying was, by her own account, a rebel from a young age. Though her father was interested in modern ideas, her mother was a traditionalist, and as well as insisting on binding her daughter's feet, made several serious attempts to force an arranged marriage on her. Xie Bingying did, however, manage to go to school; she was apparently expelled from a missionary school, after which she enrolled in the First Women's Normal School in Changsha. In 1926 she left to enroll in the newly established Central Political and Military Academy in Wuhan, which was set up to train activists.

The background to the establishment of the Wuhan Academy and Xie Bingying's military training was the First United Front, in the 1920s, between the Nationalist Party (Guomindang) and the Chinese Communist Party. They were allied, with Stalin's blessing, in order to try and end the domination of warlords in China. From their base in Guangzhou (where the highly successful Whampoa Military Academy had trained a new generation of efficient soldiers), Chiang Kai-shek's Guomindang troops in 1926 embarked upon the Northern Expedition—intending to defeat the major warlords of the north. The Whampoa Academy was moved to Wuhan, to be reestablished as the Central Political and Military Academy. While attending the Wuhan Academy, Xie Bingying joined the Academy's Women Students' Brigade in 1927. Soon after, Chiang Kai-shek turned on the local Communists in the Shanghai massacre of April 12, 1927: hundreds of workers, who had taken over the city for his troops, were killed and the Communist Party forced temporarily underground. Xie Bingying's brigade was dispersed, presumably viewed as too close to the Communists. She returned to her family's village but was treated like a prisoner by her parents. Eventually she moved to Shanghai, then to Beijing.

In 1930 Xie Bingying married a fellow student from Wuhan, but he left her soon after their daughter was born. (This daughter, Fu Bing [1930–1966], later worked at the Beijing Academy of Dramatic Art and was "persecuted to death" at the beginning of the Cultural Revolution.) Xie Bingying left to study in Japan in 1931 but was soon asked to leave. When she returned to Japan under a false name in 1935, she was imprisoned and tortured for not obeying the Japanese government's order that all Chinese students celebrate the enthronement of Puyi (who had been the last emperor of the Qing dynasty) in Manchukuo, a Japanese-controlled state in Manchuria. She regarded him as a traitor.

With the Japanese invasion of China in 1937, Xie Bingying joined a Women's Battlefields Service Group working on the frontline. She later worked in Beijing as an editor and journalist, and as a teacher in various schools including Beijing Normal University. After a brief second marriage in the later 1930s, she married for a third time in 1946, and two years later left for Taiwan. In 1974 she settled in San Francisco. Though she continued to write articles for newspapers in America and Taiwan, she remains best-known for her autobiographical work.

Xie Bingying's *Autobiography of a Girl Soldier* (*Yige nübing de zizhuan*; in English also entitled *Girl Rebel*, or *A Woman Soldier's Story*) begins with her childhood and describes her battles with her mother—which were somewhat alleviated by her grandmother's description of how her mother suffered from Xie Bingying's difficult birth but nevertheless declared right away that girls were just as good as boys. Still, she was determined to raise her daughter according to traditional principles. "Mother heard much gossip about me, saying that I was so big and had not yet had my feet bound and that in future, surely no mother-in-law would accept me. Besides, although a girl of seven, I was still often with the boys, throwing stones and making Buddhas from mud." On the question of bound feet, "Mother felt her own feet were too short and difficult to walk on. My sister's feet had been bound by mother herself and they were like a pair of red peppers. Though she thought they were pretty, after two steps she had to lean on the wall, like a cripple. So mother decided to bind my feet later, to avoid breaking the bones as she had in my sister's case. But when I was ten years old she thought that if she did not start soon, the bones would grow too much and it would be impossible to achieve small feet." In front of a statue of Guanyin, the compassionate Bodhisattva, her mother hung up a tiny pair of red, embroidered shoes and burned incense and paper money before bringing out the strips of blue cloth. In the traditional way, she filled her mouth with holy water and spat it out in a fine spray over Bingying's feet and put red-hot ashes between her toes as the girl roared in pain. Held down by her sister-in-law, Bingying's left leg was squeezed under her mother's knee as she bound the right foot tightly. "After that I could only sit beside the fireplace and spin or walk about the house slowly."

Bingying's brother suggested that she should go to school, but this was at first refused by their parents, and Bingying contemplated suicide. "In our village, all the ways I knew of committing suicide were: hanging by a rope; jumping into the river; swallowing matches [since the phosphorus was poisonous]; eating opium; swallowing a ring; cutting my throat with a knife." She rejected the first as she had seen a woman who had hanged herself with her tongue hanging out; and jumping in the river would lead to a death equally "inelegant," as she put it. "Matches smelled awful . . . there was no way of buying opium . . . I had no rings . . ."

Finally allowed to go to school, she cut off her foot-bindings, and after reading *The ABC of Communism* (by Bukharin and Preobrazhensky)—and with her brother's help—she enrolled in the new Wuhan Academy. Enrollment was a huge hurdle because thousands of students applied, and "there were too many from Hunan province." Ten of the determined Hunanese students, including Bingying, presented a petition: "Can you imagine anyone trying to limit the number of revolutionaries? The fact that so many Hunan students threw down their pens to join the army only proves that Hunanese are more advanced in thought, have more fighting spirit, and understand the revolution!" Unfortunately, the ten petitioners (perhaps a trifle threatening in their determination) were all rejected. Xie Bingying's second brother noticed that the quota for students from the north had not been filled, and so she renamed herself, declared that she was from Beijing, and managed to get a place, justifying her determination by coming top in the first round of exams.

She describes the bugle calls, the capture and execution of "wicked gentry and rich landlords," the death of fellow cadets in battle, and the pleasures of marching at night; but eventually, with the bloody break between Chiang Kai-shek and the Communists, the revolutionary Academy was closed. "Those of you who are strong could join the Eleventh Army, the others can return home and wait patiently . . ." Xie Bingying, her hair cut very short, had to go home. There she refused an arranged marriage and found herself—like a rural equivalent of the Shanghai heroine in the novel *Half a Lifelong Romance* (*Bansheng yuan*) by Zhang Ailing (Eileen Chang)—held prisoner in a small room by her parents. She made several attempts to escape as plans for her forced marriage proceeded, and did eventually break free. She was close to her brothers but her second brother died of tuberculosis; she was close to friends, but throughout her narrative she realizes how hard it was for "a girl to stand on her own against the old forces of Chinese society. It was a very good lesson for me. However many troubles and how much suffering lay ahead, I would not escape from society to live the life of a hermit, nor would I surrender to traditional forces . . ."

The significance of this tale of female emancipation in the early twentieth century is demonstrated in the number of translations, beginning with a joint effort by Adet and Anor Lin, daughters of the well-known Chinese essayist and novelist Lin Yutang.

The Man Who Came Home on a Snowy Night

Fengxue ye guiren

(1943)

WU ZUGUANG (1917–2003)

≈ ⁄≈

Wu Zuguang, born in Beijing, was one of the best modern Chinese playwrights, and he continued to write despite considerable political problems: He was attacked as a "rightist" in 1957 by a fellow dramatist, Tian Han (1898–1968), and exiled to the "Great Northern Wilderness" (i.e., the cold northeastern extremity of China). During the Cultural Revolution (1966–1976), he and his wife, Xin Fengxia (1927–1998), were sent off for several years' labor in the countryside. Xin Fengxia was one of China's best-known *pingju* actresses, who had grown up in dire poverty and been sold to a *pingju* troupe at a very early age. *Pingju* was a popular form of opera—part-spoken, part-sung—which developed in the north of China in the nineteenth century. Where *jingju*, or Peking opera (also part-spoken, part-sung), tended to use stories from China's past, *pingju* dramas were often based on shocking and dramatic contemporary events. Wu Zuguang's familiarity with the world of the popular stage through his wife's career adds greatly to the appeal of his plays. His earliest play was an anti-Japanese drama, *Phoenix City (Fenghuang cheng)* (1937), and late in life he also wrote several film scripts. *The Man Who Came Home on a Snowy Night (Fengxue ye guiren*; in English also called *Return on a Snowy Night)* was first published in 1943 in a theatrical journal in Chongqing, then published in book form the next year.

At the time Wu Zuguang wrote *The Man Who Came Home on a Snowy Night*, the mood in China—with the Chinese capital moved from the Japanese-occupied east to the far western city of Chongqing—was one of increasing disillusionment and despair, with a feeble and corrupt government failing to resist Japan. Corruption and greed are revealed in the play, which is set around that time and centers on two weak main characters longing to escape their lives of servitude to the rich. The central male character is Wei Liangshan, a *huadan* opera actor—*huadan* parts being those of women played by men. The main female character is Yuchun, fourth concubine of Mr. Xiao, a wealthy man who is also the local chief justice—and Wei Liangshan's patron. Yuchun has been given permission to study singing with Wei Liangshan and does not know that Mr. Xiao proposes to give her to his friend Mr. Xu, the local salt commissioner, with whom he is planning various illegal deals. Secondary characters include Wang, a poverty-stricken friend of Wei Liangshan's; through Wei's recommendation, Wang finally gets a job as Mr. Xiao's house steward. There is also Mrs. Ma, who comes to appeal to Wei Liangshan to intercede with his patron, Mr. Xiao, in his position as chief justice, because her son is in trouble with the police.

The first part of *The Man Who Came Home on a Snowy Night*, a prologue to the play, is set twenty years after the main action of the play. The falling snow and the darkness of evening echo the lines from Liu Changqing's mid-eighth-century CE poem "A Snowy Night on Hibiscus Mountain," which refers to a man's return to a deserted cottage in the snow. In the play, as snow falls, two beggar boys climb into the dark and deserted garden of a mansion and make a fire to keep warm. An old man enters the garden, saying, "I'm looking for my shadow . . . I'm looking for my footprints . . ." and dies. The beggars take a gold bracelet from his wrist. From the shuttered house comes a stern shout, "Who let those tramps in?"

The opening of the first act is dramatically different. Wu Zuguang's directions are detailed: a theater dressing room with flower-patterned wallpaper, a washstand and table covered with sticks of greasepaint. Clothes hanging up, a white silk scarf, and tea things ready. Offstage we hear the sounds of an opera performance with *huqin* violins, drums, and gongs. Mrs. Ma and Wei's friend Wang are waiting as Wei Liangshan enters from the stage, dressed as a woman. "He can flirt by tilting his head and casting a glance, slowly forgetting he is a man." The ambiguity of Wei's role and of his relationship with his patron, who clearly enjoys the flirtatious aspect while maintaining no less than four concubines, recalls scenes in Wu Jingzi's eighteenth-century *Unofficial History of the Grove of Literati* (*Rulin waishi*). Wu Zuguang's detailed stage directions include character sketches. Of Wei Liangshan, he says that he is "determined to save the world but has not thought of saving himself," and "He will give a beggar lunch money, but what about his supper?"

In the second act, the beautiful Yuchun is in Mr. Xiao's drawing room, waiting for Wei to give her a singing lesson. Again the stage set is described in detail: an "Eight Immortals" table; a zither table; porcelain garden stools; a writing desk with brushes, ink, paper, and books—"have they ever been opened?" Outside the window is a crab apple tree. Mr. Xiao and Mr. Xu discuss tax evasion and fraudulent use of official vehicles, "just a little business on the side . . ."

In act 3, set in Wei Liangshan's simple room, decorated with the trappings of his operatic work—pheasant-tail feathers, a horsewhip, drum, clappers, and boots embroidered with pink flowers—Wei and Yuchun propose to run away. The idea is totally impractical, though Yuchun speaks longingly of escape from being "in a cage" and encourages Wei Liangshan to "reclaim his manhood" (a complex proposition given his profession). Wang, now house steward to Mr. Xiao, enters with some thugs. Yuchun puts a gold bracelet on Wei's wrist before Wang orders her home and threateningly says, "Mr. Wei is going on a long trip. He will not be singing 'The Tale of the Red Whisk' tomorrow . . ."

In the epilogue, twenty years later, on a snowy night seen from inside the mansion, Mr. Xiao, who is very old now and inclined to Buddhism, hears from his steward that Wei Liangshan has been acting with an itinerant opera troupe as the clown and, too poor to buy himself medicine, collapsed onstage. Mr. Xu arrives and declares that Yuchun, who has been his concubine (a gift from Mr. Xiao) for twenty years, now wants to "go home." She is waiting in his car outside. There are screams: a maid has discovered the fire started by the beggars and the corpse of Wei Liangshan. Yuchun has vanished into the night.

Wu Zuguang does not offer a director much leeway with his intensely detailed stage directions, but *The Man Who Came Home on a Snowy Night* is more complex than the melodramatic story suggests, with the ambiguity implied in the *huadan* role (which can be taken up or dropped) set against the impossibility of escape for a fourth concubine from her patron.

The tragic lives of many women in early twentieth-century China, often forced into concubinage and almost invariably prevented from achieving economic independence, are echoed by the tragedy of actors such as Wei Liangshan, also entirely dependent upon the whim of a rich patron. Wu Zuguang's anger and sense of injustice make this a forceful and memorable drama.

Little Black's Marriage
Xiao Erhei jiehun
(1943)
ZHAO SHULI (1906–1970)

~~~

Zhao Shuli's short novel *Little Black's Marriage* (*Xiao Erhei jiehun*; Xiao Erhei, literally "young second dark son," is the book's male hero) was published the year after Mao Zedong made his important speech to the Yan'an Forum on Art and Literature, in May 1942. Though few would nowadays consider *Little Black's Marriage* a great literary work, its significance lies in its date of creation, its content, and its historical contribution as one of the first works of literature to seek to follow the line of Mao's speech. Until very recent times, Mao's address to the Yan'an Forum remained the most significant directive on the subject. In his speech, Mao posed questions about the audience for cultural works and whether works of literature and art should seek popularity or aim to raise educational, ideological, and literary standards, and he concluded that literature and art should be created for the broad mass of people, for workers, soldiers, and peasants. Mao insisted that writers and artists should "know" the masses and reflect their circumstances. He intended that all art and literature should show the correct revolutionary path, helping as many people as possible to follow the Communist Party in its task of combating the Japanese and achieving national liberation.

Mao was speaking in Yan'an (in the northern province of Shaanxi), the mountain stronghold to which his Communist armies had trekked on the Long March, arriving in 1935. From then onward, for over ten years, Yan'an was the center of Communist activities, both military and political. Organizing the local peasants to resist the Japanese invasion of north China was accompanied by intense political work—which included Mao's 1942 address to writers, artists, and performers who had come from all over China to give their support to the Communists' efforts in Yan'an.

Zhao Shuli was born in 1906 in the neighboring northern province of Shanxi. His family were impoverished village landlords, his grandfather having also been a teacher and his father well-known locally for his traditional medical practice and fortune-telling. Zhao Shuli had a traditional classical education but the family was able to send him to a modern middle school in Changzhi. There he came into contact with the new literature that was appearing after the May Fourth Movement of 1919, a literature of reaction against classical Chinese, written in the vernacular and addressing contemporary themes. He joined the Communist Party in 1927, spent a year in a Nationalist prison, and later joined the Communist guerrillas in the Taihang mountains in his home province of Shanxi. He worked mainly in literature and propaganda, writing plays and ballads for local newspapers and being a reporter. In later years he wrote several novels. He may well have attended the Yan'an Forum, and certainly his published work (based on his own experience in the Shanxi countryside), together with his propaganda work among the peasants of the Taihang area, demonstrate his adherence to Mao's directives for writers.

The publication of *Little Black's Marriage* in 1943 demonstrated an almost instant adherence to the new party line, and its content was even more impressively timely, reflecting new ideas about marriage being encouraged in the Communist-controlled area around Yan'an—ideas that were finally extended to the whole of China after Mao Zedong and the Chinese Communist Party took control of the country in 1949. The Marriage Law of May, 1950, and the Land Law of June, 1950, both had a significant impact on the lives of Chinese women. The Land Law granted them equal status with men, by enabling them to be allocated land when it was seized from landlords. The equally affirmative Marriage Law was designed to outlaw the traditional practice of arranged marriage, in which young women in particular had no voice and became the chattels of the family into which they were married.

Zhao Shuli's short novel describes the difficulties encountered by two young villagers at a time of transition between feudal and "modern" ideas. Xiao Erhei is the younger son of one of the village fortune-tellers. His father (like Zhao Shuli's own father) directs the villagers' agricultural work on the basis of the almanac (*Tongshu*) and its "auspicious" and "inauspicious" days and insists that there should be no planting on the Double Fifth, regardless of weather and soil conditions—much to the fury of his wife who sees him as simply lazy. Xiao Erhei is described as a handsome young man and a fine shot who has killed two "enemies" in a mopping-up operation (presumably with the Red Army), despite the fact that his father had brought him up to read only books on divination such as "The Jade Casket Account" and "The Yinyang Retreat."

Xiao Qin (literally "Little Celery") is the only surviving daughter of the other village fortune-teller, a woman who holds séances dressed up (in defiance of her age) in trousers with embroidered hems, embroidered shoes, and dyed hair. "Only her make-up let her down, powdered over the wrinkles like hoarfrost on donkey droppings."

Xiao Qin is simply described as "pretty." "When she goes to wash clothes, all the young men go. When she climbs a tree to pluck wild berries, suddenly all the young men of the village go to pick berries."

Though she and Xiao Erhei had been going out together for a couple of years, both were faced with marriages arranged by their parents. Xiao Erhei's father could not accept Xiao Qin as a prospective daughter-in-law because not only was she born in a (bad) "dog" month, she also had a "fire" fate while Xiao Erhei's fate was "gold," and he feared that fire would overcome gold. After careful calculation of birth months and fates, the father bought a nine-year-old girl from some starving refugees as Xiao Erhei's future wife. Xiao Qin's mother, on the other hand, found her daughter a rich widower for a husband.

Xiao Erhei is undergoing Communist cadre training and knows that the new marriage law being promoted only requires the agreement of boy and girl, but their plans to marry under these new regulations are disrupted by village enmities. Local thugs, jealous of Xiao Erhei and covetous of Xiao Qin, beat him up, falsely accuse him of faking illness, and drag the two of them off. Xiao Erhei's father moans, "I knew something bad would happen! When I went to the fields the day before yesterday I met a woman on a donkey dressed in mourning clothes. This year I'm under the *luo* star and any encounter with mourning clothes is bad luck . . . and last night Xiao Erhei's mother dreamt of a drama being enacted in a temple and a black crow perched on the east end of the roof and called ten times . . ."

All ends happily when the district governor, representing the new

Communist regime, approves the young couple's marriage, orders Xiao Erhei's father to send the little girl ("born in the year of the monkey") back to her parents, and sets up an investigation into the bullying and aggression of the village louts—who, it turns out, had "accepted bribes, driven people to suicide, robbed them and raped their women, compelled the local militia to collect firewood for their own private use . . . collected and embezzled taxes . . ." They are sentenced to fifteen years' imprisonment and ordered to compensate all losses. Thus the wise and just Communist administrator ensures the happiness of Xiao Erhei and Xiao Qin, rescues the villagers from local thugs, and (under his wise, modernizing influence) Xiao Qin's mother begins to dress more soberly and removes her incense table from the house and Xiao Erhei's father acknowledges his wife's wisdom.

In 1946, Zhou Yang (1908–1989), China's foremost Marxist literary critic and a leading figure in education and the arts in Yan'an during the 1940s, wrote, "*Little Black's Marriage* recounts a rural love story. Zhao Shuli praises the new freedom of marriage choice which is part of the new society where a peasant can choose whom he loves. He celebrates the victory of the peasants. Now, peasants are in control of their own fates as they learn how to fight for a better life. He praises the rise of progressive peasants who triumph over the backward-looking, superstitious, and ignorant. Finally, he celebrates the peasants' victory over feudal village tyrants." Zhou Yang's praise extended to the success of the novel, with up to 40,000 copies sold in the Taihang mountains alone.

The story is told with warmth and some wit and a light touch, considering the political burden it carries. A pioneer of uplifting, political fiction, Zhao Shuli's simple stories of village life and struggle in the pre-Communist and early Communist eras remained popular in the 1950s, but seemed less relevant as time passed. Zhao Shuli himself died in 1970, described as having been "persecuted to death" by Madame Mao and the Gang of Four. In 1979 the writer Pan Bao'an published a tribute to Zhao Shuli entitled "Xiao Erhei's Divorce."

Biography of the First Ming Emperor
Zhu Yuanzhang zhuan
(1943–49)
WU HAN (1909–1969)

≈ ⁄≈

Biography of the First Ming Emperor (*Zhu Yuanzhang zhuan*) is a solidly researched and well-written biography of one of the most interesting characters in Chinese history. Its significance, however, goes beyond the content, involving Mao Zedong, the Cultural Revolution, and the difficulties of Chinese intellectuals in the twentieth century.

The author, Wu Han, was one of modern China's best-known historians, a specialist in the Ming dynasty (1368–1644). Born into relative poverty in Bitter Bamboo Pool Village in Zhejiang province, he was one of ten children, only four of whom survived to adulthood. His mother was illiterate although his father had passed the lowest level of the imperial examinations, but with the overthrow of the old imperial order and establishment of the Republic of China in 1912, found it difficult to find work. Wu Han's education was disrupted, often depending on charity, but he finally entered the prestigious Qinghua University in Beijing in 1931 and pursued an academic career during the Sino-Japanese War. It was during this period that he wrote the first draft of his *Biography of the First Ming Emperor*, which was first published in 1943, and in a revised edition in 1949. After the Communist victory in 1949, Wu Han was asked to take the position of Deputy Mayor of Beijing (though he was not, at the time, a member of the Communist Party), with special responsibility for culture and education.

The subject of his biography, Zhu Yuanzhang (1328–1398), was born into almost unbelievable poverty yet rose, through the ranks of bandit armies that were seeking to overthrow the Mongol rulers of China, to become the first emperor of the great Ming dynasty, in 1368. This meteoric rise from homeless orphan to all-powerful ruler of some 65 million people suggests a character of extreme force and charisma, yet opinions on the Hongwu emperor (his reign name) are divided. His poverty-stricken background seems to have encouraged him to establish free schools throughout the country early in his reign and to alleviate the tax burden on peasants, but his reign is also characterized by ruthlessness and oppression, particularly after the death of his wife in 1382.

Wu Han had difficulties with censors in 1943 when the first edition of *Biography of the First Ming Emperor* was published, because the increasingly beleaguered Guomindang government thought that in his text he was too keen in his support of bandits and was perhaps drawing parallels between Zhu Yuanzhang's suppression of opposition through his (charmingly named, but ruthlessly efficient) "brocaded guards" elite police and Chiang Kai-shek's secret police and their "white oppression." And when new versions of the book appeared after 1949 (with Mao Zedong apparently taking a close interest and making suggestions about the 1954 edition), Wu Han was increasingly suspected of drawing parallels between Zhu Yuanzhang's life and Mao Zedong's incredible rise to power from a peasant background, with the anti-Communist hint that Mao might be ambitious to become an emperor and could become as isolated and paranoid as Zhu Yuanzhang in his later years.

Wu Han's political downfall came later, as a result of yet another literary work based on Ming history. In 1961, to the surprise of many, he wrote a Peking opera, *Hai Rui Dismissed from Office* (*Hai Rui ba guan*), based on events in the career of a sixteenth-century Ming dynasty official —whose zealous defense of the local peasants against excessive land taxes and subsequent dismissal from office made him a folk hero. The opera was cancelled after a few performances; however, in 1965 Yao Wenyuan (1931–2005), editor of Shanghai's *Liberation Daily* but later to become infamous as one of the Gang of Four, published an article attacking Wu Han and *Hai Rui Dismissed from Office*. This is often seen as the opening attack of the Cultural Revolution (1966–1976). The opera was described as "a poisonous weed" and Wu Han was accused of an indirect attack on Communist Party policies, particularly with relation to the collectivization of land into "People's Communes" (such an indirect attack traditionally being described as "pointing at the mulberry to revile the ash tree"). Wu Han's denials seem disingenuous, because as vice-mayor of Beijing he was close to the center of Communist Party politics and could not be unaware of the vicious infighting that went on as Mao, almost as worried as Zhu Yuanzhang about current rivals and potential successors, crushed his opponents.

Biography of the First Ming Emperor begins with these sentences:* "In 1344, people living by the Huai River suffered disasters: drought, locust plagues, and epidemics. It had not rained for months. Young crops withered and turned yellow. The earth was cracked like a turtle shell. Everywhere, appealing to the rain gods, old people bowed to the Dragon King and children ran through the fields with wreaths of willow around their heads [celebrating the Dragon King, who brought rain]. Then, before the harvest, came a plague of locusts that cleared the fields of the feeble, dry shoots. Those who had lived there for years wept and mourned, crying that they hadn't seen a year like this for decades and this was unbearable. And this was not the end. Epidemics sprang up. People in Taiping fell, one after another. Having only eaten dried grass and tree bark, they had no resistance, weakened and vomiting, they did not last a night. At first no one paid much attention but when tens died in one village in a day, in each house, they saw it as a scourge from heaven . . .

"In Guzhuang village [in Anhui province], the Zhu family lost three members in less than a month. Another four . . . then the father and mother died, leaving only Zhu Yuanzhang and an older brother. One after one they watched them die. They could get no help, they could not get medicine, they could only weep . . ."

The poor boys could not even manage to bury their parents properly. (Once he had become the first Ming emperor, Zhu Yuanzhang made sure his parents' burial was done with pomp.) Zhu Yuanzhang entered a Buddhist monastery and begged for a living, but times were so hard that even the monastery closed, and he eventually joined a rebel band.

The last chapter, "Tragic Last Years," is as dramatic as the first. The Hongwu emperor's last years were dominated by a paranoid need to control and the failure, quite out of his hands, to establish his favored eldest son on the throne.

"Then, in 1392, his son and heir died—and he would never get over it. He didn't speak for weeks, his hair went white, and in a few months he grew bent and feeble as if life had left him, too. Yet he had not finished. He designated his [eldest] son's son as his heir . . . His two wicked sons that he had wanted to execute died in 1395 and 1398, but his other sons were also openly opposed to his choice of the future emperor . . .

"In early 1398, he could no longer leave his bed. He stayed there for thirty days and then summoned all his concubines, subjects of the empire that he had built from nothing with his own hands. He closed his eyes on this image and, for the first time, knew peace . . . But there was one last bloodletting. As soon as his death was announced, all his concubines and servants were sacrificed so that they could be buried with him in order to serve him in the other world. By way of compensation, their families were all granted state aid."

Though the Ming dynasty is celebrated throughout the world for its porcelain and palaces, the extraordinary rise of its founder is less well-known—and Wu Han's biography of the first Ming emperor deserves a wider audience.

Fortress Besieged
Wei cheng
(1947)
QIAN ZHONGSHU (1910–1998)

≈ ⁄≈

Qian Zhongshu was one of the foremost literary scholars of the twentieth century. Not only did he produce magisterial texts on traditional Chinese literature but his D.Litt. thesis from the University of Oxford, examining references to China in the English literature of the seventeenth and eighteenth centuries, is an immensely scholarly survey.*

Born into a scholarly family in Wuxi (in Jiangsu province), Qian Zhongshu's father, a professor and Confucian scholar, changed one of the boy's given names to Mocun ("Silence") because he talked so much. He was educated at missionary schools in Wuxi and Suzhou before entering the prestigious Qinghua University in Beijing (another missionary foundation). It is said that his math skills were deplorable but his knowledge of English and classical Chinese was such that he was accepted. At Qinghua he met his wife, Yang Jiang (1911–2016), who translated the novels *Lazarillo de Tormes*, *Gil Blas*, and, most notably, *Don Quixote* into Chinese; she later also wrote several autobiographical pieces including *Six Chapters from a Cadre School Life* (*Ganxiao liu ji*). When Qian Zhongshu won a Boxer Indemnity Scholarship in 1935 (funded by the reparation paid by the Chinese government after the destruction of Western life and property during the Boxer Rebellion of 1900), they both traveled to the University of Oxford, where Qian Zhongshu prepared his D.Litt. thesis and Yang Jiang gave birth to their only child, a daughter. He claimed to spend much time reading detective stories and Proust but finished his thesis in 1937, and then moved to the University of Paris with his wife and daughter. Returning to China in 1938, after the outbreak of the Sino-Japanese War, Qian Zhongshu taught in a series of universities (in Kunming, Hunan, and Shanghai), reflecting the unsettled nature of life at the time. In 1949, the year of the Communist victory, the family moved to Beijing and he became a professor at Qinghua University, though he subsequently transferred to the Chinese Literature Institute of the Chinese Academy of Sciences, and later to the Chinese Academy of Social Sciences.

Before 1949, Qian Zhongshu published some short stories and essays, but *Fortress Besieged* (*Wei cheng*), published in 1947, is his only surviving novel. After 1949 he restricted himself to literary scholarship, working on Tang poetry and, most notably, Song poetry. During the Cultural Revolution (1966–1976), his son-in-law committed suicide, and he and Yang Jiang did menial work in so-called cadre schools (set up for the political "reeducation" of officials and intellectuals).

Fortress Besieged is set in China during the late 1930s and early 1940s, during the time of the full-scale Japanese invasion of China (which began in 1937). The title of the novel is taken from a French proverb, "*Le mariage est comme une forteresse assiegée, tous ceux qui se trouvent dehors veulent y entrer, tandis que ceux qui sont à l'intérieur veulent en sortir.*" ("Marriage is like a besieged fortress: those who are outside want to get inside, while those who are inside want to get out.") Marriage is, indeed, a major theme of the novel as we follow the somewhat passive main character, Fang Hongjian,** on his picaresque trip from Europe to Shanghai and then to a dubious appointment at a newly established (or half-established) university in the interior of China, located as far away from the Japanese armies as possible.

The problem of marriage is confused by the question of education, another of the major themes in the book. While still at school in China, Fang Hongjian had been engaged to the daughter of a rich man (originally from Fang's hometown of Wuxi), but she had died before he even met her. Her parents gave Fang the money set aside for a lavish wedding to enable him to study abroad. The novel begins in 1937, on the French ship *Vicomte de Bragelonne*, bringing Fang and many other Chinese students back from their studies overseas. This linking of traditional practice (an arranged marriage and continuing family ties even after death) and contemporary innovation (from the end of the nineteenth century, many young Chinese went abroad to study "modern" subjects) is very characteristic of the novel and its setting in time. It is also, perhaps, important to note that Qian Zhongshu's broad erudition appears throughout the novel, extending even to the name of the ship:

The Vicomte de Bragelonne is the title of a novel by Alexandre Dumas, in which the *vicomte* falls hopelessly in love with Louise de la Vallière. For Fang Hongjian the series of women, or marriage prospects, begins with his dead fiancée and continues with a couple of women on the ship: the straightforwardly seductive Miss Pao, who appears in shorts and whose display of naked flesh is compared by her fellow travelers to a French *charcuterie*, and the coquettish Miss Su, who has a real French Ph.D. degree—unlike Fang, who purchased a fake diploma from one Patrick Mahoney and had himself photographed in the robes of a Ph.D. holder from the University of Hamburg. Miss Su pursues Fang, sewing his buttons and washing his handkerchiefs, and later (in Shanghai) introduces him to her friend Miss Tang, with whom he fancies he is in love. After a series of misunderstandings, some due to Zhao Xinmei (who is a newspaper editor), and Japanese bombings of Shanghai and Wuxi, Fang and Zhao escape Shanghai, having been invited to join the staff of a new university, San Lu, in the interior. Among their traveling companions is Miss Sun, a shy recent graduate on her way to her first post, in the Foreign Languages Department of San Lu University.

The long trip to San Lu involves bug-ridden hotels, a severe shortage of money, and a series of buses, one of which shudders and shakes as though suffering from malaria and another which stops dead, prompting the driver to kick it and, in a common Chinese curse, declare himself intent on sexual intercourse with the bus and its mother.

San Lu University itself is little better. The ill-assorted staff fight among themselves, and Director Gao offers little leadership but has plenty of ideas. He tries to introduce a tutorial system based on that of Oxford and Cambridge but with contemporary Chinese aspects. In accord with Chiang Kai-shek's puritanical "New Life Movement" (a moral code of life proposed in 1934 stressing healthy pursuits, cold water bathing, and saluting the flag), tutors are forbidden from smoking in front of their students (as Oxbridge dons did habitually), and— in defiance of the numbers of students, tables, and chairs—they are ordered to eat with their students. "Why not just share beds with the students?" asks Fang. Also at San Lu, a Mrs. Wang attempts to provide Zhao and Fang with wives, one being the bespectacled Miss Fan, who has personally inscribed her collection of plays with fake "dedications" from their authors, and the other the plump and silent Miss Liu. In the end, with no offer of a contract from Director Gao, Fang leaves for Hong Kong with Miss Sun and finds himself unhappily married to her.

While Fang Hongjian's entanglements with women and his eventual marriage recall the sense of helplessness of Evelyn Waugh's *Vile Bodies* (1930), Qian Zhongshu's satire extends beyond the problem of marriage. The educational system, the attempt to preserve a semblance of authority in the turmoil of a country being invaded and bombarded, and the growing contradictions between traditional ideology and modern (Western) ideas are all major subjects in his novel, which accurately depicts a country in chaos. It is told with considerable wit, satirizing the "new poetry" (with titles like "Adulterous Smorgasbord") and the passion for foreign ideas while also including a rich variety of reference to traditional Chinese beliefs and stories.

Memories of South Peking
Chengnan jiushi
(1960)
LIN HAIYIN (1918–2001)

≈ ⁄≈

Lin Haiyin's stories told in *Memories of South Peking* (*Chengnan jiushi*) are based on her childhood memories of life in Beijing in the 1920s and early 1930s. She was born in Osaka, Japan, where her father, originally a primary school teacher from Toufen in northern Taiwan, had gone to seek business opportunities. When Lin Haiyin was three, the family returned to Toufen but then moved to Beijing in 1923. When she was thirteen, her father died, and as the eldest of six children she had to support her mother. She later studied journalism in Beijing and worked as a junior reporter at the same time. In 1948, toward the end of the civil war in China, she returned with her husband, Xia Chengying, and their children to Taiwan. There she established herself as an editor, journalist, and writer, working for major newspapers and founding a literary publishing house. Her contribution to Taiwanese writing and literature was considerable, as she encouraged an important group of young writers at the time that Taiwan was just recovering from the Japanese occupation (1895–1945) and the Chinese language was reestablishing itself after being banned by the Japanese during World War II.

The question of language is significant in Lin Haiyin's life and in her work, where she frequently ridicules her parents' non-standard pronunciation. Her father, from a Hakka family settled in Toufen, used local dialect and pronunciation (the Hakka Chinese from the southern provinces of China were famous for their migrations to other parts); her mother, born and brought up near Taipei, was a speaker of the Minnan dialect originating in Fujian province. Having grown up in Beijing, Lin Haiyin spoke Beijing dialect, so when "Mandarin" Chinese was established as the official language in Taiwan (in 1945), she was naturally able to assume a leading literary position. "Mandarin" is a term of Portuguese origin applied to what might better be described as modern standard Chinese, spoken by about four-fifths of the population today. (It is not strictly Beijing dialect as that includes nonstandard pronunciations.)

Memories of South Peking was published in Taiwan in 1960 and made into a charming and successful film by the Shanghai Film Studio in 1982. The book consists of a series of linked stories, all told by Yingzi ("Little Hero") who, when we first meet her, is a girl of about ten years: an acute, wide-eyed yet innocent observer. By the end of the last story, like Lin Haiyin, Yingzi is forced to grow up and take responsibility, helping her mother when her father dies.

Yingzi's childhood home was in southern Beijing, in a series of dwellings in the narrow lanes or alleys (*hutong*) lined with courtyard houses hidden behind gray brick walls that characterized old Beijing. Though Yingzi's Beijing is that of the 1920s and early 1930s, anyone familiar with the city up until the mid-1970s will recognize her descriptions with great nostalgia, part of the reason for the popularity of the work. The narrow lanes were visited by street vendors of all sorts, banging drums and clanking cymbals, bringing water from clean wells, selling sweets and cakes, or exchanging second-hand goods. In the introductory story, "Winter Sun, Childhood, the Camel Caravan," Yingzi recalls the double-humped Bactrian camels that delivered coal. Yingzi watches her father bargaining over coal prices with a camel driver from Mengtougou, north of Beijing: "I stood in front of the camels, watching how they chewed straw. Such ugly faces, such long teeth, such calm. As they chewed, their upper and lower teeth ground together, warm breath streamed from their large nostrils, and white foam covered their beards. I stood watching, transfixed, and my own teeth began to grind . . . Winter was almost over, spring about to arrive . . . clumps of hair were beginning to fall off them, hanging under their stomachs. I wanted to take scissors and trim them, they were so untidy."

In the longest story, "Hui'an Hostel," Yingzi intervenes in the lives of two seemingly very different characters. Xiuzhen ("Elegant and Loyal") lives in the gatehouse of the Hui'an Hostel with her parents, the gatekeepers, and is known locally as "the mad woman." The hostel (like many similar "hometown" establishments in Beijing) was built to provide cheap accommodation for students and travelers originating in Hui'an, in distant Fujian province. Xiuzhen's "madness" lies in her obsessive search for her lost baby, Little Cassia, who would have been about the same age as Yingzi. It transpires that Xiuzhen had become pregnant by a student from Hui'an who left the hostel because he was ill and poor, but he promised to return. As soon as the baby was born, Xiuzhen's outraged parents took it and abandoned it by one of the city gates, without telling Xiuzhen. Frequently passing the Hui'an Hostel with the family nursemaid (and local gossiper), Song Ma ("Mother Song"), Yingzi becomes friendly with Xiuzhen, as well as making friends with a little girl of her own age, Niu'er ("Little Girl"), who is trained as a street singer by her parents, and beaten. There is much for Yingzi to observe, understand, and misunderstand as she walks through the lanes with Song Ma who is, like the camels, part of old Beijing.

"Her horrible black cotton padded trousers, so thick, so baggy, were tightly tied at her ankles. People had told my mother that maids in Beijing liked to steal things and when they stole rice, they'd pour it into their trousers at the waist so it filled the legs but it could not trickle out. I wondered whether Song Ma's trousers were full of our rice?"

Worried about Niu'er's beatings by her father and hearing that she is, in fact, a foundling, Yingzi finds a distinctive birthmark on Niu'er's neck, a feature described by Xiuzhen when talking about Little Cassia. Already suffering from a fever, Yingzi steals a gold bracelet from her mother and helps Xiuzhen and Niu'er to run away, before she herself collapses. It appears that the flight ended in tragedy. Still weak in hospital, Yingzi overhears Song Ma talking to her mother: "'It's all so strange, how would she have managed to kidnap two children? If we'd got back a little later, Yingzi could have gone with them. The more I think about it, the more frightening it is. Sweet little Niu'er! That train! The two of them together! I've always said that Niu'er was very pretty but somehow ill-fated . . .'"

Another of Yingzi's plans to sort people out is more complex and more successful, and reflects her growing maturity. Her father is generous, offering hospitality to distant cousins come to study in Beijing and also (despite warnings) to Lan Yiniang, the rejected (or rejecting, depending on whose version one believes) concubine of Mr. Shi. Yingzi's mother is yet again pregnant, suffering in the summer heat, and when Yingzi sees her father holding Lan Yiniang's hand, she plots (successfully) to get her student cousin to run off with Lan Yiniang.

In "Let's Go to the Sea," Yingzi is a more passive observer of life in the lanes. There is much talk among the grown-ups of a series of burglaries in the neighborhood. Looking for a lost soccer ball on an overgrown plot, Yingzi encounters a strange man. They converse about school and her lessons, which include a poem in chapter 26 of her schoolbook:

Let's go to the sea, let's go to the sea!

On the great blue sea is a boat with white sails

The golden-red sun rises from the sea

Shining on the sea and shining on the boat

Let's go to the sea, let's go to the sea!

At her primary school's graduation ceremony, in front of an audience that includes her father, Yingzi performs as a sparrow in a dance and is proud of her success. When she leaves the stage, she sees the strange man among the seated parents. A few days later he is arrested at the overgrown plot where he has been hiding the stolen goods. In between fretting about the pain of eating with wobbly teeth, Yingzi has decided that the strange man is a good man. After the arrest, her mother remarks, "'Little Yingzi, did you see that wicked man? You like to write, don't you? When you grow up you can write a book about what happened today, telling how a bad man became a thief and how he came to such an end.'" But Yingzi decides otherwise. "No! I shan't do as mother says. When I grow up I will write a book but it won't be what mother wants me to write. I want to write about 'Let's Go to the Sea.'"

A child's view of the world, combined with descriptions of old Beijing, create an atmosphere of charming nostalgia.

From Emperor to Citizen
Wode qian ban sheng
(1964)
PUYI (1906–1967)

≋ ⟆

Puyi, the last emperor of the Qing dynasty (1644–1911), only reigned for about three years, from late 1908 to the beginning of 1912. He ascended the Dragon Throne as a little boy, as a result of a long series of political maneuvers by the Dowager Empress Cixi (1835–1908). The Qing emperors, who were Manchus from the northeast of China, only married other Manchu or Mongolian women; Cixi was a Manchu who entered the court as a low-ranking concubine of the Xianfeng emperor (1831–1861), who came to the throne in 1850. She was raised in status when she bore the emperor's only surviving son, the future Tongzhi emperor (1856–1875). By the middle of the nineteenth century, the Qing emperors seemed almost incapable of producing sons, despite having a number of consorts. The Tongzhi emperor and the succeeding Guangxu emperor (1871–1908) had no sons at all, which facilitated the Dowager Empress's machinations. When the Xianfeng emperor died, Cixi's son was only six years old (by Chinese calculation); she got rid of the courtiers appointed as regents and proclaimed herself and Cian (1837–1881), who was the senior consort of the Xianfeng emperor, as joint regents—although it was well known that Cixi herself held all power.

When Cixi's son, the Tongzhi emperor, died in 1875, she chose her sister's son (one of the Tongzhi emperor's cousins) as the Guangxu emperor, breaking with the tradition that held that a new emperor should be of the next generation. The Guangxu emperor, despite attempts to break free and begin some of the modernization and reform that China desperately needed, remained a virtual prisoner of his aunt until he died in November 1908. Although she herself died the next day, Cixi had already nominated his successor, Puyi, a son of Prince Chun. (Puyi's father, Prince Chun, was the fifth son of the first Prince Chun, seventh son of the Daoguang emperor [1782–1850].)

Despite his relative closeness to imperial power, the child Puyi howled his way through his enthronement in the Forbidden City. In February 1912, after the Wuhan uprising by imperial soldiers that set off the ultimate fall of the Qing dynasty, his parents signed the act of abdication and China became a republic. Puyi was allowed to live on in the Forbidden City as the republican central government broke down and regional warlords fought for power, but his position was problematic—as could be seen in 1917, when Zhang Xun, a general, led a short-lived coup to try and restore him to the throne. When the "Christian warlord" Feng Yuxiang (1882–1948) seized Beijing in 1924, he ordered Puyi's expulsion from the Forbidden City. Assisted by his Scottish tutor Reginald Johnston (1874–1938), Puyi fled first to his father's house but then moved to the Japanese Legation, embarking on closeness to Japan that was to lead to disaster. He moved to the nearby city of Tianjin, regarded as much safer than Beijing, and for several years lived in the Japanese concession there. In 1932 he unwisely agreed to become head, and later "emperor," of Manchukuo, a Japanese puppet state on Chinese soil that marked one of the first steps toward Japan's full-scale invasion of China in 1937. When Japan was defeated at the end of World War II, Soviet troops moved into northeastern China and Puyi was taken prisoner and held in the Soviet Union. He was handed over to the Chinese authorities in 1950 and imprisoned to be "remolded" ("reeducated") until 1959. In 1960 he became a worker in the Beijing Botanical Gardens. He died in 1967, which was probably fortunate as the Cultural Revolution (1966–1976) would almost certainly have been a very difficult period for him.

Puyi had no children despite having five wives. He married both Wanrong (1906–1946) and Wenxiu (1909–1953) in 1922, seemingly because he was shown an album of suitable girls and lacked interest in choosing. Wanrong was apparently addicted to opium, and Wenxiu left him in 1931. In 1937 he married Tan Yuling (1920–1942), who died in slightly suspicious circumstances, and in 1943 he married Li Yuqin (1928–2001); she divorced him in 1958 but suffered during the Cultural Revolution for her association with him. His last wife was a nurse, Li Shuxian (1925–1997), who seems to have been appointed to look after him.

Puyi's autobiography was published in Chinese in 1964, in an edition that was very restricted in circulation, which was a common practice in China. However, the "official" English edition, in a fine translation, was published soon after (in two parts, in 1964 and 1965). The text must have been based upon many "self-criticisms" that Puyi would have written while in prison, because rhetorical self-criticism is a major part of the Chinese political process. There have been many arguments about the veracity of the text and the question of whether Puyi wrote it himself, which are discussed in the translator's introduction to the English-language edition published in 1985.

As it stands, the book has much to offer. It describes the conditions in which this special prisoner was held in prisons in the Soviet Union and China and the attempts to "remold" him through study and through practical work. For those interested in the dying days of the Qing dynasty and life in the Forbidden City, it is fascinating. The accounts of his education at the hands of Reginald Johnston as of 1919, seconded from the British Colonial Service to guide the young ex-emperor in British ways, are amusing. Puyi and his fellow pupils, his brother Pujie (1907–1994) and cousin Pujia, chose English names (Henry, William, and Arthur) and wanted to assume European dress, which Johnston— who was delighted with his own flowery Chinese titles and great sable-lined silk robes—rather discouraged. However, he taught the boys how to take tea the English way, which included not greedily stuffing themselves with cakes, and diagnosed Puyi's nearsightedness; this resulted (much against the wishes of the palace eunuchs) in Puyi wearing glasses for the rest of his life.

Puyi's memory of his early childhood was of "a yellow mist," since yellow, associated with "earth" (one of the Five Elements), was chosen as the imperial color by the Ming dynasty (1368–1644) and seen most obviously in the yellow roofs of the Ming Forbidden City. (The Qing should have chosen an alternative color on taking power but they continued to use the Ming yellow.) "The glazed tiles were yellow, my sedan chair was yellow, my chair cushions were yellow, the lining of my hats and clothes were yellow, the girdle round my waist was yellow, the dishes and bowls from which I ate were yellow, the padded cover of the rice-gruel saucepan, the material in which my books were wrapped, the window curtains, the bridle of my horse . . . everything was yellow."

In late 1922, the dominant color in Puyi's life changed briefly. "According to tradition, the emperor and empress spent their wedding night in the Palace of Earthly Peace . . . This was a rather peculiar room; it was unfurnished except for the bed-platform which filled a quarter of it and everything about it except the floor was red. When we had drunk the nuptial cup and eaten sons-and-grandsons cakes and entered this dark red room I felt stifled. I looked around me and saw that everything was red: red bed-curtains, red pillows, a red dress, a red skirt, red flowers, and a red face . . . it all looked like a melted red wax candle." Puyi decided that he preferred the Mind Nurture Palace and went back there, abandoning his bride.

There are also interesting descriptions of the food in the palace and how it was served, and of Puyi's attempts to cut down the number of eunuchs and control their stealing, and smuggling out, palace treasures.

However, in the end, the author remains an enigma: he confesses to considerable cruelty, to a complete lack of interest in his wives, while he himself seems, in part, to be a victim of his large and complex family. Despite the difficulty of his character, Puyi's account of his life reveals the extraordinary circumstances of the end of imperial rule in China and the advent of republicanism and, eventually, Communism.

Quotations from Chairman Mao Tse-tung
Mao Zhuxi yulu
(1964–66)

MAO ZEDONG (1893–1976)

≈ ⁄≈

The compilation *Quotations from Chairman Mao Tse-tung* (*Mao Zhuxi yulu*; the English title gives his name in the then current form of romanization [in the present form, the name is Mao Zedong]) was originally undertaken for the People's Liberation Army in 1964. By 1965 a definitive edition had been established, and it was released for mass distribution from late 1965 and reprinted in vast numbers, with a bilingual Chinese-English edition appearing in 1966. It was translated into eight Chinese minority languages and several dozen foreign languages. A Braille edition was also produced. It is estimated that some 720 million copies in Chinese had been printed by the end of 1967. In the West, the *Quotations* came to be known as the "Little Red Book."

The 1964 compilation, a set of quotations from Mao Zedong's longer and more complex works written between 1926 and 1963, was prepared for use in the army, where semiliterate soldiers might have struggled with some of Mao's more difficult theoretical writings, which were published in his five volumes of *Selected Works* (*Mao Zedong xuanji*) (1951–1977).

Early editions of the *Quotations* were prefaced with a calligraphic exhortation from Lin Biao (1907–1971), a long-time military leader, later minister of national defense, whose position was supported by his control of the People's Liberation Army, particularly during the Cultural Revolution (1966–1976). He was apparently very close to Chairman Mao and widely regarded as his probable heir. After his disgrace and apparent death in 1971, however, this page was removed from subsequent printings and also physically removed by many panic-stricken owners of the *Quotations*.

Though early editions of the book were mostly issued in paper covers, editions from 1966 onward were frequently covered in red plastic, which, together with its small size, made it handy to carry around and wave at mass demonstrations during the Cultural Revolution. There are 427 quotations, arranged in 33 sections, several of which seem specifically directed at the army.

The *Quotations* contains many well-known slogans, taken from the hundreds of essays and speeches by Mao. Every individual in China was expected to own a copy, and the text was used in political study groups, at political meetings, and in schools and other educational institutions. People had to be careful about handling their copy because damaging it could lead to severe criticism. The significance of the book during the Cultural Revolution was huge, as shown in the photographs of thousands of excited students and soldiers waving their copies. Streets and buildings were plastered with slogans taken from the book, and many of the more violent quotations were used to justify the terrifying violence that erupted in many of China's cities as young students swarmed across the country determined to show their revolutionary fervor.

Some of Mao's quotations refer back to traditional Chinese works, such as the reference to the great Han historian Sima Qian, author of *The Grand Scribe's Records* (*Shi ji*) (first century BCE), in Mao's 1944 essay "Serve the People"—a short section of which was included in the *Quotations*. Mao referred to Sima Qian's description of human lives as being more weighty and significant than the great Mount Tai, as long as these lives were lived in the service of others and the Communist cause.

Another quotation refers to the story in the ancient Daoist text *Zhuangzi* (c. fourth century BCE) that notes that it is not worth talking to a frog in a well about the universe, as the frog's world view is so confined. Mao used this example of narrow experience to discuss the need for Marxists to fully understand facts and events.

Some of Mao's quotations, particularly with respect to military matters, echo the pronouncements of *Master Sun's Art of War* (*Sunzi bingfa*) by Sun Wu (c. 544–c. 496 BCE).

In one long passage, Mao retells the Chinese fable of "The Foolish Old Man Who Removed the Mountains." This relates to a popular Chinese fable about an old man, who, in spite of the difficulty and his neighbors' derision, set about digging up two mountains that stood in front of his house. His determination moved the gods who carried the mountains away. Mao wrote that the "two mountains" of imperialism and feudalism, which were crushing the Chinese people, could be removed through similar hard work and determination.

Much included in the *Selected Works* comes from speeches, and Mao was a considerable orator, as well as a witty conversationalist (as can be seen in the account of his life story he gave to the American journalist Edgar Snow when they met in Yan'an in 1936; Snow's book *Red Star Over China* was published the following year).

Mao was impatient with the overelaborate writings of others. These he described as being as pointless as playing the flute to an ox, in a reference to the many traditional paintings of small boys sitting on the backs of water buffaloes. The clarity and effectiveness of his writing had a profound effect on China. Though the little red books are no longer flourished and Mao's legacy is beginning to be questioned, his pithy statements were echoed in the pronouncements of Deng Xiaoping (1904–1997), and even today, the Chinese government continues to issue slogans to encourage the people to follow government policies.

Half a Lifelong Romance
Bansheng yuan

(1969)

Lust, Caution
Si, rong

(1979)

ZHANG AILING (EILEEN CHANG) (1920–1995)

≈ ⁄

Zhang Ailing (or Eileen Chang, the part-romanized name by which she is known to English-language readers) was a prolific and successful writer of short stories, novellas, novels, and film scripts. She was born in Shanghai but died in Los Angeles. Her great-grandfather was Li Hongzhang (1823–1901), one of China's greatest nineteenth-century statesmen and modernizers, but her father was a traditionalist somewhat out of his time, an opium addict and concubine-keeper with a very autocratic attitude to his daughter. Her mother was completely different, a modern woman who had studied in London and traveled in Europe, even skiing despite her bound feet. When her parents divorced, Zhang Ailing had to live with her father, who treated her with great cruelty when he felt she had been insolent to her stepmother. When she was seventeen and fell ill, he locked her in her bedroom for six months; she subsequently left to live with her mother.

Zhang Ailing had hoped to go to London to study English literature, but the Japanese invasion of China made this impossible, so she followed the same course of study in Hong Kong. In 1942 she returned to Shanghai; her first story was published there in 1943, and she enjoyed success with a subsequent collection of short stories.

She left for Hong Kong in 1952, moving to the United States in 1955. There, in 1956, she married an American screenwriter, Ferdinand Reyher, who died in 1967.

Lust, Caution (Si, rong) was begun in the 1950s but not published until 1979. It is a subtly told story, set in Shanghai during the Japanese occupation. After fierce fighting for three months in late summer and autumn of 1937, Shanghai was abandoned by the Chinese army and Chiang Kai-shek and his Nationalist government retreated to Chongqing in Sichuan. Despite the Japanese presence, many rich Chinese continued to lead comfortable lives in Shanghai. Wang Jingwei (1883–1944), formerly a left-wing politician, accepted an invitation from the Japanese to form a collaborationist government in 1940. In this context it is significant that in 1943, Zhang Ailing married the writer Hu Lancheng, also considered a collaborationist. At the time, he was still married to his third wife and also had several concubines (and a fourth wife) before he and Zhang Ailing divorced in 1947.

Lust, Caution, a beautifully crafted novella, begins with a noisy, gossipy afternoon session of mah-jong, played by a group of rich Shanghainese ladies. Their sapphire earrings and diamond rings, their elegant cheongsams and velvet capes with gold clasps, the room with its heavy curtains printed with phoenix-tail fern patterns, are all described in detail. Their conversation is of jewelry, dinner parties, and fashionable restaurants. They are watched by Jiazhi, a young woman who is equally beautifully dressed, but who is not Shanghainese. She had met her hostess and her husband, Mr. Yi, sometime earlier in Hong Kong. As Jiazhi leaves for a clandestine assignation with Mr. Yi, it becomes apparent that she is having an affair with him, but also that she is part of a loose and somewhat ineffective group of students attempting to combat the Japanese occupation and its collaborators. In order to seduce Mr. Yi, who collaborates with the Japanese, Jiazhi has had to learn about sex from one of her group. The main action of the story is an extremely tense, drawn-out scene in an Indian jeweler's shop in Shanghai where Jiazhi has led Mr. Yi, in order for him to be assassinated. The unravelling comes suddenly and sharply.

The film director Ang Lee made a wonderful film of *Lust, Caution* that was released in 2007. Closely based on the novella, which only lightly touches on the background to the story, it successfully develops this background.

Lust, Caution is an unusually political work from Zhang Ailing. More typical is the novel *Half a Lifelong Romance* (*Bansheng yuan*), which—though set partly at the same time and briefly reflecting the deaths and upheavals of the 1937 Battle of Shanghai and its aftermath—is a more characteristic romantic tale. Though it existed in a variant form (published in 1950–51), the final version, published in Taiwan in 1969, like so many of Zhang Ailing's stories, illuminates a complex period in China's recent history when traditional morals and practices, particularly around love and marriage, were beginning to be challenged. (Both Zhang Ailing's father and her first husband, Hu Lancheng, had concubines, and their right to be considered as a legal, second wife [or third or fourth wife], while not enshrined in law, was part of the tradition.) Though the main protagonists of the story are ostensibly modern, working young people in the modern city of Shanghai, they constantly come up against traditional values that threaten their own freedom of action.

The story begins with three young people who work in an engineering factory. Gu Manzhen is a modern young woman, earning her living as a secretary, and Xu Shuhui and Shen Shijun are two young engineers with whom she shares lunch most days. (Shuhui later moves away to study in America.) A particular friendship develops between Manzhen and Shijun, although they are still bound by traditional codes of behavior. They take care not to be seen together too much as this would be compromising, and Shijun, bound by tradition, is unable to fully express his love for her. A serious complication in Manzhen's life is the poverty of her family, since her father died young. Manzhen is determined to support her family honestly through secretarial work and tutoring, rather than remaining financially reliant on her elder sister Manlu (who in effect had been a high-class prostitute, until she settled with a Mr. Zhu as his concubine, or second wife).

The complications of second wives also affects Shijun, whose family lives in Nanjing. His rich father left his mother to live with a second wife, and as the father's health deteriorates, Shijun's mother becomes more and more determined that he should return to die in her home. She takes braised lettuce (stuffed with roses) to his bedside and lures him back home by "steeping and curing and pickling and fermenting everything in sight: bamboo hearts, sausages, vegetables, noodles." Unfortunately for Shijun, his father's return and death mean that he has to leave his job in Shanghai and take over the family business in Nanjing.

Another difficult aspect of traditional China was the interference of one's family in marriage. Shijun's attempts to keep in touch with Manzhen by letter are thwarted by his mother, partly because of the discovery of Manlu's past (which is seen to sully Manzhen), and Shijun eventually marries Shi Cuizhi, a cousin of his sister-in-law whom he has known from childhood but never loved. Cuizhi is reminiscent of the Shanghai wives in *Lust, Caution*, obsessed with appearances both social and physical. Meanwhile, as Manlu becomes sick and fails to produce an heir for Mr. Zhu, he rapes Manzhen and imprisons her in his house until she gives birth to a son. This horrible sequence may owe something to Zhang Ailing's own imprisonment by her father. While it seems unlikely that such things could happen in a modern city like Shanghai, with its telephones and trams, Manzhen's attempts to bribe servants to help her (or at least to pass messages) fail, as their greatest fear is of their master.

Though it does not end well, *Half a Lifelong Romance* is enlivened by characters such as Manzhen's younger brother, a stolid boy, protective of Manzhen yet a witty observer of the characters around him; by the light-hearted relationship of Shijun, Shuhui, and Manzhen at the beginning of the story; and by Zhang Ailing's descriptions of places and, especially, fabrics, shoes, jewelry, and interior decor, illuminating the Shanghai of the late 1930s and its inhabitants, torn between past and present.

Mayor Yin

Yin xianzhang

(1976)

CHEN RUOXI (CHEN JO-HSI) (born 1938)

≈ ⟋

For much of the turbulent decade of the Cultural Revolution (1966–1976), internal events in China were concealed from the outside world. Even during the early 1970s, when a few outsiders were allowed in, the scale of control and concealment was hidden from them. While pioneering intrepid journalists reported on well-stocked shops and markets and the neat and tidy flats they were invited to visit, they remained unaware of the machinery of control involved. Only an insider could reveal the lengths to which the Chinese government went to present a positive picture of a successful revolutionary society. Chen Ruoxi's collection of short stories *Mayor Yin* (*Yin xianzhang*), first published in 1976, enabled her readers to understand what it was really like to live in Cultural Revolution China.

The Cultural Revolution (or Great Proletarian Cultural Revolution) was so called because it sought to "revolutionize" the "cultural superstructure" of society. Mao Zedong considered that industry and agriculture had been "revolutionized" under socialist ownership, but the "cultural superstructure" needed to be transformed and remolded. By this he meant not only "culture" as we would understand it, but also the whole bureaucracy and system of government and the educational structure. In education and research, he deplored a stress on expertise at the expense of supporting the correct political line. This attempt to transform the "cultural superstructure" arose from a proposal by Lin Biao, head of the People's Liberation Army.

In his call to young people to criticize the authorities, Mao unleashed an anarchic movement of youth activists (called the Red Guards), who, in many places, created a regime of violence and terror. He saw the Communist Party as complacent and corrupt, and teachers and specialists of all kinds as "ivory-tower" individualists, unconcerned with the masses and the correct political line. All over the country, specialists—whether surgeons or teachers, researchers or professors—were ordered to take part in manual labor, often of the lowest kind, or spent months away in so-called May 7 cadre schools, carrying out physical labor and working in fields, in order that they might understand the hard lives of peasants and manual workers.

Chen Ruoxi (or Chen Jo-hsi, in her personal romanization) was already a published writer in Taiwan (where she was born) when she went to America to study in 1961, first at Mount Holyoke College and then at Johns Hopkins University. There she met her husband, Duan Shiyao, also from Taiwan, studying for a Ph.D. in hydraulic engineering. Though both had grown up in fiercely anticommunist Taiwan, in America they were introduced to a different view of Communist China, and in 1966 they responded to the outbreak of the Cultural Revolution by applying to go to China. At the time, no one knew where the Cultural Revolution would lead, and it was a brave, but in the end somewhat foolhardy, move. Overseas Chinese, though officially described as patriotic compatriots, were regarded in mainland China with suspicion as possible spies or saboteurs, particularly if they came from Taiwan. Chen Ruoxi and her husband waited in Beijing for two years before being sent to Nanjing, where Duan Shiyao was assigned to the waterworks (although he spent three years simply shoveling coal there), before being sent to a May 7 cadre school for "reform through labor." (As several of Chen Ruoxi's stories demonstrate, these cadre schools meant hard manual labor and also represented a great waste of talent and money.) Chen Ruoxi and her family lived in China for seven years before leaving for Hong Kong and subsequently North America.

Chen Ruoxi herself looked after children in Nanjing who were left behind when their parents had to go off to cadre school. She lived in the crammed dormitory housing provided for the workers at the Nanjing Institute of Hydraulic Engineering. Her experiences, as related in her collected stories (of which "Mayor Yin" is the first in the volume) offer an insider's view of what life was really like during the Cultural Revolution. "Jingjing's Birthday," set in the claustrophobic dormitory where anything could be overheard and neighbors spy on neighbors, centers on the innocence (or guilt) of children accused of saying, "Chairman Mao is a rotten egg." The mother of young Jingjing (his father is away at the May 7 cadre school) hears about this from Aunty Wang, who works in the kindergarten. Aunty Wang has to write a self-criticism, and four-year-old Xiaohong is interrogated late into the night (about what she might or might not have said about Chairman Mao), and the (inconclusive) results are included in her file. "Fortunately, I thought, [Xiaohong's father] Professor Shen is from an impeccable social origin, but apparently her mother is from an old landlord family, and in order to clear herself politically she's always terribly zealous. Poor things! And poor Xiaohong! Only four and she's already got a file with her confessions. She's sure to encounter political difficulties when she grows up . . . 'an intractable reactionary since infancy!' I could understand why Aunty Wang couldn't sleep. Though it had nothing to do with me directly, her account upset me and I found it difficult to sleep that night. I couldn't stop seeing Xiaohong's little round face and shining eyes."

But Jingjing's eight-year-old friend and neighbor, Dongdong, then claims that it was Jingjing all along. Jingjing's mother, heavily pregnant and devastated, hits her son; Dongdong's father beats Dongdong; and Jingjing explains that Dongdong wanted him to say, "Chairman Mao is a rotten egg." Jingjing is absolved but the atmosphere of suspicion and whispers cannot be dispelled. Jingjing's mother cautions her husband: "'When you buy books for Jingjing, be careful. Don't get any with too many portraits of Chairman Mao.' 'Don't worry,' he said, with a smile, 'My colleagues already warned me . . . Lots of children coloring their books run the risk of scribbling on the face of the Leader . . . don't ever let Jingjing do any coloring unsupervised, don't let him play with pencils and chalks . . .'"

A couple of Chen Ruoxi's stories illustrate the illusion of prosperity and harmony deliberately created by the authorities to deceive visiting foreign journalists. In "The Big Fish," an elderly man with a sick wife hears that the markets—usually rather bare in late February, and anyway beyond the purse of most except high officials in the government or the People's Liberation Army—were to be well-stocked before the arrival of foreign journalists. He hurries to see for himself and, to his delight, spends a lot of money on a big fish. As he leaves the market he is told, "that fish isn't for sale," and he must return it, because "If they're all sold out what will be left to show the foreign journalists when they arrive?"

In the story "The Journalists Accompanying President Nixon," Chen Ruoxi describes the lengths to which the authorities were prepared to go to present a perfect image to U.S. President Richard Nixon and his entourage on the groundbreaking visit he made to China in 1972. The narrator describes how she and her husband are ordered to take down the clothes-drying contraption they have constructed out of bamboo and wire outside the window of their cramped flat in a university dormitory block. Such arrangements were commonplace, everywhere, but the local "street commissar" had orders to clear them all away and neaten the dormitories, just in case the party of journalists passed by on the one day they might spend in Nanjing. The narrator refuses to make this "little sacrifice for the revolution," explaining that her accommodation was three blocks back from the road, and even if the journalists were traveling on the top of their cars they would not be able to see her window and self-built clothes dryer.

"We had made our clothes dryer, a superb structure of bamboo and iron wire, with love and sweat two years ago. My husband had to go all the way to Fuzimiao to get the bamboo canes and I had found the wire. [Raw materials were incredibly difficult to come by during the Cultural Revolution.] You couldn't buy it anywhere, but a colleague gave me a small roll of wire and we had spent a long time making it. The result was a triple-decker construction at the window that was strong enough to take the weight of two heavy cotton quilts. In the two years it had been up, exposed to the elements, the wire had rusted and if we dismantled it now, the wire would break and be unusable."

In the end, most of the journalists accompanying Nixon decided to go to Hangzhou instead of Nanjing, apart from "two French journalists who stopped for a moment and made a short visit to Xinjiekou [in the center of Nanjing, far from the dormitories], before rejoining the others that same evening. As a result, the sound of hammering resounded through the dormitory blocks as people hurried to put back together their clothes dryers. Nixon was long back in America as the work continued."

Six Chapters from a Cadre School Life
Ganxiao liu ji
(1981)
YANG JIANG (1911–2016)

~≈ ⁄≈

Yang Jiang was married for more than sixty years to Qian Zhong-shu (1910–1998), the author of *Fortress Besieged* (*Wei cheng*) (1947). Born in Beijing, she studied at Suzhou University and in 1932 moved to the graduate school of Qinghua University in Beijing, where she met her husband. They spent the years between 1935 and 1938 mainly at the University of Oxford (where their daughter, Qian Yuan, their only child, was born) and at the University of Paris. While Qian Zhongshu became a leading specialist in Chinese and English literature, Yang Jiang is famous for her translations of Spanish and French literature including *Don Quixote, Lazarillo de Tormes*, and *Gil Blas*. She taught at Qinghua University and carried out literary research in the Chinese Academy of Sciences and at Peking University, as well as writing a couple of plays and several pieces of fiction. Both Yang Jiang and Qian Zhongshu suffered along with their intellectual colleagues during the Cultural Revolution (1966–1976), but after they were rehabilitated, both worked in the Chinese Academy of Social Sciences.

Beginning in 1968, all universities and government institutions set up their own May 7 cadre schools ("cadre" in this context referring to officials and experts), as a result of a letter of May 7, 1966, from Mao Zedong to Lin Biao, head of the People's Liberation Army, advocating the transformation of officials and specialists through manual labor and ideological reeducation. May 7 cadre schools were often far away in poor parts of the countryside, where almost all members of each institution were meant to spend a considerable amount of time away from home, "learning from the peasants." Students also spent part of their time away in specially established agricultural schools. For instance, in the early 1970s virtually all Peking University students spent their first year on such farms and were also sent off to work in factories and live in army units as part of their political education.

Conditions in May 7 cadre schools could be very hard, as there was often no proper accommodation in the countryside for this sudden influx of long-term urban interlopers, who were also unfitted to support themselves, let alone help the peasants from whom they were expected to "learn." Not only were these urban experts forced to abandon their specialized work, their arrival also interrupted the lives of the peasants, and the cadre schools were rarely able to produce enough to feed themselves, let alone anyone else.

In 1969 Qian Zhongshu was sent to the Chinese Academy of Sciences Cadre School in Henan province, and Yang Jiang followed her husband in 1970. They had both reached retirement age, and though in good health, were not ideally suited to heavy manual labor. For much of the time in the countryside they were separated, Qian Zhongshu working for the local post office and Yang Jiang in the vegetable garden. Writing about her experience in *Six Chapters from a Cadre School Life* (*Ganxiao liu ji*), Yang Jiang chose the format established by Shen Fu (1763–after 1807) in *Six Records of a Floating Life* (*Fusheng liu ji*), the apparently straightforward recollections of his life and travel, which yet offer a deeper insight into difficult experiences.

The Chinese Academy of Sciences Cadre School was located in rural Luoshan, in Henan, hundreds of miles away from Beijing. Yang Jiang describes Qian Zhongshu's arrival, which he recounted to her in his letters. "They had to sweep the earth and dirt out of an old army barracks. That evening they still sweltered, even though they were sleeping on rush mats. A sudden snowstorm turned the earth to mud and the weather was freezing . . . On the 19th, the rest of the group arrived, so there were eighty gentlemen squeezed into one hut, sleeping on several *kang* [brick platform beds]."

"On rest day, everyone went into town to buy food. Mocun [Qian Zhongshu] told me there was roast chicken and boiled tortoise. I asked him what tortoise tasted like but he wrote back that he hadn't eaten any. He sent me a few doggerel verses."

Yang Jiang reveals some of the careless planning in the "rustication" of intellectuals: "There was no land that was suitable for tilling in Luoshan and there was nothing to do, so the whole Cadre School, together with family members and dependents, packed everything into suitcases and baskets and moved to Dongyue in Xi county. I managed to find Xi county on the map, but Dongyue was too small to be marked. The people there were poor and in winter there was no fuel for the stove, so many women had chilblains on their faces. To wash clothes, they had to crouch by the pond and pound them. Mocun gave a new shirt to an old lady to wash but he never saw it again. I was worried that he'd fall into the pond [if he did the washing himself], so it was worth losing the odd item of clothing." [Yang Jiang recounts unemotionally other examples of theft by the poor peasants, which recall Chen Ruoxi's stories of cadre school life in *Mayor Yin* (*Yin xianzhang*).]

Yang Jiang's colleagues, still in Beijing, were keen to hear what the cadre school was like from Qian Zhongshu's letters. "The story everyone liked best was He Qifang and the fish." He Qifang (1912–1977) was a poet, literary critic, expert on Cao Xueqin's novel *Dream of the Red Chamber* (*Hongloumeng*), and director of the Chinese Literature Institute. "They'd drained a pond to get the fish and the cooks decided to make the most of this bounty and serve *hongshao* fish [i.e., braised in soya sauce and rice wine, which would have been a great treat]. He Qifang quickly grabbed the large enamel mug in which he kept his toothbrush and toothpaste, to buy a portion [of fish], but it tasted very odd and got odder and odder. When he scooped out the largest morsel, he saw that it was a bit of old soap that had been at the bottom of the mug, and that he had not tipped out. People laughed, but they were very sympathetic."

Yang Jiang describes one of the worst times for her family in an unemotional and straightforward manner. Despite the leftist fervor of the Cultural Revolution, Yang Jiang's son-in-law, Deyi, had always said that he was slightly right-wing and disliked ultra-leftists. He taught in a university that, like so many others, engaged in frequent political campaigns and purges. During a purge of the ultra-left so-called May 16 activists (a group, aiming to eliminate "bourgeois elements," that went too far even by the "standards" of the Cultural Revolution), Deyi was accused of being a May 16 leader and of possessing a list of members. Alone, since his wife, Qian Yuan, was working in a factory elsewhere, the false accusations drove him to suicide.

"The last time I saw him he said, 'Ma, I can't let them accuse me of having the wrong attitude to the masses, and I can't beat the Revolutionary Propaganda Team. But I definitely won't make up a list and harm others. I can't lie.' He was locked up at the university. The Cultural Revolution was a blazing inferno. Yuan and her teammates were sent back to the university and the Propaganda Team ordered every unit to struggle against Deyi, to force him to hand over the list of names. So he killed himself."

Yang Jiang describes her work in the fields, planting wheat and beans from before dawn till dusk, and in the vegetable garden, as well as her attempts to keep in touch with her husband.

She downplays the discomfort and despair of her own experience, preferring to recount stories that amused and offered some hope that the spirit of the intellectuals was not entirely crushed by the cold, the mud, and the hopelessness of their situation. She does not complain, nor does she remind her readers that she is one of China's foremost specialists in foreign literature.

Stones of the Wall
Ren a ren!
(1981)
DAI HOUYING (1938–1996)

≫ ⁄≪

Dai Houying was born in a poor area of Anhui province. She studied Chinese literature at East China Normal University in Shanghai, graduating in 1960, when she was assigned to a job as a literary critic in the Institute for Literary Research in the Shanghai Writers' Association. Her first novel, *Death of a Poet* (*Shi ren zhi si*), about the suicide of her lover, the poet Wen Jie (1923–1971), was published in 1978, followed by the novel *Stones of the Wall* (*Ren a ren!* The literal translation is "Oh Humanity!"), published in 1981 but apparently suppressed until 1983.* Her novel *The Sound of Footsteps in the Air* (*Kongzhong de zuyin*) appeared in 1985. Dai Houying continued to write and teach literary theory at Shanghai and Fudan universities, until she was murdered (together with her nineteen-year-old niece) at her apartment in Shanghai in 1996. She was a very controversial figure, not just because she wrote about radical ideas but because she had, apparently, been a particularly fierce Red Guard during the Cultural Revolution (1966–1976), feared by elderly intellectuals. In later life she seems to have tried to make amends, donating much of her money to good causes in her home province, and it was apparently her rumored wealth that led to her murder.

The construction of *Stones of the Wall* is unusual, especially for China. Apart from the use of dreams and surreal nightmares, it makes use of the stream of consciousness. It is told by ten separate characters, each reflecting their own point of view as they describe the relationship between the novel's three major characters and a political battle over the publication of a controversial book. The time in which the story is set, in the 1970s, after the Cultural Revolution, is significant. All but the two youngest characters grew up through the 1950s, the first campaigns against "rightists" and the great famine of the early 1960s, and they saw the devastating violence of the Cultural Revolution. The place, a university, is also significant, because many intellectuals since 1949 had thrown themselves enthusiastically, and often idealistically, into campaigns that they thought would purge China of mistakes and improve society. Unfortunately, it was only too easy to find oneself on the "wrong" side, to be attacked instead of attacking—and in the late 1970s, when things had ostensibly returned to "normal," many people found themselves back at work and sitting next to those who had attacked them, whether for ideological reasons or motives of self-protection. For all the characters in *Stones of the Wall*, history—whether their own or that of the state—is ever-present.

The central character in the novel is a woman, Sun Yue, a teacher and departmental (Communist) party secretary of the university's literature department. She is divorced and raising her teenage daughter, Hanhan, on her own. Many of the ten characters were once her fellow students. Soft-hearted, Sun Yue helps one of these, Xu Hengzhong (now also a teacher, who struggles to care for his little son after his wife's death), although her assistance causes gossip. The second major character is Sun Yue's former husband, Zhao Zhenhuan, a childhood friend and then a fellow student, who divorced her when she was under attack during the Cultural Revolution, remarried very quickly, and has a second daughter. He now works as a journalist in another city. The other major character is He Jingfu, who was also a fellow student of Sun Yue, Xu Hengzhong, and Zhao Zhenhuan, and who has been in love with Sun Yue since their student days. His background was one of extreme poverty, and when he was sent away from the university—branded as a "rightist" for his perennial interest in humanity and humanitarianism—he spent ten years wandering and working as a laborer. He has now returned to the university, in poor health after his years of hardship. He is a passionate character, but open and kind, and much admired by Sun Yue's daughter and other young students. He has produced a book on "Marxism and Humanity," arguing that Marxism was fundamentally humane, that it was about improving the lives of people—and not, as claimed in the Cultural Revolution, only about class struggle. This, it seems, remains a dangerous political view that is opposed by the university party secretary, Xi Liu, and his shrewish second wife, although their student son, Xi Wang, is a keen supporter of He Jingfu.

There is much in *Stones of the Wall* that is quite universal: middle-aged, educated people, divorced or separated, trying to sort out their daily life and their love lives, worrying about the effects of parental unhappiness and divorce on their children while often unable to protect them. There is also much that is specifically Chinese within these universal concerns. For instance, in China it is common for people to arrange marriages in a much less subtle way than in the West, because the unmarried state is seen as unhappy and unnatural. During the Cultural Revolution, primary school children are made to eat their lunch next to a dung heap in order to understand the suffering of peasants. The stories told by Sun Yue's fellow students of the university classes of 1959 and 1960, as they cram into her apartment for a reunion, include such particularly Chinese experiences.

The writing is emotional and personal. Child of a divorce, Sun Yue's teenage daughter writes, "Why is it the first thing history loads on my shoulders is a burden?" and she continues:

"The simple noun 'Daddy' has become a possessive, 'my Daddy.' Ever since Ma showed me the letter, I've been hating him inside. He left Ma and he left me and I hate him. He's with some woman that I don't know and I hate him. He's made it so that whenever I think of him, I blush, and I never dare talk about him in front of my classmates. I hate him.

"He says his hair has gone white, it serves him right. But what does his white hair look like? Does it look like an old person's? I'll call him the old person. If he's become an old person, is he still good-looking?

"He says he's got a daughter called Huanhuan. That used to be my name. Why didn't he call her something else? He says he thinks about me every day but I don't believe it: if he misses me why hasn't he come to see me?

"Today 'my Daddy' has suddenly arrived. Should I see him? This Daddy? This sort of Daddy? Of course I shouldn't see him. But I'd love to see if his hair is really white. And I'd like to ask him why he came.

"Ma said it was up to me to decide. Why does she want me to decide? Can't she take charge? 'I can't forgive him'—she's made her position clear. Should I forgive him? She doesn't want to force me. But what does she want? 'I won't see him, Ma.' That was how I finally answered.

Her eyes shone suddenly as if she was pleased. She didn't want me to see him, I was right."

Thus Hanhan's ideas revolve as the novel's characters revolve around one another with no clear resolution.

There is a long passage about the Great Wall of China in *Stones of the Wall*, in which one of the characters says, "I loved the Great Wall. The first time I climbed to the beacon at the 'greatest pass in the world' [a gate in the Wall near Beijing], I forgot my low status. Each brick seemed like a person; the Wall, snaking off into the distance, seemed like an endless mass of people. I felt like a new recruit in an enormous army."

Thus the Great Wall, a universally recognized symbol of China, stands as a representative of Chinese humanity, created by an army of mortals over thousands of years. It is a symbol of power, marking the border of the massive Chinese empire, yet it failed to hold back the invading Mongols and Manchus. It commemorates the suffering of those who built it centuries ago, going back to the reign of the First Emperor, continuing with the massive rebuilding in the Ming dynasty. It has seen the unfolding of the history of imperial China and remains a major attraction today.

"People had scratched their names on almost every brick on the beacon, as if like me, they wanted to broadcast the fact that they had joined this army, as if the Wall was our roll of honor . . ."

Chronology

Defining a chronology, particularly of the distant past, is a complex matter involving texts, archaeological sites, academic debates, and politics. The sequence of more recent dynastic changes is easier to establish, but sources often vary by a year or two. As the chronology here is intended to help readers, rather than explore historical arguments, I have used standard reference works to compile a brief list.

Shang dynasty c. 1600–1046 BCE

Zhou dynasty 1046–221 BCE
   Western Zhou 1046–771 BCE
   Eastern Zhou 770–256 BCE
      Spring and Autumn period 770–476 BCE
      Warring States period 475–221 BCE

Qin dynasty 221–206 BCE

Han dynasty 206 BCE–220 CE
   Western (or Former) Han 206 BCE–9 CE
   Wang Mang interregnum 9–23 CE
   Eastern (or Later) Han 25–220 CE

Three Kingdoms 220–280 CE
   Wei 220–265 CE
   Shu Han 221–263 CE
   Wu 222–280 CE

Western Jin dynasty 265–316 CE

Eastern Jin dynasty 317–420 CE/**Sixteen Kingdoms** 304–439 CE

Northern and Southern dynasties 420–581 CE
   Southern dynasties
      Song 420–479 CE
      Southern Qi 479–502 CE
      Liang 502–557 CE
      Chen 557–589 CE

Northern dynasties
    Northern Wei 386–534 CE
    Eastern Wei 534–550 CE
    Northern Qi 550–577 CE
    Western Wei 535–556 CE
    Northern Zhou 557–581 CE

Sui dynasty 581–618 CE

Tang dynasty 618–907 CE

Five Dynasties & **Ten Kingdoms** 907–960 CE

Song dynasty 960–1279
    Northern Song 960–1127
    Southern Song 1127–1279

Liao dynasty 916–1125

Western Xia 1038–1227

Jin dynasty 1115–1234

Yuan dynasty 1279–1368

Ming dynasty 1368–1644

Qing dynasty 1644–1911

Republic of China 1912–

People's Republic of China 1949–

Notes

Introduction

* See John DeFrancis, *The Chinese Language* (Honolulu, 1984), and William G. Boltz, *The Origin and Early Development of the Chinese Writing System* (New Haven, 1994).

** Administrative boundaries, and the names of provinces and places in China, have changed over the centuries. The modern names are used, with earlier names provided where needed.

*** Victor H. Mair, Sanping Chen, Frances Wood, *Chinese Lives* (London, 2013), p. 132.

† Jacques Pimpaneau, *Anthologie de la littérature chinoise classique* (Arles, 2004), p. 5.

Book of Songs • Shi jing

* An interesting version of this poem is that of Ezra Pound (1885–1972), whose Chinese translations, made through the Japanese translations of Ernest Fenellosa (1853–1908), have been as controversial as anything connected with Pound. He reverses and exaggerates the repetition in the first stanza and fails to reflect it in the next two, and in the central section, with no textual basis, he hints at the medicinal use of the plantain. See Ezra Pound, *The Classic Anthology Defined by Confucius* (London, [1954] 1974), p. 7.

Reading:

Apart from Ezra Pound, there is the translation by the great British pioneer of Chinese translation, Arthur Waley, *The Book of Songs* (London, 1937); and a translation by the Swedish scholar Bernhard Karlgren, *The Book of Odes* [includes Chinese text] (Stockholm, 1950).

Book of Changes • Yi jing

The *Book of Changes* was first translated into English by James Legge in 1865, and into German by Richard Wilhelm in 1923. Wilhelm's German version was translated into English by Cary F. Baynes and published in 1950, with an additional preface by Carl Jung. Jung was greatly taken by "this oracle method," or "method of exploring the unconscious." He proclaimed, "Let it go forth into the world for the benefit of those who can discern its meaning," and noted that "the less one thinks about the theory of the *I-ching*, the more soundly one sleeps."

Reading:

The Wilhelm/Baynes translation (with Jung's foreword) is titled *The I Ching, or Book of Changes* (Princeton, 1977); and there is a more recent translation by John Blofeld, *I Ching: The Book of Change* (London, 1965).

Classic of the Way and of Virtue • Daode jing
Zhuangzi

* The "Way" is transliterated as *dao* in the modern pinyin romanization system. In the older Wade-Giles romanization, it is rendered *tao*.

Reading:

There are a number of translations, including by Victor H. Mair, *Tao Te Ching* (New York, 1990); Victor H. Mair, *Wandering on the Way* (Honolulu, 1998); Robert G. Henricks, *Te-Tao Ching* (New York, 1989); A. C. Graham, *Chuang-tzu* (London, 1981); D. C. Lau, *Tao Te Ching* (Harmondsworth, 1963); and Burton Watson, *The Complete Works of Chuang Tzu* (New York, 1968).

Analects • Lun yu

* The reference to Confucius's mat is a reminder that until the Tang dynasty, the Chinese sat on mats, not chairs (and in Chinese, "Chairman Mao" means "Mao, the person sitting on the chief mat").

** Raymond Dawson, *Confucius* (Oxford, 1981), p. 76.

Reading:

The *Analects* was translated by James Legge (1815–1897) of the London Missionary Society in *The Four Books* (1861); a fine modern version is the translation by D. C. Lau, *The Analects* (Harmondsworth, 1979).

Mencius • Mengzi

Reading:

There is a fine translation by D. C. Lau, *Mencius* (London, 2004). An early translation, first published in 1861 by James Legge, has been surpassed but is often published in useful bilingual editions including the Chinese text.

Master Sun's Art of War • Sunzi bingfa
Reading:
The two best current translations of *Master Sun's Art of War* are slightly different in approach: Roger T. Ames's *Sun-tzu: The Art of Warfare* (New York, 1993) includes much discussion of the discovery and significance of the Yinqueshan bamboo slips, the Chinese text, and an annotated translation; it illuminates the history of the text itself as well as providing a fine translation. John Minford's *Sun-tzu: The Art of War* (London, 2009) provides a translation and much of the commentary that has accrued over a thousand years, demonstrating the history of the work within the Chinese tradition.

Almanac • Tongshu
* See Susan Whitfield, "Under the Censor's Eye: Printed Almanacs and Censorship in Ninth-Century China," in *British Library Journal*, vol. 24, no. 1, 1998.
** This almanac, Or.8210/P.6, can be seen on the website of the International Dunhuang Project (IDP) at the British Library, http://idp.bl.uk.
Reading:
There is a translation of a contemporary almanac revealing its traditional sources by Martin Palmer, *T'ung Shu: The Ancient Chinese Almanac* (London, 1986).

Proper Ritual • Yi li
* See Evelyn S. Rawski and Jessica Rawson, *China: The Three Emperors, 1662–1795* (London, 2005), p. 55, p. 90–91, p. 118–19.
** The order of ritual vessels is given using the cardinal directions (north, south, east, west) rather than "left" and "right." These are in fact clearer, and were traditionally used widely, for example in street directions.
Reading:
There is a fairly early translation, which conveys the complexity of ritual, by John Steele, *The I-Li, or Book of Etiquette and Ceremonial* (London, 1917). There is also a detailed description of the work by William G. Boltz, in Michael Loewe, *Early Chinese Texts: A Bibliographical Guide* (Berkeley, 1993).

The Grand Scribe's Records • Shi ji
* Quoted in Wm. Theodore de Bary et al., *Sources of Chinese Tradition*, vol. 1 (New York, 1960), p. 228.
Reading:
Translations include William H. Nienhauser's fine version in several volumes, *The Grand Scribe's Records* (Bloomington, 1995–), and Edouard Chavannes, *Les Mémoires Historiques de Se-ma Ts'ien* (Paris, 1895–1905).

Nineteen Old Poems • Gu shi shijiu shou
* Wonderfully translated by David Hawkes, *The Songs of the South* ([Oxford, 1959], Harmondsworth, 1985).
Reading:
Arthur Waley included most of the *Nineteen Old Poems* in his *One Hundred and Seventy Chinese Poems* (London, 1918); a more recent version of the full complement is Jean-Pierre Diény, *Les Dix-neuf Poèmes anciens* (Paris, 1974). Waley left the poems to speak for themselves, but Diény includes very useful notes.

Records of the Buddhist Kingdoms • Foguo ji
* The great pillar, or stupa, of Ashoka at Sanchi was discovered by British officers out hunting tigers in 1819. More systematic explorations of Buddhist sites of significance in India, such as the excavation of the Maha Bodhi Temple in Bodh Gaya in the 1880s by General Alexander Cunningham, were partly inspired by translations of Chinese pilgrim accounts of India many centuries earlier, particularly that of Faxian, which offered the only clues to the survival of great Buddhist temples by then forgotten and hidden by jungle.
** These are listed in Soothill and Hodous's *A Dictionary of Chinese Buddhist Terms* (London, 1937) as the *sapta ratna* or seven treasures: gold, silver, lapis, crystal, agate, ruby, and cornelian.
Reading:
Records of the Buddhist Kingdoms was first translated into French by Rémusat, Klaproth, and Landresse and published in 1836. Translations into English followed, by Samuel Beal (1869), Herbert Allen Giles (1877), and James Legge (1886).

On the question of translation, Herbert Allen Giles (1845–1935) worked on several editions of his *Travels of Fa-Hsien or Records of the Buddhistic Kingdoms,* published between 1877 and 1923, and was characteristically scathing about the works of others. In a preface to his edition of 1923, he wrote of Beal's translation, "An English translation, really of Rémusat's works . . . In which he reproduced all of Rémusat's mistakes while adding many more of his own . . . In 1886, Dr Legge published a fresh translation, in which he borrowed largely, without acknowledgement, from my corrections of Beal and managed to contribute not a few mistakes of his own."

Lotus Sutra • Saddharmapundarika sutra
Diamond Sutra • Vajracchedikaprajnaparamita sutra
* For a brilliant overview of the process see Erik Zürcher, *The Buddhist Conquest of China* (Leiden, [1959] 2007).
** See Nicholas Poppe, *The Diamond Sutra* (Wiesbaden, 1971).
*** Frances Wood and Mark Barnard, *The Diamond Sutra* (London, 2010). For the discovery of the Dunhuang documents see Frances Wood, *The Silk Road* (London, 2002), p. 88–110.
Reading:
Translations of Buddhist texts into English began in the nineteenth century, but more recent versions are better. There is a translation of the *Lotus Sutra* by Burton Watson (New York, 1993); and a translation of the *Diamond Sutra* is by Red Pine, *The Diamond Sutra* (Berkeley, 2001).

Poems (Li Bai)
Poems (Du Fu)
Reading:
All of Du Fu's poems included in the *Three Hundred Tang Poems* (*Tang shi sanbai shou*) have been translated (with Chinese text, transcription, a literal version, and notes) by David Hawkes in *A Little Primer of Tu Fu* (Oxford, 1967), a marvelous volume that enables anyone to more fully understand how Chinese poetry works, what it looks like, and what it sounds like.
    Apart from Hawkes on Du Fu, there are many translations of Li Bai and Du Fu, including *Li Po and Tu Fu* by Arthur Cooper (Harmondsworth, 1973); by various translators, in John Minford and Joseph S. M. Lau (eds.), *Classical Chinese Literature,* vol. 1 (New York, 2000); and Stephen Owen, *The Great Age of Chinese Poetry* (New Haven, 1981).

Poems (Li Shangyin)
Reading:
Translations are by James J. Y. Liu, *The Poetry of Li Shang-yin* (Chicago, 1969), and Stephen Owen, *The Late Tang* (Cambridge, MA, 2006).

The Story of Yingying • Yingying zhuan
Master Dong's Western Chamber Romance • Dong shi Xi xiang ji zhugongtiao
Romance of the Western Chamber • Xi xiang ji
Reading:
The *Story of Yingying* has been translated as "Golden Oriole" in *The Golden Casket* (Harmondsworth, 1967). This is a translation from the German by Christopher Levenson; the original translations were by Wolfgang Bauer and Herbert Franke. Other translations are by James Hightower, "The Story of Yingying," in John Minford and Joseph S. M. Lau (eds.), *Classical Chinese Literature,* vol. 1 (New York, 2000); and by Arthur Waley, "The Story of Ts'ui Yingying," in *More Translations from the Chinese* (London, 1919).
    There is a fine translation of *Master Tung's Western Chamber Romance* by Li-li Ch'en (New York, 1994), and a less satisfactory translation of Wang Shifu's *Romance of the Western Chamber* by the Chinese writer and dramatist S. I. Hsiung (London, 1935).

Poems (Li Qingzhao)
* According to tradition, a rhino horn in a gold dish could warm a whole room.
Reading:
Li Qingzhao's enduring popularity is reflected in a number of translations: Kenneth Rexroth and Ling Chung, *Li Ch'ing-chao: Complete Poems* (New York, 1979); Jiaosheng Wang, *The Complete Ci-poems of Li Qingzhao,* Sino-Platonic Papers, no. 13, October 1989 (www.sino-platonic.org). A translation into the French is *Li Qingzhao: Oeuvres poétiques complètes,* translated by Liang Paitchin (Paris, 1977).

The Orphan of Zhao • Zhao shi guer
* This was a common method of female suicide; see Wang Ping, *Aching for Beauty* (Minneapolis, 2000), p. 69.

Reading:
Translations include Prémare's version included in du Halde, *Description de la Chine* (1735); Voltaire's in his *Oeuvres Complets* (1784); Stanislas Julien, *Tchao-chi-kou-eul, ou l'Orphelin de la Chine* (1834); James Fenton, *The Orphan of Zhao* (London, 2012).

Three-Character Classic • Sanzi jing
Reading:
Herbert Allen Giles's original translation is *San Tzu Ching, or Three Character Classic, and Ch'ien Tzu Wen, or Thousand Character Essay* (Shanghai, 1873), and there are several later editions.

Twenty-Four Exemplars of Filial Piety • Ershisi xiao
* I am working here from an illustrated edition published in Shanghai (c. 1920). The order in which the exemplars are listed seems to vary in different editions.

** Instead of saying that he was "eight years old," a better translation would probably be "nine years old," as Chinese children are considered to be one year old at the time of birth.
Reading:
A number of the stories are included in Wm. Theodore de Bary and Richard Lufrano, *Sources of Chinese Tradition*, vol. 2 (New York, 2000).

The Water Margin • Shuihu zhuan
* Reign periods were used from the Tang dynasty (618–907 CE) onward to designate specific periods within a reign. They were selected and changed to reflect events, and were invariably positive.

** Roderick MacFarquhar and Michael Schoenhals, *Mao's Last Revolution* (Cambridge, MA, 2006), p. 402–404.

*** See Patricia Buckley Ebrey, *Emperor Huizong* (Cambridge, MA, 2014).
Reading:
The Water Margin was translated into English by Sidney Shapiro and published under the title *Outlaws of the Marsh*; and, less helpfully, as *All Men Are Brothers* by Pearl S. Buck.

The Story of the Three Kingdoms • Sanguo zhi
Reading:
There is a fine translation by Moss Roberts, *Three Kingdoms: A Historical Novel* (London, 2013; this is a reprint of an earlier edition).

The Story of the Lute • Pipa ji
Reading:
An early translation is by A. P. L. Bazin, *Le Pi-pa-ki ou l'histoire du luth* (Paris, 1841); a fine translation and study is Jean Mulligan's *The Lute: Kao Ming's P'i-p'a chi* (New York, 1980).

The Classic of Lu Ban • Lu Ban jing
* See Wolfram Eberhard, "Chinese Building Magic," in Wolfram Eberhard, *Studies in Chinese Folklore and Related Essays* (Bloomington, 1970).
Reading:
There is an English translation by Klaas Ruitenbeek, *Carpentry and Building in Late Imperial China* (Leiden, 1993).

Journey to the West • Xiyou ji
* For Xuanzang, see Sally Hovey Wriggins, *Xuanzang* (Boulder, 1996); Arthur Waley, *The Real Tripitaka* (London, 1952); and Samuel Beal, *Si-Yu-Ki: Buddhist Records of the Western World* (London, 1884).
Reading:
There are two good recent translations: W. J. F. Jenner, *Journey to the West* (Beijing, 2003), and Antony C. Yu, *The Journey to the West* (Chicago, 2012).

Plum in a Golden Vase • Jinpingmei
The Carnal Prayer Mat • Rou putuan
Reading:
An English translation of *Plum in a Golden Vase* is by David Tod Roy, *The Plum in the Golden Vase, or, Chin P'ing Mei* (Princeton, 1993–2013). There is a brilliant French translation of *Plum in a Golden Vase* by André Lévy, *Fleur en Fiole d'Or: Jin Ping Mei cihua* (Paris, 1985).

There is a fine translation by Patrick Hanan of *The Carnal Prayer Mat* (London, 1990).

Travels of Xu Xiake ◆ *Xu Xiake youji*
Tracks of a Wild Goose in the Snow ◆ *Hongxuan yinyuan tuji*
* See E. O. Reischauer, *Ennin's Travels in T'ang China* (New York, 1955).
Reading:
Xu Xiake's travels have been translated by Li Chi, *The Travel Diaries of Hsü Hsia-K'o* (Hong Kong, 1974). Some episodes in Linqing's memoirs are translated in T. C. Lai, *A Wild Swan's Trail: The Travels of a Mandarin* (Hong Kong, 1978).

The Craft of Gardens ◆ *Yuan ye*
* Comparisons between photographs of gardens in Suzhou taken by Osvald Siren in the early twentieth century (see Osvald Siren, *The Gardens of China* [New York, 1949]) and present-day pavilions reveal changes in roof profile; and there is a Ming painting of the Zhuo zheng yuan (Garden of the Artless Administrator) in Suzhou that reveals earth banks lining a pool where there are now piled rocks.
Reading:
There is a very fine translation of *The Craft of Gardens* by Alison Hardie with useful photographs and diagrams to supplement the original illustrations (New Haven, 1988).

Exploitation of the Works of Nature ◆ *Tiangong kaiwu*
* See Tsien Tsuen-hsuin, *Paper and Printing*, in Joseph Needham, *Science and Civilisation in China*, vol. 5, part 1 (Cambridge, 1985).
Reading:
There is a translation by E-tu Zen Sun and Shiou-chuan Sun, *T'ien-kung k'ai-wu: Chinese Technology in the Seventeenth Century* (University Park, PA, 1966).

Mustard Seed Garden Manual of Painting ◆ *Jieziyuan huazhuan*
* Li Yu's humorous essays have been translated in part by Lin Yutang, in *The Importance of Living* (1937) and *The Importance of Understanding* (1960).
** Since Mount Sumeru, the central mountain of Buddhist cosmology, is defined as being about 800,000 miles above sea level and reaching a further 800,000 miles below the sea, this Buddhist paradox describes the inconceivable achievements of the enlightened Buddha, but the comparison of a garden with a tiny mustard seed is also part of the traditional Chinese self-deprecation in which one's possessions or achievements are politely diminished. The same figure of speech can be seen in the name of Linqing's Half-Acre Garden depicted in his memoirs, *Tracks of a Wild Goose in the Snow* (*Hongxuan yinyuan tuji*).
Reading:
The work has been translated by Mai-mai Sze, *The Tao of Painting: A Study of the Ritual Disposition of Chinese Painting. With a Translation of the Chieh tzu yuan hua chuan, or Mustard Seed Garden Manual of Painting* (New York, 1963).

The Peach Blossom Fan ◆ *Taohua shan*
Reading:
A translation of almost all of the drama was made by Sir Harold Acton, a British writer who lived in Beijing between 1932 and 1939, working with Chen Shixiang in the 1950s. It was finished and revised by Cyril Birch and published as *The Peach Blossom Fan* (Berkeley, 1976). Lynn Struve, with some justification, described the translation as inaccurate and "anomalously Shakespearian in tone," and there is a better translation, but only of scene 4, by Richard E. Strassberg in *Renditions* (Hong Kong, number 8, 1977).

Poems/Essays (Yuan Mei)
* See Jacques Pimpaneau, *Anthologie de la littérature chinoise classique* (Arles, 2004).
Reading:
Though Yuan Mei's poetry and literary criticism has recently been translated in full, by J. D. Schmidt, some of his more interesting and esoteric writing can only be found in fragmentary versions; see for example Herbert Allen Giles, *Gems of Chinese Literature* (London, 1923), for Yuan Mei writings on eating. Arthur Waley's biography *Yuan Mei: Eighteenth Century Chinese Poet* (London, 1956) introduces the very varied elements of Yuan Mei's personality.
J. D. Schmidt, *Harmony Garden: The Life, Literary Criticism, and Poetry of Yuan Mei* (London, 2003).

Unofficial History of the Grove of Literati • Rulin waishi
* Benjamin A. Elman, *A Cultural History of Civil Examinations in Late Imperial China* (Berkeley, 2000), p. 143.
** There is a crib sheet, a tiny square of silk covered with quotations from the Confucian classics, in the British Library collection, and an undervest similarly covered in tiny script in the Gest Library, Princeton.
Reading:
Unofficial History of the Grove of Literati has been translated by Gladys Yang and Yang Xianyi as *The Scholars* (Beijing, 1957).

Three Hundred Tang Poems • Tang shi sanbai shou
* Li He's poetry has been translated by J. D. Frodsham, *The Poems of Li Ho* (Oxford, 1970).
Reading:
Translations include Witter Bynner (from the texts of Kiang Kang-hu/Jiang Kanghu), *The Jade Mountain* (New York, 1929), and Peter Harris, *Three Hundred Tang Poems* (New York, 2009).

Strange Stories from the Liao Studio • Liaozhai zhiyi
Reading:
Though there is as yet no complete translation into English, the first selections translated by C. F. R. Allen were published in the *China Review* in 1873–74, followed by Herbert A. Giles, *Strange Stories from a Chinese Studio* (London, 1880). John Minford's larger selection, *Pu Songling: Strange Tales from a Chinese Studio* (London, 2006), is a wonderfully readable version with copious scholarly notes.

Dream of the Red Chamber • Hongloumeng
* See Jonathan Spence, *Ts'ao Yin and the K'ang-hsi Emperor* (New Haven, 1966).
** See Frances Wood, *Blue Guide China* (London, 2001), p. 144–46. The garden is open to the public but the mansion is still occupied by the Central Conservatoire of Music.
*** David Hawkes, *Cao Xueqin: The Story of the Stone*, vol. 1 (Harmondsworth, 1973), p. 44.
Reading:
David Hawkes gave the overall title *The Story of the Stone* to his translation of *Hongloumeng*, and it refers to the magical jade stone, *bao y*, found in the mouth of the newborn Jia Baoyu, named for his jade. Hawkes gave the subtitle *The Golden Days* to this first volume, and it was followed by four more volumes, *The Crab-Flower Club*, *The Warning Voice*, *The Debt of Tears*, and *The Dreamer Wakes* (the last two volumes were translated by John Minford). The sequence of titles hints at the arc of the complex novel.
The translation by David Hawkes and John Minford is a triumph. I can only marvel at Hawkes's ability to translate the doggerel verses—retaining rhyme, rhythm, and sense—and the sustained quality of the work is outstanding.
David Hawkes, *Cao Xueqin: The Story of the Stone*, vols. 1–3 (Harmondsworth, 1973–1980).
John Minford, *Cao Xueqin and Gao E: The Story of the Stone*, vols. 4–5 (Harmondsworth, 1982, 1986).

Six Records of a Floating Life • Fusheng liu ji
Reading:
There is a translation by Leonard Pratt and Chiang Su-hui, *Shen Fu: Six Records of a Floating Life* (Harmondsworth, 1983).

Poems (Qiu Jin)
Reading:
On Qiu Jin, see Ono Kazuko, *Chinese Women in a Century of Revolution, 1850–1950* (Stanford, 1989), and Kang-i Sun Chang and Haun Saussy, *Women Writers of Traditional China* (Stanford, 1999).

The Travels of Lao Can • Lao Can youji
* The description of Lao Can himself and how he chose his nickname raises questions of translation. In Yang Xianyi and Gladys Tayler's (later Yang) *Mr. Decadent* (published in Nanjing in 1947), the version is straightforward and amusing, catching the eccentricity of the character: "His family name actually was Tie and his personal name Ying but he had taken the pen-name 'Patcher of Decadence' after the monk 'Lazy and Decadent' of the Tang dynasty, whose name was associated with baked potatoes." Harold Shadick, in his scholarly version, *The Travels of Lao Ts'an* (Ithaca, 1952),

writes, "He chose Ts'an as his *hao* because he liked the story of the monk Lan Ts'an roasting taros." This is accompanied by a footnote describing the prophecy of the lazy monk. Baked potatoes are anachronistic because there were no (South American) potatoes in China in the Tang dynasty—so Shadick's version is more accurate but potatoes are funnier than taros.

Reading:
Harold Shadick's translation, *The Travels of Lao Ts'an* (Ithaca, 1952), has lots of useful footnotes and photographs of the translator with Liu E's son. The translation (with a Chinese text) by Yang Xianyi and Gladys Tayler (later Yang), *Mr. Decadent* (Nanjing, 1947), is different and more amusing and lively. A later version by Yang Xianyi and Gladys Yang, *The Travels of Lao Can*, was published in Beijing in 1983.

"My Old Home" (in *Call to Arms*) ◆ "*Gu xiang*" (in *Nahan*)
Old Tales Retold ◆ *Gushi xinbian*
Reading:
There are translations by Julia Lovell, *The Real Story of Ah-Q and Other Tales of China: The Complete Fiction of Lu Xun* (London, 2009), and Gladys Yang, *Silent China: Selected Writings of Lu Xun* (Oxford, 1973).

Miss Sophie's Diary ◆ *Shafei nüshi riji*
Reading:
There are a number of translations of *Miss Sophie's Diary*, notably that by W. J. F. Jenner (Beijing, 1985). *The Sun Shines over the Sanggan River* was translated by Gladys Yang and Yang Xianyi (Beijing, 1954).

Mr. Ma and Son ◆ *Er Ma*
Camel Xiangzi ◆ *Luotuo xiangzi*
Beneath the Red Banner ◆ *Zheng hongqi xia*
* Lao She's mixed group of students possibly included the writer Graham Greene, whose employer, the British-American Tobacco Company, in the end did not send him to China.
Reading:
There is a fine translation of *Mr. Ma and Son* by William Dolby, *Mr Ma and Son* (London, 2013). See also Anne Witchard, *Lao She in London* (Hong Kong, 2012). Don Cohn translated *Beneath the Red Banner* (Beijing, 1982). There is a translation of *Camel Xiangzi* by Shi Xiaoqing (Beijing, 1988).

Family ◆ *Jia*
Reading:
Translations are by Sidney Shapiro, *The Family* (Beijing, 1958), and Olga Lang, *Family* (New York, 1972).

Midnight ◆ *Ziye*
* W. H. Auden and Christopher Isherwood, *Journey to a War* (London, 1939).
Reading:
Midnight was translated by A. C. Barnes (Beijing, 1957).

Autobiography of a Girl Soldier ◆ *Yige nübing de zizhuan*
Reading:
Translations of *Autobiography of a Girl Soldier* include *Girl Rebel*, translated by Adet Lin and Anor Lin (New York, 1940); *Autobiography of a Chinese Girl*, translated by Tsui Chi (London, 1943); *A Woman Soldier's Own Story*, translated by Lily Chia Brissman and Barry Brissman (New York, 2001).

The Man Who Came Home on a Snowy Night ◆ *Fengxue ye guiren*
Reading:
There is a translation by Thomas Moran, *Return on a Snowy Night*, in Xiaomei Chen (ed.), *The Columbia Anthology of Modern Chinese Drama* (New York, 2010). Background to *pingju* opera can be found in John Chinnery, *The Memoirs of Xin Fengxia* (Hong Kong, 2001).

Little Black's Marriage ◆ *Xiao Erhei jiehun*
Reading:
Translations are included in *Modern Chinese Stories*, translated by W. J. F. Jenner and Gladys Yang (Oxford, 1970), and *Rhymes of Li Yu-tsai* (Beijing, 1954).

Biography of the First Ming Emperor • Zhu Yuanzhang zhuan
* I first read *Biography of the First Ming Emperor* in 1976, during the Cultural Revolution. I was following a Chinese history course and the biography, despite being a "poisonous weed," was grudgingly loaned as "negative teaching material" by Peking University Library for an essay I was due to write on taxation policies at the beginning of the Ming. It was so fascinating and well-written that I sat up all night reading it, and my Chinese roommate did the same the next night, because the book was so different from our usual Cultural Revolution fare. From the first sentences, I was fascinated.
Reading:
There is a good translation into French (though it does not state from which edition of the book) by Nadine Perront, *Wu Han: L'Empereur des Ming* (Arles, 1991).

Fortress Besieged • Wei cheng
* Adrian Hsia (ed.), *Qian Zhongshu: The Vision of China in the English Literature of the Seventeenth and Eighteenth Centuries* (Hong Kong, 1998).
** I am using the pinyin romanization of the Chinese names in the novel. The translation by Jeanne Kelly and Nathan K. Mao uses the older Wade-Giles romanization, which is listed here in parenthesis: Fang Hongjian (Fang Hung-chien); Zhao Xinmei (Chao Hsin-mei); Director Gao (Kao).
Reading:
The translation by Jeanne Kelly and Nathan K. Mao, *Fortress Besieged*, first published by Indiana University Press (Bloomington, 1979), has recently been reissued by Penguin Books (London, 2006).

Memories of South Peking • Chengnan jiushi
Reading:
Memories of Peking: South Side Stories has been translated by Nancy C. Ing and Chi Pang-yuan (Hong Kong, 2002).

From Emperor to Citizen • Wode qian ban sheng
Reading:
From Emperor to Citizen: The Autobiography of Aisin-Gioro Pu Yi was translated by W. J. F. Jenner (Oxford, 1987). See also Reginald Johnston, *Twilight in the Forbidden City* (London, 1934).

Quotations from Chairman Mao Tse-tung • Mao Zhuxi yulu
Reading:
Mao's writings and speeches survive in his *Selected Works*, and in some interesting unofficial compilations such as Stuart Schram's *Mao Tse-tung Unrehearsed: Talks and Letters, 1956–71*, translated by John Chinnery and Tieyun (Harmondsworth, 1974).

Half a Lifelong Romance • Bansheng yuan
Lust, Caution • Si, rong
Reading:
Eileen Chang, *Half a Lifelong Romance*, translated by Karen S. Kingsbury (London, 2014).
Eileen Chang, *Lust, Caution and Other Stories*, translated by Julia Lovell et al. (London, 2007).

Mayor Yin • Yin xianzhang
Reading:
These stories are translated by Nancy Ing and Howard Goldblatt, *The Execution of Mayor Yin and Other Stories from the Great Proletarian Cultural Revolution* (Bloomington, 1978).

Six Chapters from a Cadre School Life • Ganxiao liu ji
Reading:
There are translations of *Six Chapters from a Cadre School Life* by Howard Goldblatt, *Six Chapters from My Life "Downunder"* (Seattle, 1988), and Geremie Barmé, *A Cadre School Life: Six Chapters* (Hong Kong, 1982).

Stones of the Wall • Ren a ren!
* I translated *Ren a ren!* into English in 1985. I changed the title because I felt that "humanity" was too broad a word, that the novel was specifically about China, and because there is a long passage in the novel about the Great Wall of China. Thus *Stones of the Wall* seemed a more fitting title for a translation.
Reading:
Translated by Frances Wood, *Stones of the Wall* (London, 1985).

Index